Bureaucracy
and
Rural Development in Mizoram

About the Author

Harendra Sinha obtained his MA (Political Science) and Ph.D. degrees from Gauhati University, Guwahati, Assam. He is presently working as Associate Professor and Head of the Department of Political Science, Government J. Buana College Lunglei, Mizoram. He is actively engaged in teaching and research works. He has contributed number of research papers and regularly contributes articles to various journals and present papers at seminars. He has written books on Indian Government and Politics, Major Political System, Political Theory, Western Political Thought and Public Administration (co-authored) published by Research and Publications Committee, Government J. Buana College.

Dr. Sinha is currently a member of Board of Studies of the Department of Political Science, Mizoram University, Mizoram Academic Forum (MAF), Mizoram Political Science Association (MIPSA), Mizoram College Teachers Association (MCTA) and the Secretary of MCTA Branch.

Bureaucracy and Rural Development in Mizoram

Harendra Sinha

Associate Professor & Head
Department of Political Science
Government J. Buana College
Lunglei (Mizoram)-796701

CONCEPT PUBLISHING COMPANY PVT LTD.,
NEW DELHI-110059

ISBN-13 : 978-81-8069-830-9

First Published 2012

Published and Printed by

Concept Since 1974

Concept Publishing Company Pvt. Ltd.
A/15-16, Commercial Block, Mohan Garden
New Delhi-110059 (India)
T: 25351460, 25351794, *F*: 091-11-25357109
E: publishing@conceptpub.com, W: www.conceptpub.com
Editorial Office: H-13, Bali Nagar, New Delhi-110 015, India.

Cataloging in Publication Data--*Courtesy:* D.K. Agencies (P) Ltd. <docinfo@dkagencies.com>

Sinha, Harendra.
Bureaucracy and rural development in Mizoram / Harendra Sinha.
p. cm.
Originally presented as the author's thesis (Ph. D.)—Gauhati University.
Includes bibliographical references (p.) and index.
ISBN 9788180698309

1. Bureaucracy—India—Mizoram. 2. Rural development—India—Mizoram.
I. Title.

DDC 352.630954166 23

Dedicated
to
my beloved wife
Late Nandita Sinha
(1976-2003)

Preface

Rural development has been one of the abiding concerns among policy-makers and planning experts as an apposite answer to the problems of poverty all-over the world. It is advocated as an essential strategy for social justice and economic development especially in developing countries. In a developing country like India where majority of population live in rural areas, rural development assumes immense significance. Hence, soon after Independence, the focal point of the planners both at the Centre and State levels was to eradicate poverty and to improve the standard of living of rural masses. The launching of Community Development Programme in early fifties and the introduction of the Panchayati Raj Institutions (PRIs) later were the significant measures undertaken by the Government of India towards rural reconstruction.

The implementation of the Community Development (nomenclature changed) later as Rural Development Programme was characterised by division of the entire country into small manageable 'blocks' and a new bureaucratic model created in the form of 'block level functionaries' consisting of a generalist kingpin of the block—the Block Development Officer with a team of Extension Officers and Village Level Workers. With the exception of some good results at the preliminary periods, this model failed in discharging multiple rural reconstruction activities and to induce people's participation in the programme as was expected. Thus, a Committee on Plan Projects popularly known as Balwantrai Mehta Committee, after the name of its Chairman, was set up to enquire the working of the community development. The committee recommended the introduction of three-tier system of PRIs to involve people in the development processes. Various committees, later on, headed by Ashok Mehta, V.P. Naik, P.B. Patil, G.V.R. Rao, L.N. Singhvi refurbish these institutions which gave necessary momentum to the 73rd Constitutional Amendment Act 1992 which revolutionise the Panchayats. The 73rd Amendment granted the Panchayats constitutional status and entrusted considerable number of functions and responsibilities in ensuring genuine participatory development process at the village level.

With the introduction of PRIs in almost all the States of India, rural development programme is undertaken and implemented by PRIs as well as with the coordination of the block level functionaries. In case of Mizoram, rural development programmes are being implemented by the block functionaries only as Mizoram has not introduced PRIs as local self-government. The State of Mizoram has been exempted from the 73rd Constitutional Amendment due to the existence of traditional local self-government bodies—the Village Councils. As the Village Councils are not as intense as PRIs, block level functionaries are vital for planning, implementation and to stimulate people's participation in the rural development programme.

There has several works on rural development and PRIs been done in various parts of the country. However, the remote and hilly State of Mizoram has been neglected in this manner by researchers on this very aspect. This study is the first of its kind in the disciplines of public administration and rural development which is focused on the block level functionaries and their role in rural development in the absence of PRIs, their role in planning and implementation, performance in motivating and encouraging people's participation in rural development programmes, their problems and the perceptions of the people towards these functionaries.

This book is organized in eight chapters. The first chapter deals with brief introduction, objectives and methodology and introduction of the study area. The second chapter deals conceptual framework of bureaucracy and rural development. The third chapter includes the democratic decentralisation in Mizoram, the District Councils and Village Councils. Chapter four is devoted to bureaucracy and rural development in Mizoram. In chapter five the author explained the problems and prospects of rural development in Mizoram. The sixth chapter deals with the role and functions of the block functionaries and relationship between the generalist head of the block and his team of extension officers. The seventh chapter covers the role performance of the block functionaries and the perceptions of the people towards the rural functionaries. The last chapter presents the summary of major findings, suggestions and conclusions.

The present book "Bureaucracy and Rural Development in Mizoram" is mainly based on my Ph.D. thesis. This research would be of enormous help to the common people, policy-makers, government officials, future researchers and the non-governmental organisations who are engaging themselves in the upliftment of the rural poor in Mizoram.

Harendra Sinha

development in Mizoram. The sixth chapter deals with the role and functions of the block functionaries and relationship between the grassroot level staff—VLWs and BDOs and extension officers. The seventh chapter covers the role performance of the block functionaries and the perceptions of the people towards the rural functionaries. The last chapter presents the summary of major findings, suggestions and conclusions.

The present book "Bureaucracy and Rural Development in Mizoram" is mainly based on my Ph.D. thesis. This research would be of enormous help to the common people, policy makers, government officials, future researchers and the non-governmental organizations who are engaging themselves in the upliftment of the rural poor in Mizoram.

Harendra Sinha

Acknowledgements

First of all, I express my gratitude to my beloved wife Late Nandita Sinha at whose constant encouragement I undertook this study. It is unfortunate that she did not live to see the completion of this work and breathed her last during the course of my field work. Her encouragement and love will remain an invariable source of inspiration to me.

I am highly indebted to my Supervisor Dr. Alaka Sarmah, Associate Professor, Department of Political Science, Gauhati University for her able guidance, valuable suggestions, affectionate encouragement and good wishes without which the work could not be completed. I also owe a deep sense of gratefulness to large number of officials who granted me interviews, answered my queries and also allowed me access to files and other official documents. I am immensely grateful to Mr. Lalsiama Fambawl. AI & PRO and Dr. Lalnilawma, Rural Planning Officer, Directorate of Rural Development, Aizawl, Mr. F.L. Thansiama, Statistical Inspector, Lunglei RD block, the BDOs, EOs, VLWs of Lunglei district for their support. I also thank the respondents of the questionnaires, answered my queries and for excellent hospitality I received from the sample villages during field work. I am extremely grateful to James R. T. Khuma, Assistant Professor, Govt. J. B. College, and Madika of Compu Arts, Lunglei who helped me with enormous patient in editing and typing the manuscript.

I am also immensely grateful to Dr. Debendra Kr. Sinha, President, NBMMS, my close friends particularly Samir Sinha, President BMGSP, Late Gopikanta Sinha and Raj Chandra Sinha, Anukul Sinha and my brother-in-laws Bipin, Ramen and

Kartiksena Sinha, MLA Patharkandi Constituency, Assam, Er. A. Goswami and Pu. Chalchhunga of Electric Veng Lunglei, and the Principal and other faculty members of Govt. J. B. College, for their good wishes throughout the course of my study.

I am highly indebted to my parents, my father Sri Mohan Sinha, my mother Late Ratharani Sinha, my uncles Sri Rajkumar Sinha and Sri Rajbabu Sinha, my adorable father-in-law Sri Sadananda Sinha and mother-in-law Smt. Ketaki Sinha my sisters Kumari, Sandhya, Anjana, Anjuli, brothers Binode, Mangal, Kalasena, Subhas, Rajib, Rajen, Subendu and all the natives of my village Parugaon, Karimganj, Assam for their full cooperation, mental support, their love and affection and good wishes.

During the course of the study, my wife Sunita, son Ishan and daughters Shaini and Simran were always supportive. I deeply express my heartfelt gratitude to them –especially my wife for managing all the domestic chores and sharing equally all my trepidations. I am also thankful to Mr. A.K. Mittal and Mr. S.P. Sinha of Concept Publishing Company Pvt. Ltd., New Delhi, for their support and cooperation in bringing out the book in a short time and elegant manner.

Finally, I am deeply indebted to many eminent scholars and researchers of India and other countries whose valuable works I have drawn upon for this work. The blessing of information technology is highly acknowledged through which much information and materials were gathered. I am alone responsible for all the shortcomings in the book, if any and would welcome suggestions for future guidance.

Lunglei, Mizoram **Harendra Sinha**
Monday, 29 November, 2010

Contents

List of Tables/Charts/Maps

Chart

Map

Glossary

Bawi: Dependants of the Mizo Chief

Chakma: A tribe belongs to eastern group of the Tibeto-Burman group and Budhists in religion having their own dialect

Chichhiah: Salt due payable to the chief

Fathang: Paddy due payable to the chief

Gramin Awaas: Village housing

Gram Panchayat: Village council

Gram Sevak: Village level worker

Gram Sevika: Lady village level worker

Gram Swaraj: Village self-sufficiency

Hnatlang: Rendering services for the community

Indira Awaas Yojana: Indira Housing Scheme

Mizoram Intodelhna Project: Project for Self-sufficiency in Mizoram

Jawahar Rojgar Yojana: Jawahar Employment Scheme

Jhum: Slash and burn method of cultivation

Khuaichhiah: A honey-due payable to the chief

Lal: A Mizo chief

Lakher: A particular clan also known as Maras of Mizoram inhabiting the southern part and having their own dialect.

Mandal: A revenue unit with a population of about 35000-50000.

Mautam: Mautam is a natural famine appears in Mizoram at an interval of about 50 years.

Mizo Hmeichhe Insuihkhawm Pawl: Mizo Women's Organisation

Mizo Hnam Dan: Mizo Customary Law

Mukhya Sevika: Block level female development functionary

Pawis or Pois: A particular clan known also as Lai dwelling in the south and south eastern part of Mizoram having their distinct dialect.

Panchayat Samiti: Block level council

Panchayati Raj: Rural democratic decentralisation pattern in India

Puithiam: Village Priest

Ram: The chief's land

Ramhual: Privileged villagers who had the first choice of the jhum site thereby paying more paddy dues to the chief

Pradhan Mantri Gramodaya Yojana: Prime Minister Village Upliftment Scheme

Sailos: Ruling clan of the Lushais (Mizos).

Sampoorna Grameen Rozgar Yojana: Complete Village Employment Scheme

Sachhiah: A flesh due payable to the chief

Sarvodaya: Well being of all

Swarnajayanti Gram Swarozgar Yojana: Golden Jubilee Village Self-Employment Scheme

Swarozgari: Self-employed individual

Thirdeng: A village blacksmith

Thirdengsa: A flesh due payable to the village blacksmith

Tlangau: A village crier

Tlawmngaihna: The Mizo social and moral code by which every individual discharge his responsibility to the society

Upas: Chief's Council of Elders

Upa Pawl: Elders Association

Zalen: Priviledged villagers who were exempted from paying paddy due to the chief but have to support him in times of need.

Zawlbuk: Bachelor's dormitory

Zila Parishad: District Level People's Council

Abbreviations

AAP	:	Annual Action Plan
AARDO	:	Afro Asian Rural Development Organisation
AEO	:	Agriculture Extension Officer
AMDP	:	Accelerated Maize Development Programme
ANP	:	Applied Nutrition Programme
ARWSP	:	Accelerated Rural Water Supply Programme
BAC	:	Block Advisory Committee
BADP	:	Border Area Development Programme
BAFFACOS	:	Bamboo Flowering and Famine Combat Scheme
BDC	:	Block Development Committee
BDO	:	Block Development Officer
BPL	:	Below Poverty Line
BRTF	:	Border Road Task Force
CADC	:	Chakma Autonomous District Council
CADP	:	Command Area Development Programme
CDP	:	Community Development Programme
CIRDAP	:	Centre on Integrated Rural Development of Asia and the Pacific
COPP	:	Committee On Plan Projects
CRSP	:	Central Rural Sanitation Programme
CSRE	:	Crash Scheme for Rural Employment
CSS	:	Centrally Sponsored Schemes
DDP	:	Desert Development Programme
DIC	:	District Industries Centre
DESBAPP	:	Development of Sustainable Base for Pig Production
DLMC	:	District Level Monitoring Cell

DLPC : District Level Project Committee
DPAP : Drought Prone Areas Programme
DRDA : District Rural Development Agency
DVMC : District Vigilance and Monitoring Committee
DWCRA : Development of Women and Children in Rural Areas
EAS : Employment Assurance Scheme
EO : Extension Officer
FFWP : Food For Work Programme
GA : Gramin Awaas
GoI : Government of India
GoM : Government of Mizoram
GNP : Gross National Product
HYV : High Yielding Varieties
Ha : Hectares
IAAP : Intensive Agricultural Area Programme
IADP : Intensive Agricultural Development Programme
IAS : Indian Administrative Service
IAY : Indira Awaas Yojana
ICDS : Integrated Child Development Programme
IDDP : Integrated Dairy Development Programme
IEO : Industry Extension Officer
IRDP : Integrated Rural Development Programme
ITDP : Integrated Tribal Development Programme
JRY : Jawahar Rojgar Yojana
IWDP : Integrated Wasteland Development Project
KBIB : Khadi and Village Industries Board
KVIC : Khadi and Village Industries Commission
LAD : Local Administration Department
LADC : Lai Autonomous District Council
MADC : Mara Autonomous District Council
MCS : Mizoram Civil Service
MDMP : Mid-Day Meal Programme
MFAL : Marginal Farmers and Agricultural Labourers
MHIP : Mizoram Hmeichhe Insuihkhawm Pawl
MIP : Mizoram Intodelhna Project
MLA : Member of Legislative Assembly
MNP : Minimum Needs Programme
MUP : Mizo Upa Pawl
MWS : Million Wells Programme

NAEP	:	National Adult Education Programme
NABARD	:	National Bank for Agriculture and Rural Development
NES	:	National Extension Service
NEHU	:	North Eastern Hill University
NFBS	:	National Family Benefit Scheme
NGO	:	Non-Governmental Organisation
NLUP	:	New Land Use Policy
NIRD	:	National Institute of Rural Development
NES	:	National Extension Service
NOAP	:	National Old Age Pension
NREGS	:	National Rural Employment Guarantee Scheme
NSAP	:	National Social Assistance Programme
NREP	:	National Rural Employment Programme
NWDP	:	National Watershed Development Project
OFWM	:	On-Farm Water Management
OPP	:	Oilseed Production Programme
PDS	:	Public Distribution System
PHC	:	Primary Health Centre
PIREP	:	Pilot Intensive Rural Employment Programme
PMGY	:	Pradhan Mantri Gramodaya Yojana
PO	:	Project Officer
PRI	:	Panchayati Raj Institution
PWD	:	Public Works Department
RLEGP	:	Rural Landless Employment Guarantee Programme
SC	:	Schedule Caste
ST	:	Schedule Tribe
SEO	:	Social Education Organiser
SFDA	:	Small Farmers Development Agency
SGSY	:	Swarnajayanti Gram Swarozgar Yojana
SHG	:	Self-Help Group
SITRA	:	Supply of Improved Toolkits to Rural Artisans
SLCC	:	State Level Coordination Committee
SLMC	:	State Level Monitoring Cell
SNP	:	Supplementary Nutrition Programme
SUBACS	:	Sustainable Development of Sugarcane Based Cropping System
TSP	:	Total Sanitation Programme
TRYSEM	:	Training of Rural Youth for Self-Employment

US	:	United States
VC	:	Village Council
VCP	:	Village Council President
VDC	:	Village Development Committee
VEO	:	Veterinary Extension Officer
VLMC	:	Village Level Monitoring Cell
VLW	:	Village Level Worker
VO	:	Voluntary Organisation
WVDP	:	Whole Village Development Programme
WRC	:	Wet Rice Cultivation
WDPSCA	:	Watershed Development Project in Shifting Cultivation Area
YMA	:	Young Mizo Association
YMCA	:	Young Men Christian Association
ZENICS	:	Zoram Electronics Industries Corporation
ZIDCO	:	Zoram Industrial Development Corporation
ZOHANDCO	:	Zoram Handloom and Handicraft Development Corporation
ZP	:	Zila Parishad

1
Introduction

Statement of the Problem

Rural development has specifically been given prime importance in the development plans as 75 per cent of the worlds poor live in rural areas.[1] Any attempt at bringing overall development should lay greater importance on rural development especially in developing countries, which are characterised by high incidence of rural poverty. The increasing height of rural poverty in these countries is a matter of grave concern. Therefore, the primary goal of planning and development strategies in these countries has been directed towards tackling under-development and rural poverty. Bureaucracy occupies an important role in the formulation and implementation of these development plans and programmes even in the new economic order in which a reduced governmental intervention in the economic sector, thus implying a reduced role for the bureaucracy in the process of development is expected. However, at any rate, bureaucracy is a considerable segment of it, an inescapable obligation to inculcate a disposition towards work in the field—more especially in the rural areas and amongst the vulnerable sections of the population.[2] The vital requirement for bureaucracy now is to get away from the sluggishness to give a thorough response to the challenges posed by the new economic order.

The role of state intervention in the overall development of the population in developing countries are indispensable where the challenges of mass poverty, lack of infrastructure, unemployment, ill-health, illiteracy and inequality needs to be dealt with. For this, good governance through e-governance, transparency, democratic decentralisation, accountability, efficiency and productivity and people's participation has now been acknowledged to be the basic requirements of administration in improving the quality of life of the people—especially the rural poor. In India, rural development has been one of the important objectives of planning since independence. The launching of Community Development Programme (CDP) in early fifties and the introduction of the Panchayati Raj Institutions (PRIs) later were the significant measures undertaken by the Government of India towards rural reconstruction.

The implementation of the CDP was characterised by division of the entire country into small manageable 'blocks' and a new bureaucratic model created in the form of 'block level functionaries' consisting of a generalist kingpin of the block—the block development officer with a team of extension officers and village level workers. With the exception of some good results at the preliminary periods, this model failed to discharge multiple rural reconstruction activities and to induce people's participation in the programme as expected. Thus, a Committee on Plan Projects popularly known as Balwantrai Mehta Committee was set up to enquire the working of the community development. The committee recommended the introduction of three-tier system of PRIs to involve people in the development process. Various committees, later on, headed by Ashok Mehta, V.P. Naik, P.B. Patil, G.V.R. Rao, L.N. Singhvi refurbish these institutions which gave necessary momentum to the 73rd Constitutional Amendment Act 1992 which revolutionise the Panchayats. The 73rd Amendment granted the Panchayats constitutional status and entrusted considerable number of functions and responsibilities in ensuring genuine participatory development process at the village level.

With the introduction of PRIs in almost all the states of India, rural development programme is undertaken and implemented by PRIs as well as with the coordination of the block level functionaries. In case of Mizoram, the programme has been implemented by the block functionaries only as Mizoram has not introduced PRIs as local self-government. The State of Mizoram has been exempted from the 73rd Constitutional Amendment due to the existence of traditional local self-government bodies—the Village Councils. As the Village Councils are not as intense as PRIs, there is heavy reliance on grassroots bureaucracy in the overall upliftment of the rural poor and it is, in fact, vital for planning, implementation and to stimulate people's participation in the rural development programme.

In this context, it is important to focus attention on the role of grassroots bureaucracy in rural development in this remote underdeveloped state.

Importance of the Study

In India where about 72 per cent of the population lives in rural areas, the development and progress of the country lies in the development of its villages. Any progress of growth and development that does not fulfil the needs of rural area and its people, especially the poor cannot be claimed as development. Mizoram is an under-developed state. It is highly mountainous with rugged topography, is a primary producing state. Shifting cultivation (*jhum*) has been widely practiced in the state causing soil erosion, damage soil fertility, creates environmental and socio-cultural problem, denudation of forest cover, etc. Agriculture (*jhum*) is the sole occupation but the local agricultural products could substantiate only about 25 per cent[3] of the states requirements despite about as much as 70 per cent of the workers engagement in agricultural activities. The region is at an infantile stage in the field of industry. Whatever industry, it may be called; at present is only small-scale industry, fed by indigenous agricultural produce covering only a small market zones.[4] The situation in respect of allied sector is in no way better. The potential in animal husbandry, a common subsidiary activity, is grossly under utilised and meat, eggs, fish come from outside the state.[5]

In Mizoram, facilities like transport, communication, irrigation, industry, etc. are not adequate. The state depends largely on other states for essential commodities. In spite of the massive efforts of the government to develop the rural area, the success has been minimal. According to the 1990 Survey Report of the Rural Development Department, 52 per cent of people in the state were living below poverty line. It is a paradoxical situation that, more than ever the threats of poverty loom large in the hearts of the working class despite the fast growth in developmental expenditures since 1972.[6] With the existing structure of Mizoram economy, precarious state of agriculture (no fertile, intensive type of crop-land easily amenable), slow growth of alternative employment avenues in rural areas, lack of industries, poor communication facilities, there is low possibility of absorbing the fast expanding labour force. The cultivable land and other traditional rural enterprises have a limited scope for supporting the fast emerging population. This has forced more people to seek their fortunes in the urban areas, which have its own repercussions on the economy.[7]

Inequality in economic status in Mizo society has been very much evident with the emergence of elite rich class. One of the main reasons is unequal distribution of the fruits of development in the state. While launching New Land Use Policy (NLUP) by dissolving the Mizoram Intodelhna Project (MIP), the Chief Minister Lal Thanhawla sounded a warning that if the present trend of widening gap between the rich and the poor is not reversed, there may be discontent amongst the poorer sections leading to social tensions, disharmony and violence to the extent of causing bloodshed in Mizoram.[8]

Under these circumstances, the state is facing with the uphill task of elimination of shifting cultivation (*jhum*) and in achieving self-sufficiency in foodgrain production. Therefore, development strategies of the Government of Mizoram has been mainly towards agricultural development and to protect the land from degradation, to protect burning of forests for jhuming, encouraging permanent cultivation in achieving sustainable development in eco-friendly manner vis-à-vis to find out alternative way of livelihood for the jhumia families. The Government of Mizoram launched various programmes for rural development other than the Centrally Sponsored Schemes like NLUP in 1990-91, revived in 2009-2010 and MIP during 2002-2003, BAFFACOS during 2005-2006, etc. to wean away the jhumia families from shifting cultivation by providing them alternative means of livelihood. Bureaucracy is the focal point of administration, planning, and actual ground implementation of these rural development programmes. The present position of the Village Councils in Mizoram may be compared with the Panchayats of Indian States before the Constitution (73rd Amendment) Act 1992. Socio-economic development is beyond the scope of the Councils due to lack of financial and political power. Although the Councils are being involved in the process of rural development, their role is limited by the fact that the bureaucracy assumes more power and influence. It is bureaucracy that made the actual ground implementation of all the schemes of rural development in the absence of PRIs.

The study of bureaucracy especially at the block level and its role in rural development in Mizoram assumes significance in the above context.

Review of Literature

The present study is concern with the role of bureaucracy at the grassroots level in the rural development in Mizoram where the Panchayati Raj Institutions not introduced. There is enormous trust vested on bureaucracy in the implementation of rural development programmes as the existing local governing institutions are not intense and bureaucracy easily overrides the local democratic bodies in Mizoram. Researches on bureaucracy and rural development in a state where the Panchayati Raj Institutions not introduced are few although there have been numerous studies carried out on the various facets of bureaucracy and rural Development.

R.K. Sapru[9] (2003) in his book '*Development Administration*' suggested that a developing country like India can realise its developmental goals only through its instrument of action, namely, the civil service and there is need of bringing about reforms in the civil service system through better recruitment procedures, sustained training, more rational organisation and improved administration capacities. The state should have a clear developmental programmes for the future not only in terms of goals and objectives in various spheres of socio-economic development and nation-building and policies required to achieve these goals, but also in terms of a civil service system with such organisation, personal and procedures as would help it implement those programmes and policies and enable the state to achieve its developmental goals.

N.R. Inamdar[10] (1992) in his book '*Development Administration in India*' pointed out the need of modifications in the Indian model of development administration and politics in practice. Both political and bureaucratic components have to be more active taking more energetic efforts to reach the development outputs to the marginal and poorer peasants, artisan and labourers.

Debidas M. Muley[11] (1987), in his book '*Rural Development Administration*' suggested realistic plan formulation and the effective implementation of plans depends on sound and viable local government structure, which at the same time needs smaller and larger units to reconcile democratic aspirations a strong executive to carry out development programmes and policies.

In their book '*Village Development in India: A Sociological Approach*' G.R. Madan and Tara Madan[12] (1988), given emphasis on the problem of village development from a sociological point of view in all the major aspects of the problem—economic, technological, social, religious, cultural, political and administrative so as to understand the problem in proper perspective.

S.R. Maheshwari[13] (1985) in his book '*Rural Development in India*', opines that a large amounts of public funds are presently disbursed under the various programme of rural development, leakages and seepages have become noticeable and corruption in rural development administration has become a serious problem today. The media and the opinion leaders in India are, as a rule, notoriously urban oriented both by training and temperament, and happenings in the rural sector are not reported at any great length or discussed.

B.S. Khanna[14] (1991), in his book '*Rural Development in South Asia, India*', opines that block development administration began to be weakened from about the middle of the decade of sixties onwards with the decline of community development programme and rise of separate sectoral programmes of rural development.

A.K. Agarwal[15] (1991), in his article 'Dynamics of Rural Development in Mizoram', stated that administrative infrastructure for programme planning and implementation is weak in the state as it is found in the North East as a whole. Lack of training facilities within the region is to a great extent responsible for poor motivation of grassroots staff.

S.G. Deogaonkar[16] (1980), in his book '*Administration for Rural Development in India*' opines that success and failure of the rural development depended on village level workers at the grass root level and hence selecting the right man and equipping him suitably and sufficiently to do his work was the crux of the problem.

In their book '*Problems in Rural Development*' (1985),

Ramashray Roy, T.M. Vinod Kumar and V.B. Singh[17] gave importance on developing planning process at the block level.

E.D. Setty[18], in his book *'New Approaches to Rural Development'*, (2002), evolved some guidelines for the block staff in assisting the Panchayat Samiti and the Village Panchayats in diagnosing village problems and in developing plans and programmes for village improvement.

Shiv Raj Singh[19] (1989), in his book *'Bureaucracy and Rural Development'* evaluated and made an assessment of the performance of all the bureaucrats at block level including bureaucrats of development departments, peoples participation in Panchayat, IRD Programme at the Pachhad Block and Chopal Block of the districts of Shimla and Sirmour of Himachal Pradesh and opined that block bureaucracy should be committed to rural development. This can be possible in case the block bureaucracy has its social roots in the rural soil.

In his book *'Development Administration in An Indian State Guide Book Evolved for Block Development Officer in Orrisa'* (2002), Dr. Taradatt[20], suggested number of guidelines and duties of the block development officer in relation to Panchayat, relation to block level functionaries.

Kalpana Das[21], in her book, *'Rural Development in Mizoram'* (2004), focusing on the various ramifications of the IRDP administration and suggested to build motivation of the personnel at the cutting edge through a system of continuous appraisal, performance based rewards, and special postings in remote areas and need to build professionalism.

The above studies on bureaucracy and rural development are different from the present study. Because of the absence of Panchayati Raj Institutions and its geographical location where the villages are scattered with different socio-economic structure, the policy recommendations that are applicable to other parts of the country may not necessarily be suitable for the state. It is in this background that an assessment towards block level bureaucracy and their role on rural development has been carried out.

Objectives of the Study

The present study aims to focus mainly on bureaucracy at the block level which is involved in the implementation of rural development programmes in Mizoram. In the absence of Panchayati Raj Institutions, where the existing local self-government system is irrelevant today, grassroots bureaucracy is the key in overall development of rural Mizoram. Accordingly, the specific objectives of the study have been set:

1. To make an assessment on the performance of the grassroots bureaucracy and their role in the execution of rural development programmes.
2. To highlight the implementation of various rural development programmes towards upliftment of the rural poor in Mizoram, its impact and the role of bureaucracy in it.
3. To obtain the perceptions of the people—the beneficiaries and non-beneficiaries of rural development programmes towards the rural bureaucratic functionaries as well as the perceptions of the rural bureaucrats, their difficulties and challenges.
4. To explore the problems and prospects of rural development in the study area and to suggest suitable measures.

Hypothesis

To meet the objectives of the study, the following hypotheses are formulated for empirical verification in the study.

1. The existing rural bureaucracy at the block level has failed to execute the task of rural development to the extent needed.
2. There is lack of motivation of rural bureaucracy to the extent required and belongingness in their department, hence, failed in the task of motivating the village people.
3. The existing local self-government is irrelevant and its role in rural development is insignificant in the absence of Panchayati Raj Institutions.
4. There is very modest impact of rural development programmes initiated in the blocks.

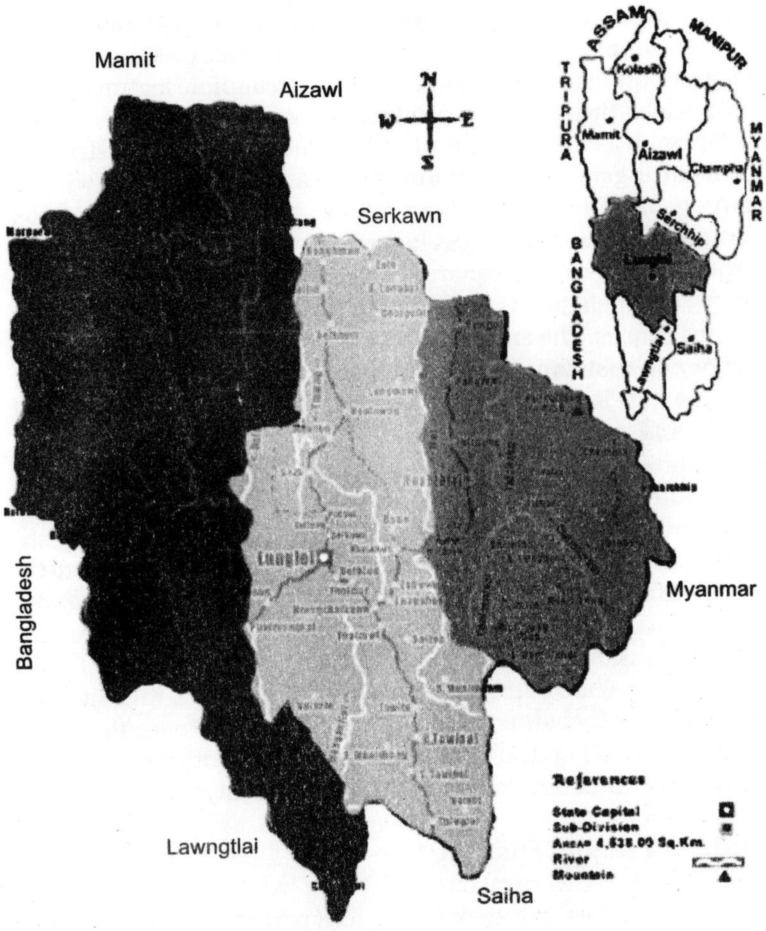

Map 1.1: Mizoram with the Study Area—Lunglei district blocks.

Source: Economics and Statistics Department, Lunglei, 2010.
Red = Lungsen block, Yellow = Lunglei block
Blue = Hnahthial block, Green = Bunghmun block

Study Area

For an in depth study of this nature requires limiting the geographical parameter of the study. This was done taking up four rural development blocks—Lunglei, Lungsen, Hnahthial, Bunghmun rural development blocks in the Lunglei district of Mizoram.[22] A brief description of the physical and socio-economic features of the area in which the study was conducted is given below.[23]

Mizoram located in the northeast corner of India has a strategic significance geographically and politically for it is sandwiched between Myanmar and Bangladesh; and shares a common international boundary of 585 kilometers with these two countries. Its total area is 21,081 square kilometers having a population of 888,573 of which 50.35 per cent rural and 49.65 per cent urban, as per 2001 census. The erstwhile Lushai Hills District became Union Territory on 21st January 1972 and got statehood on 20 February 1987. The state is geographically located between 21.58°N to 24.35°N latitude and 92.15°E to 93.29°E longitude.[24] The state is highly mountainous and has rugged topography with high ranges trending north south direction. Barring few patches of flat land along the valleys and the area bordering the plains of Cachar and Bangladesh, the topography of Mizoram is composed of steep hills and deep gorges.[25] Mizoram is divided into eight districts now (earlier three districts—Aizawl, Lunglei and Chhimtuipui before the reorganisation of administration in late 1990's)—Aizawl, Lunglei, Saiha, Mamit, Kolasib, Champhai, Serchhip, Lawngtlai. The state is inhabited by ten main tribes including the Lusei, the Ralte, the Hmar, the Paite, the Pawi, the Lakher, the Chakma, the Riang and others. There are twenty-three rural development blocks at present.

Profile of Lunglei District[26]

Lunglei district lies on the south-western part of Mizoram situated between 22.30N-23.18N Latitude and 92.15E-93.10E Longitude. The 'South Mizoram' has been used to refer to Lunglei Division which comprises the present three districts of southern Mizoram, namely, Lunglei, Lawngtlai and Saiha. It is bounded on the north by Mamit district, on the east by the district of Aizawl and Saiha on the South by Myanmar and on the west by bordering Bangladesh. The district has international borders of 35 kilometers with Myanmar and 107 kilometers with Bangladesh and the total area of the district is 4,536 square kilometers. It is the largest district of Mizoram in terms of area. The district derives its name from the town of Lunglei which is also the district headquarter. As per the 2001 census, the total population of this district is 1,37,223. The male population is 71,403 and female 65,821. The rural population of the district is 79,2672 and urban 57,956. The density of population per square kilometer is 30 and the literacy is 84.20 per cent. The present Lunglei district has three sub-divisions Lunglei, Hnahthial, and Tlabung and four rural development blocks--Lunglei, Lungsen, Hnahthial and Bunghmun. Lunglei is 235 km (via Hnahthial) and about 165 km. (via Thenzawl) far from Aizwal. Agriculture is the predominant activity in the district. The general condition of rural population is poor.

Profile of Blocks and Villages[27]

(a) Lunglei is one of the biggest rural development blocks in Lunglei district which covers inside and neighbouring villages of Lunglei town. The number of rural population is 20904 with 4227 households. The number of cultivator *(jhum)* is 3282 and 161 wet rice cultivators. The block office is located at Chanmari, in Lunglei town. Dawn (85 households, population of 367) which is 25 kms away from Lunglei town, Thualthu (227 households, population of 588)—31 kms, Tawipui (143 households, population of 620)—40 kms, Mualthuam N (271 households, population of 1253)—70 km and Mamte (100 households, population of 524)—80 km and Thingfal (254 households, population of 1374)—68 kms away, were selected from this block for the present study.

(b) Lungsen is one of the backward blocks in Lunglei District with a rural population of 38814 with 8104 households. The number of cultivator *(jhum)* is 6236 and 912 wet rice cultivators. The block office is located at Lungsen which is 58 km away from Lunglei town. Hmunthar (36 households and population of 177) which is 118 kms away from Lunglei town, Belthei (102 households and population of 429)—42 kms, Lungsen (475 households and population of 2218)—58, Tuichawng (1521 households and population of 2750)—95 km and Rangte (125 households and population of 746)—59 kms, Tipperaghat (155 households and population of 911) 100 kms away, were selected from this block for the present study.

(c) Hnahthial block is situated 60 kms away from Lunglei town. Under this block total number of rural households is 4268 and total population is 23351. The number of cultivator (*jhum*) is 3210 and 210 wet rice cultivators. The block office is located at Hnahthial. Thingsai (452 households with population of 2801) which is 227 kms away from Lunglei town, Leite (177 households and population of 885)—47 kms, Darzo (243 households and population of 1417)—79 kms, Rotlang E (127 households and population of 696)—53 kms away, were selected from this block for the present study.

(d) Bunghmun block is one of the most backward blocks in Mizoram. Under this block total number of rural households is 3657 and total population is 18768. The number of cultivator (*jhum*) is 3297 and 129 wet rice cultivators. The block office is located at Bunghmun which is 140 kms away from Lunglei town. Serte (85 households with population of 450) which is 40 kms away from Lunglei town, Bunghmun (242 households and population of 2019)—140 kms, Belkhai (153 households and population of 773)—167 kms, Dengsur (71 households and population of 402)—56 kms away, were selected from this block for the present study.

The four blocks of the Lunglei district and the sample villages almost shares the same characteristics. Out of the four blocks, Lunglei block, being nearest to the district headquarter is relatively in a better position due to the facilities available. The economic status and the standard of living of the villages which are located nearby block headquarters are also relatively better than those remote villages because of the market accessibility and other facilities like health, education etc. which are available near to them in the towns. Otherwise, the overall economic condition—dependence on agriculture (mostly jhum), communication constraints, market accessibility, scarcity of essential commodities and lack of facilities like irrigation, power supply, etc. are almost the same.

Methodology

The present study requires both primary and secondary data. The primary data has been collected from the fieldwork through questionnaire and interview schedule. Total of 20 villages—10 nearby and 10 remote villages (six villages each from Lunglei and Lungsen block, four villages each from Hnahthial and Bunghmun block) from the block headquarters were selected. A previously prepared schedule was used to acquire information from the respondents of both beneficiaries and non-beneficiaries of rural development schemes. A stratified sampling method was used in selecting individuals. Total of 240 individual (including SHG) members was obtained. Detail interview with block functionaries was done with a previously prepared schedule with total of 19 functionaries selected. A simple tabulation method in terms of percentage was made to analyse the data collected for the study.

The secondary data is mainly collected from published and unpublished works on the related topics, books, articles, journals, souvenir, Potential Linked credit Plan of NABARD, Mizoram, publications of the Government of India and Government of Mizoram, records available in the Directorate of Rural Development Department and concerned block offices, Mizoram and Reports, Acts, Rules and Regulations. In addition, web sources were also an important source of secondary information. In addition, personal interviews and informal discussions were also done with government officials to know their reactions and suggestions related this study.

Chapterisation

The introductory chapter deals with a brief introduction on the topics, importance of the study, objectives of the study, hypothesis, brief introduction of the study area and methodology applied. It also reviewed a number of literatures on the subject, limitations of the study and the organisation of materials.

Chapter 2 deals with conceptual framework of bureaucracy and rural development, approaches and strategies of rural development in India.

Chapter 3 deals with democratic decentralization—the PRIs, District Councils and Village Councils in Mizoram.

Chapter 4 deals with the bureaucracy and rural development in Mizoram.

Chapter 5 deals with the problems and prospects of rural

development in Mizoram.

Chapter 6 deals with the block level bureaucracy and their role, duties and responsibilities in rural development.

Chapter 7 presents an assessment of the block level bureaucracy in Mizoram.

Chapter 8 presents the findings and suggestions.

Limitations of the Study

Researchers generally come across many constraints and barriers in the course of their studies. The present study on the role of bureaucracy and rural development in Mizoram is not a straightforward task where the villages are scattered over a wide geographical area. The following are the main limitations of the study:

1. Almost all the four rural development blocks in the Lunglei district do not maintain proper and uniform record. Moreover, there is shortage of officials in all the blocks. Gathering of adequate information is difficult although the researcher managed to draw together as much information as possible for the purpose of data analysis. Here, the researchers very good command in Mizo language (the researcher a non-Mizo) as well as the supportive and sociable nature of the Mizo people helped.
2. The conclusions drawn from the present study may not be applicable to other states where Panchayati Raj Intuitions are introduced as local self-governing institutions which are involved in the implementation of rural development programmes in coordination with the rural bureaucracy.
3. As the study was carried out mainly in the sample villages of Lunglei district blocks, some of the generalisations may be at variance with other parts of the state. Moreover, all the aspects relating to bureaucracy and rural development in the state cannot be covered in the present study leaving scope for further research in the field. However, genuine efforts have been made to make the study meaningful—which may serve as a highlight for further studies in the field.

Notes and References

1. http://www.worldbank.org, viewed on 27.08.2010
2. Avasthi, Amreshwar, Maheshwari, Shriram (1999): *Public Administration*, Lakshmi Narain Agarwal, New Delhi, p. 316.
3. In reply to the Assembly House Members, Agriculture Minister of Mizoram, H. Liansailova said that the production of rice could substantiate only about 25 per cent of the states requirements (huge decrease in production due to famine (mautam) during 2007-2008 (*Virthli Daily*, Lunglei 25 March 2010: 1)
4. Pachuau, Rintluanga. (1994): *Geography of Mizoram*, R.T. Enterprise, Aizawl, p. 73.
5. Das, Kalpana. (2004): *Rural Development in Mizoram*, Mittal Publications, New Delhi, p. 34.
6. Thangchungnunga, (2003): "Agrarian Change and Social Transformation Among the Mizos" in Prasad, R.N. and Agarwal, A.K. (ed.) *Modernisation of The Mizo Society*, Mittal Publications, New Delhi, p. 143
7. Thansanga, H. (2003): "Poverty and Unemployment in Mizoram" in Prasad, R.N. and A.K. Agarwal (ed.) *Modernisation of Mizo Society op. cit.* p. 215-216.
8. Minute, Matter of Dissolution of MIP and Launching of NLUP, Aizawl 5 February 2010, Dept.of Agriculture, Govt. of Mizoram
9. Sapru, R.K. (2003): *Development Administration*, Sterling Publishers Pvt. Ltd., New Delhi.
10. Inamdar, N.R. (1992): *Development Administration in India*, Rawat Publications, Jaipur, New Delhi.
11. Muley, M. Devida (1987): *Rural Development Administration*, Chugh Publications, Allahabad.
12. Madan, G.R. and Tara Madan (1988): *Village Development In India: A Sociological Approach*, Allied Publishers Private Limited, New Delhi,
13. Maheshwari, S.R. (1985): *Rural Development in India*, Sage Publications, New Delhi.
14. Khanna, B.S. (1991): *Rural Development in South Asia India*, Deep and Deep Publications, New Delhi.
15. Agarwal, A.K., (1991): Dynamics of Rural Development in Mizoram in Samanta, Dr. R.K., (ed.), *Rural Development in North East India—Perspective, Issues and Experiences*, Uppal Publishing House, New Delhi.
16. Deogaonkar, S.G. (1980): *Administration for Rural Development in India*, Concept Publishing Company, New Delhi.
17. Roy, Ramashray, Vinod Kumar, T.M., and Singh, V.B. (1985): *Problems in Rural Development*, Discovery Publishing House, Delhi.

18. Setty, E.D. (2002): *New Approaches to Rural Development*, Anmol Publications Private Limited, New Delhi.
19. Singh, Shiv Raj. (1989) *Bureaucracy and Rural Development*, Mittal Publications, New Delhi.
20. Taradatt, (2002): *Development Administration in An Indian State Guide Book Evolved for Block Development Officer in Orrisa*, Uppal Publishing House, New Delhi.
21. Das, Kalpana (2002): *Rural Development in Mizoram*, Mittal Publications, New Delhi.
22. Field work for the study was carried out during 2003-2005.
23. The detail physical and socio-economic profiles of the rural development blocks of the study area are given in chapter six and the data are hereby updated as far as possible from available sources.
24. Government of Mizoram (2008): Statistical Handbook of Mizoram, Directorate of Economics and Statistics, Aizawl, p. 1.
25. Singh, S.N. (1994): *Mizoram*, Mittal Publications, New Delhi, p. 2.
26. Government of Mizoram (2008): Statistical Handbook of Mizoram, District Research Officers Office, Lunglei, 2007 p. IV-V.
27. Government of Mizoram (2009): The Prospect of Rural Village, Department of Economics and Statistics, Lungei, Mizoram.

2
Bureaucracy and Rural Development

This chapter is divided into three sections. Section-I look at the conceptual framework of bureaucracy. Section-II explores the conceptual aspects of 'rural development'. Section-III outlines the approaches and strategies of rural development in India'. In this section, recommendations of various committees' on Panchayati Raj, 'its organisation and functions' are also briefly summarised.

INTRODUCTION

Most of the Third World countries have been facing gigantic problems of rural poverty, illiteracy, poor health, low agricultural productivity, lack of industrial development, etc. The urgent need is to bring about speedy socio-economic transformation and nation-building through planned development. Therefore, these countries have undertaken various development strategies in the economic and social spheres of life with special emphasis on the development of rural areas. In order to achieve these objectives, states are mainly to depend upon the bureaucratic structure. Obviously, qualitative bureaucracy different from its past colonial bureaucratic structure and attitude is vital. The role that the bureaucracy can play is varied and significant. In fact, it has been recognised as the central point to give direction and dynamism to the pace of nation building, modernisation, growth and development. The success of great number of rural development programmes and socio-economic transformation as a whole largely depends on bureaucracy. Despite the coming out of new public management movement in most countries which sought to slim down the role of bureaucracy, it cannot be completely abolished and its importance in development administration all over the world is still intact, although the experiences in most third world countries shows that bureaucracy has not been able to deliver goods as effectively as the theorists on bureaucracy had expected. Public administration therefore, should undergo structural and attitudinal changes to develop the right type of vision, change-orientedness and administrative skills for the success of developmental programmes.[1] Development administration needs an administrative structure which can meet the developmental requirements of the developing countries.

Bureaucracy: Conceptual Framework

The term 'bureaucracy' may be traced to the French word 'bureau' meaning a writing table or desk. It is usually regarded as a modern phenomenon. Four structural concepts are central to any definition of bureaucracy:[2]

1. A well-defined division of administrative labour among persons and offices.
2. A personnel system with consistent patterns of recruitment and stable linear careers.
3. A hierarchy among offices, such that the authority and status are differentially distributed among actors, and
4. Formal and informal networks that connect organisational actors to one another through flows of information and patterns of cooperation.

While the concept as such existed at least from the early forms of nationhood in ancient times, the word "bureaucracy" itself stems from the word "bureau", used from the early 18th century in Western Europe not just to refer to a writing desk, but to an office, i.e., a workplace, where officials worked. The original French meaning of the word *bureau* was the baize used to cover desks. Thus, bureaucracy simply means 'desk government'. The term bureaucracy came into use shortly before the French Revolution of 1789 and from there rapidly spread to other countries. The Greek suffix-*kratia* or *kratos*—means "power" or "rule". *Encyclopedia Britannica* defines bureaucracy as a professional corps of officials organised in a pyramidal hierarchy and functioning under impersonal, uniform rules and procedures to secure the goals of their organisations. According to *Microsoft Encarta Encyclopedia*, bureaucracy is an administrative system, especially in a government, that divides work into specific categories carried out by special departments of non-elected officials. It is an "integrated hierarchy of specialised offices defined by systematic rules—an impersonal routinised structure wherein legitimised authority rests in the office and not in the person of the incumbent."[3] Bureaucracy is also defined as a systematic organisation of tasks and individuals into a pattern which can most effectively achieve the ends of collective efforts.[4] Laski applied to a system of government, the control of which is so complete in the hands of the officials that their power jeopardises the liberties of the ordinary citizens."[5] Dimock identified bureaucracy with institutions and large scale organisations in society. For him "bureaucracy is the state of society in which institutions overshadow individuals and simple family relationships: stage of development in which division of labour, specialisation, organisation, hierarchy, planning and regimentation of large groups of individuals either by voluntary or involuntary methods, are the order of the day....Bureaucracy is simply institutionalism written large. It is not some foreign substance which has been infused into the life—blood of an institution; it is merely the accentuation of characteristics found in all. It is a matter of degree, of the combination of components, and of the relative emphasis given to them"[6] Pfiffner and Presthus defined bureaucracy as "the system of authority, men, offices and methods that the government uses to carry out its programmes.[7] It may be used in the sense of a type of administrative organisation, or government by civil servants for its aggrandisement, or just plain professional civil service.[8] Thus, the term bureaucracy may be defined as a professional body technically skilled, recruited rather than elected and organised in a hierarchical way under different departments to serve the people under certain rules and regulations.

Max Weber on Bureaucracy [9]

It was Max Weber (1864-1920), the German sociologist, who gave the modern concept of bureaucracy in a systematic manner. His theories on legitimacy and domination have shaped the basis for a number of further studies. His writing on bureaucracy is more important than the sum total of the contributions of countless scholars.[10] He is well-known for his study of bureaucratisation of society; many aspects of modern public administration go back to him; a classic, hierarchically organised civil service of the continental type is—if perhaps mistakenly—called Weberian civil service. However, "bureaucracy" was an English word before Weber; the Oxford English Dictionary cites usage in several different years between 1818 and 1860, prior to Weber's birth in 1864.

Weber described the ideal type bureaucracy in positive terms, considering it to be a more rational and efficient form of organization than the alternatives that preceded it, which he characterized as *charismatic domination* and *traditional domination*. According to his terminology, bureaucracy is part of *legal domination*. He classified authority on the basis of its claim to legitimacy, because on that would depend largely the type of obedience, the kind of administrative staff suitable to it, and the ways of exercising authority. The classification is threefold.[11]

Traditional Authority: Legitimated by time by its existence in the past. It rests on an established belief in the sanctity of memorial traditions and the legitimacy of the status of those exercising authority under them.

Charismatic Authority: Legitimated by outstanding personal leadership characteristics of the bearer. It rests on devolution of the specific and exceptional sanctity, heroism or exemplary character of an individual person and of the normative order ordinated by him.

Legal Rational Authority: Legitimated by being in accordance with formally correct rules and by the right of those in authority to issue commands under such rules. It rests on a belief in the legality of these rules.

In designing the legal-rational authority system, Weber devised the following structural propositions:[12]

1. Official tasks are organised on a continuous, regulated basis.
2. These tasks are subdivided into functionally distinct spheres, each furnished with the requisite authority and sanctions.
3. Offices are arranged hierarchically, the rights of control and complaint between them being specified.
4. Official work is conducted according to the rules which are neither necessary.
5. The resources of the organisation are quite distinct from those of the members as private individuals.
6. The holder of an office cannot appropriate the office.
7. Administration is based on written documents or files. This tends to make the office the hub of the modern organisation.
8. Legal authority systems can take many forms, but are seen at their purest in a bureaucratic administrative staff.

The above principles of authority informed the organisation of the bureaucratic administrative staff in Weber's view. Following this line of thought, the defining characteristics of the bureaucracy in its most rational form were identified as follows:

1. The administrative staff members are engaged in the discharge of only the impersonal duties of their offices; they are personally free.
2. There is a clear hierarchy of offices.
3. The functions of the offices are clearly specified.
4. Officials are appointed on the basis of a contract.
5. They are selected on the basis of professional qualifications, ideally substantiated by a diploma gained through competitive examination.
6. They have a money salary, and usually pension rights. The salary is graded according to position in the hierarchy. The official can always leave the post, and under certain circumstances it may also be terminated.
7. The official's post is his sole or major occupation.
8. There is a career structure, and promotion is possible either by seniority or merit, or according to the judgement of superiors.
9. The official may appropriate neither the post nor the resources that go with it.
10. He is subject to a unified control and disciplinary system.

Criticism of Weber's Bureaucracy

Weberian model of bureaucracy has evoked much criticism. Competences can be unclear and used contrary to the spirit of the law; sometimes a decision itself may be considered more important than its effect. Nepotism, corruption, political infighting and other degenerations can counter the rule of impersonality and can create a recruitment and promotion system not based on meritocracy but rather on oligarchy.

Even a non-degenerated bureaucracy can be affected by common problems:

- Over specialisation, making individual officials not aware of larger consequences of their actions;
- Rigidity and inertia of procedures, making decision-making slow or even impossible when facing some unusual case, and similarly delaying change, evolution and adaptation of old procedures to new circumstances;
- A phenomenon of group thinking-zealotry, loyalty and lack of critical thinking regarding the organisation which is perfect and always correct by definition, making the organisation unable to change and realise its own mistakes and limitations;
- Disregard for dissenting opinions, even when such views suit the available data better than the opinion of the majority;
- As bureaucracy creates more and more rules and procedures, their complexity rises and coordination diminishes, facilitating creation of contradictory and recursive rules, as described by the saying "the bureaucracy is expanding to meet the needs of the expanding bureaucracy"; and
- Not allowing people to use common sense, as everything must be as is written by the law.

Robert K. Merton[13], who is among the first sociologists to emphasise systematically dysfunctional aspects of bureaucracy, redtapism and inefficiency, pointed out that conformity can be detrimental because it reduces flexibility. Rules and regulations become so emphasised that they take on a symbolic meaning of their own. The rules become more important than the ends that they were designed to serve, the result being goal displacement and loss of organisational effectiveness. Occasionally you will see this phenomenon in large retail clothing stores. Rules about keeping shelves fully stocked and neat, instituted to increase sales, can be followed so compulsively by the sales personal that customers are ignored. Weberian model of bureaucracy is opposed to democracy. Weber recognised that bureaucracy concentrates power in the hands of those who are in charge of bureaucratic machinery and that such a concentration of power is against the basic premises of democracy.[14]

The features like hierarchy, rules, etc. which Weber incorporated into his model of bureaucracy, may not really make for maximum effectiveness. They may equally make for strain, ineffectiveness, avoidance of responsibility, compulsive obsession with rules, ritualism replacing organisational rules, etc.[15] The bureaucratic form of organisation has been quite useful at a certain point of time in history. But its capacity for adaptation to change is, however, rather low. In the developing countries where the speedy change is needed to bring about socio-economic transformation, bureaucracy is a misfit.[16] Weberian model of bureaucracy has not been found to respond adequately to the task of socio-economic transformation in the developing countries. These tasks require quick changes whereas the capacity of the Weberian model for adaptation to change is rather slow.[17] The rule-bond bureaucratic system in a developing country is thus incompatible with the many-faceted and complex tasks of socio-economic development. Organisational rationality and systemic rationality will be at loggerheads in a situation of speedy social reconstruction. Most post-colonial societies are faced with this dilemma, and any attempt to innovate new modes of administration is often frustrated by bureaucratic dominance.[18] Weber does not take notice of the pattern of interaction of bureaucracy with its environment—social, cultural, economic, and political. In recent times, writers like F.W. Riggs have drawn attention to the continuing interaction between public bureaucracy and the environment within which it functions. Since bureaucracy has been greatly influenced by its environment, one cannot understand its real nature without understanding its relationship with ecology. Moreover, bureaucracy is criticised as an essentially self-seeking institution. It develops the tendency to become an interest group itself and places its own at the centre of things. When its own objectives displace the goals of administration, bureaucracy subverts the intended purposes of a government agency and its offices as well as the essential public aspirations.[19] The developing countries like India had inherited a colonial bureaucracy which is characterised by centralisation of authority, hierarchical, generalist administrators which is elitist and authoritarian in nature. Bureaucracy with such characteristics and the rational legal organisation prescribed by Max Weber cannot be effective in playing a role in multi-development process.

In India, the British legacy was totally accepted at the time of freedom, a generalist higher civil service, not used to any tasks of nation-building, trained in the traditions of law and order machinery based on fear and awe, and without any institutionalised system of accountability to the people. It was an irresponsible, unresponsive, autocratic, bureaucratic structure which operated in the context of a poor, backward economy.[20] It has been argued that the administrators of the post-independence India were as elitist and west-oriented as their counterparts during colonial rule. Many of them continued to be alienated from the poor sections of the community and did not possess requisite behavioural traits to administer the developmental tasks initiated by government.[21] The present bureaucratic structure in India has also been criticised for being highly urban oriented, came from the middle and upper strata of society, unable to adjust to the needs of rural areas where majority of the people live. Today bureaucracy of India needs to devote its energies and time to the tasks of planning and implementation of plans and programmes, mobilisation of resources towards sustainable rural development. A developing state like India can realise its developmental goals only through its instrument of action, namely, the civil service. The role of the civil service in development fields such as health, education, agriculture and industrial promotion should enjoy greater priority and regard than those in the traditional order maintenance fields such as collection of revenues, maintenance of internal security and ceremonious activities of the state.[22] For this, one thing that requires vigorous effort is how to ensure the accountability of the administrative system.[23]

RURAL DEVELOPMENT: A BRIEF CONCEPTUAL FRAMEWORK

Before we seek to analyse the concept of rural development, it is imperative to make an attempt to explore the two terms of which this phrase is composed: 'rural' and 'development'.

"Rural" Defined

International Encyclopedia of the Social Sciences defines the term "rural" to 'the area(s) whereby people are usually engaged in 'field activities', involving production of food, fiber, ores and raw materials'.[24]

Encyclopedia Britannica states: "rural society is a low ratio of inhabitants to open land and in which the most important economic activities are the production of foodstuffs, fibres, and raw materials".[25]

Wikipedia English—The Free Encyclopedia states: Rural areas (also referred to as "the country", countryside) are sparsely settled places away from the influence of large cities. Such areas are distinct from more intensively settled urban and sub-urban areas; the inhabitants live in villages, hamlets, on farms and in other isolated houses.[26]

Webster's Online Dictionary defines the term "rural" as "that which is pertaining to the country, as distinguished from a city or town, suiting the country or resembling it; as rural scenes; a rural prospect; a rural situation, an economy that is basically rural." It adds, rural areas can have an agricultural character, though many rural areas are characterised by an economy based on logging, mining, petroleum and natural gas exploration, wind or solar power or tourism. Lifestyles in rural areas are different from those in urban areas depending on the area, mainly because limited services, especially public services, are available. Governmental services like police, schools, fire stations, and libraries are generally available, but may be limited in scope, or unavailable in remote communities. Utilities like water, sewerage, street lighting, and public waste management are generally present in the larger settlements. Public transport is usually limited or absent and many people use their own vehicles. If this is impractical, they may walk or ride an animal such as a horse, donkey, or camel depending on where they live. Establishing and maintaining telecommunications and internet access in rural areas are often more difficult than urban areas, due to the greater distance that requires coverage.[27]

According to Official US Census Bureau definitions, rural areas comprise open country and settlements with fewer than 2,500 residents. Urban areas comprise larger places and densely settled areas around them. Urban areas do not necessarily follow municipal boundaries. They are essentially densely settled territory as it might appear from the air. Most counties, whether metropolitan or non-metropolitan, contain a combination of urban and rural populations. Rural areas consist of all territory located outside of urbanized areas and urban clusters.[28]

Thus, rural is dissimilar from urban. It includes shelter, territory not included within an urban area and population with a distinct social environment, mostly depends on primary production.

"Development" Defined

Encyclopedia Britannica states: "development as an act, process, or result of developing, the state of being developed".[29] Webster's Online Dictionary defines the term 'development' the act of developing or disclosing that which is unknown; a gradual unfolding process by which anything is developed. It also adds development as a plan or method, or an image upon a photographic plate; gradual advancement or growth through a series of progressive changes; also, the result of developing, or a developed state.[30] Longman's Dictionary of Contemporary English defines 'development' as growth, the process of gradually becoming bigger, better, stronger or more advanced. In economic activity, it adds, development as the process of increasing business, trade and industrial activity.[31] Wikipedia English—The Free Encyclopedia states: Development is "improvement in a country's economic and social conditions". It refers to improvements in ways of managing an area's natural and human resources in order to create wealth and improve people's lives. This definition is based on the more obvious distinctions in living standards between developed and less developed countries.[32] According to R.K. Sapru, "Development in the ultimate analysis is about improving the well-being of the people, which is often measured in terms of providing facilities and services that could give them a chance for a better life." Sapru also adds that raising standards of living, improving education and health and opening out new and equal opportunities for a richer and varied life are all essential components of development.[33] Thus, development is a multi-faceted progression of economic growth with distributive justice, social well-being that includes health, education, housing and equality of opportunities in the process of decision-making. The essence of development is to remove poverty, concentration of wealth, unemployment, illiteracy, social injustice, malnutrition and to build scientific technology in providing wide range of goods and services creating an environment where human beings lead an enhanced way of life.

Concept of Rural Development

Rural development in general is used to denote the actions and initiatives taken to improve the standard of living in non-urban neighbourhoods, countryside, and remote villages. These communities can be exemplified with a low ratio of inhabitants to open space. Agricultural activities may be prominent in this case whereas economic activities would relate to the primary sector, production of foodstuffs and raw materials.[34] World Bank defines rural development as "the strategy designed to improve the economic and social life of the specific group of people—the rural poor. It involves extending the benefits of development to the poorest among those who seek a livelihood in rural areas—the group includes small scale farmers, tenants and landless."[35]

Robert Chamber[36] incorporated some alterations in the definition of World Bank and defined rural development as "a strategy to enable a specific group of people, poor rural women and men, to gain for themselves and their children more of what they want and need. It involves helping the poorest among those who seek a livelihood in the rural areas to demand and control more of the benefits of development. The group includes small-scale farmers, tenants, and the landless". Copp[37] has defined rural development as a process through collective efforts, aimed at improving the well being and self-realisation of people living outside the urbanised areas. He further contends that the ultimate target of rural development is people and not infrastructure and according to him one of the objectives of rural development should be to "widen people's ranges of choices". According to Ensminger,[38] "Rural development seeks to involve a process of transformation from traditionally oriented rural cultural towards an acceptance and reliance on science and technology". Lele[39] defines it as "an improvement in the living standard of the masses of low income population residing in rural areas and making the process of self-sustaining". Katar Singh[40] defines rural development as "a process leading to sustainable improvement in the quality of life of rural people, especially the poor". Andrew Shepherd[41] defines rural development as "the set of activities and actions of diverse actors—individuals, organisations, groups—which taken together, lead to progress in rural areas". He gives importance on people's initiative and their collective action as the key to success. Patel[42] gave importance on every aspect of human development and defines rural development as "integrated development of area and the people through optimum development and utilisation (and conservation where necessary) of local resources—physical, biological and human and by bringing about necessary institutional, structural and attitudinal changes by delivery of a package of services to encompass not only the economic field i.e. agricultural, allied activities, rural industries, but also establishment of required social infrastructure and services in the area of health and nutrition, sanitation, housing, drinking water, literacy, with ultimate objective of improve quality of life of 'rural poor' and the rural weak". Thus, rural development means to the process of improving living conditions, providing minimum needs, increasing productivity and employment opportunities and developing potential of rural resources through integration of spatial, functional and temporal aspects".[43]

In the light of these definitions and the meaning of the term 'rural' and the 'development' as above, we can define rural development as a strategy to improve the socio-economic, cultural and political conditions of the rural people particularly the poor and the area. The development includes fuller utilisation of physical and human resources to raise the standard of living. It also implies involvement of voluntary organisations, rural development functionaries and institutions and strategic interventions to help the rural community to enhance sustained increases in production, productivity and employment generation, communication, education and health, field activities and equity in the distribution of the fruits of development to bring about a positive and constructive change in their attitude and psychic levels of rural people.

The broadly shared view of the definitions above on rural development is to reduce poverty by sustained increase of production, improve of the living standard, ensure equality of opportunities and to involve rural people in planning and development through decentralisation of power. The World Bank approach to rural development now is multi-sectoral and focused on improving the well-being of rural poor by building their productive social and environmental assets.[44]

The goals pursued by European Union for rural development include:

- modernising farms;
- producing safe, quality products;
- ensuring fair and stable incomes for farmers;
- meeting environmental challenges;
- fostering supplementary or alternative job-creating activities, in a bid to halt the drift from the country and to strengthen the economic and social fabric of rural areas; and
- improving living and working conditions and equal opportunities.

RURAL DEVELOPMENT IN INDIA: APPROACHES AND STRATEGIES

Early Experiments

Rural development has a long history in India. The perception of uplift at securing synchronised development of rural life, as a whole owes its origin to a period long before independence. Mahatma Gandhi had realised that political freedom alone will not be of advantage unless the rural masses had felt that they can improve their lot by their own efforts and can shape their destiny they like. Therefore, his constructive programme covered khadi and village industries, basic and adult education, removal of untouchability, rural sanitation and health.[45] Similarly, Rabindranath Tagore started his first experiment in rural reconstruction (in 1908) at

Sailadaha (Bangladesh), a village in his estate and at Patisar Rajashahi District. In these two earlier experiments, the initiative was from the poet and the villagers only obeyed or agreed to his suggestion. Tagore was not satisfied within his earlier attempts and wanted to make a more intensive and comprehensive experiment in rural reconstruction. Therefore, in 1921, he started an Institute of Rural Reconstruction at Sriniketan (Birbhum District) with the help of Mr. and Mrs. L.K. Elmhirst.[46] Tagore's interest was in economic, educational and aesthetic development of village people. He believed in both self-help and mutual help and recognised the need for a change in the outlook of rural people as a precondition for improvement. Gandhi too gave importance on the role of people themselves in any constructive programme through his idea of '*Gram Swaraj*' which emphasised self-rule, equity and self-sufficiency.[47] Sir V.T. Krishnamchari, the then Prime Minister of erstwhile princely state of Baroda was the live wire behind the Baroda rural development programme. The Gurgaon experiment under F.L. Brayne (Deputy Commissioner under the British Government in India) emphasised agriculture development, sanitation, education and cooperation. While Gandhiji propagated *Sarvodaya*, non-violence, dignity of labour, the Firka Development Scheme of Madras made headway in attaining Gandhian idea of *Village Swaraj*.[48] At this time, another extremity of India—Spencer Hatch of Young Men's Christian Association was doing similar work at Marthandam in South India. As a true Christian he dedicated himself 'in the service of God through service of man'.[49]

As early as 1928, the Royal Commission on Agriculture stressed that no lasting improvement in rural life is possible if its different aspects are treated in isolation.[50] In broader sense, even the passing of the Indian Co-operative Societies Act in 1904 can be taken as a rural development measure. Legislation regarding tenancy rights and rents, consolidation of land holdings, regulation of money lending and marketing of agriculture products can as well be stated as rural development measures.[51] Attention to India's villages becomes more or less organised and systematic with the enforcement of the Government of India Act 1919 and 1921. It placed the nation-making activities including rural development under the popularly elected ministers in the provinces. Rural development from now onwards became an important concern of the nation even though it did not occupy that high priority in the colonial administration.[52]

Post-Independence Experiments

At the time of independence, India was primarily an agrarian economy and majority of the population resides in rural areas, and interference of the government in rural development was considered vital. Therefore, rural development has been one of the central objectives of planning in India since independence. In fact, successive Five-Year Plans has been focusing largely on development of agriculture and allied activities to improve the living conditions of the rural population. Extensive measures were undertaken as strategies for rural development on a nation-wide basis. The Community Development Programme initiated in 1952, National Extension Service in 1953 and the setting up of the Panchayati Raj Institutions later were the significant measures undertaken with the objective of coordinated rural development by the Government of India. The First Five Year Plan[53] gave recognition to this approach in the following words, "Community development is the method and the rural extension, the agency through which the Five Year Plan seeks to initiate a process of transformation of the social and economic life of the villages".

The Community Development Programme

The Community Development Programme (CDP) was the first major rural development programme initiated after independence. It was launched to synchronise the birth anniversary of Mahatma Gandhi which was inaugurated on 2nd October, 1952 by Jawaharlal Nehru at Alipur. "The work that we are starting today not only in Alipur but also in many parts of India is of supreme importance, not merely an occasion for pomp and pageantry. You have to work to run your homes. The affairs of the country are managed by work and not idle talk".[54] It was variously described as the Magna Charta of hope, happiness for two-thirds of India's population, the testament of emancipation, the declaration of war on poverty, ignorance, squalor and disease under which million have been groaning. It was remarkable because it was a conscious effort to bring about an all-round development in living standard of millions of rural people. The main objective is to take development to villages through fast increase in agricultural produce and material and human resources in rural areas, to raise the standard of living and to generate employment opportunities, to bring the villagers in the mainstream with their active participation and effort. Hence, "the purpose of the community development project shall be to serve as a pilot in the establishment, for men, women and children, covered by the project area of the right to live, food—the principal item in the wherewithal's for this purpose receiving the primary emphasis in the initial stages of the programme".[55] It may be noted that the aim of the CDP was not merely to provide ample food, clothing, shelter, health and sanitation facilities but also to bring about a change in the outlook of the village people.

Initially, the CDP covered 55 Community Projects, in 15 Districts comprising 27,388 villages having a population of 16.17 millions. The development programmes launched under CDP were development of agriculture and allied activities with modern technology, rural industries and communication, establishment of agriculture credit societies, schools, hospitals, etc. It was meant to be a pilot scheme in order to see how the people reacted to the programme. Each project area was divided into three development blocks. Each block comprised of a population of 60,000 to 70,000 and each blocks was divided into groups of 5-10 villages. A project was expected to be over in three years. The period of the project was divided into five stages of work. The first stage was 'conception stage' of three months duration. This was intended for selection of area, survey and planning. The second stage was 'initiation stage' spread over six months in which arrangement for housing of personnel, establishment of communication within the project area and collection of required material were made. During the 18 months of 'operation stage', approved activities were taken up. The fourth stage was 'consolidation stage' lasting six months and the last stage was 'finalisation stage' of three months meant for finishing touches.[56]

National Extension Service

The experience gained in the CDP projects and the huge interest involved by people stressed the need for a rapid extension of the programme. Hence, the Government of India launched National

Extension Service (NES) on 2nd October 1953 with a lesser number of personnel and minimum financial provision, which eventually cover the entire country by around 5,000 community development blocks. "The service was intended to give scientific and technical help to the village people so that they could improve their lives. While the stress on agricultural schemes remained, the work programme in National Extension Service blocks was less than in the Community Development Blocks...the two programmes were, however, complementary".[57] The main function of the NES was to make the people understand what change or innovation will benefit them, why it will benefit them and how it can be introduced. It is for the community to participate in all the activities which will lead to such change of innovation.[58] The CDP and NES had a uniform unit of operation known as a development block. From among NES blocks, selection was made periodically for intensive development work under the CDP and such blocks were called CD blocks. Subsequently, the distinction between NES blocks and CD blocks was removed and with effect from April 1, 1958 all NES blocks became CD blocks.

Special Multipurpose Tribal Blocks

To cover the areas of tribal concentration known as Special Multipurpose Tribal Blocks were also initiated in 1956 by the Ministry of Home Affairs, Government of India in accordance with the principle of giving particular attention to hitherto neglected areas and populations in the country, as laid down in Article 46 and 275 of the Constitution.[59] The object was to make the programme of development more intensive in character than that undertaken in the normal CD blocks.[60] Forty-three Special Multipurpose Tribal Blocks were started and the average coverage for each block works out at 182 villages each with a population of 39,193 spread over an area of 547,45 square miles.[61]

Organisation of the Community Development Programme[62]

The administration of the CDP was entrusted to a newly created agency called the Community Projects Administration located in the Planning Commission. In September 1956, this agency was raised to the status of a separate independent Ministry of Community Development. This Ministry was merged into the Ministry of Food and Agriculture in January 1966. In October 1974, the Department of Rural Development came into existence as a part of Ministry of Food and Agriculture. On 18th August 1979, the Department of Rural Development was elevated to the status of a new Ministry of Rural Reconstruction. That Ministry was renamed as Ministry of Rural Development on 23rd January 1982. In January 1985, the Ministry of Rural Development was again converted into a Department under the Ministry of Agriculture and Rural Development which was later rechristened as Ministry of Agriculture in September 1985. On July 5, 1991 the Department was upgraded as Ministry of Rural Development. Another Department viz. Department of Wasteland Development was created under this Ministry on 2nd July 1992. In March 1995, the Ministry was renamed as the Ministry of Rural Areas and Employment with three departments namely Department of Rural Employment and Poverty Alleviation, Rural Development and Wasteland Development. Again, in 1999 Ministry of Rural Areas and Employment was renamed as Ministry of Rural Development. This Ministry is a nodal department for the two international organizations viz., the Centre on Integrated Rural Development of Asia and the Pacific (CIRDAP) and the Afro-Asian Rural Development Organisation (AARDO).

The Ministry consists of the following three Departments:

1. Department of Rural Development
2. Department of Land Resources
3. Department of Drinking Water Supply

The Department of Rural Development implements schemes for generation of self-employment and wage employment, provision of housing and minor irrigation assets to rural poor, social assistance to the destitute and rural roads. Apart from this, the department provides the support services and other quality inputs such as assistance for strengthening of District Rural Development Agency (DRDA) administration, Panchayati Raj Institutions, training and research, human resource development, development of voluntary action, etc. for the proper implementation of the programmes. The major programmes of the Department of Rural Development are

Pradhan Mantri Gram Sadak Yojana, (PMGSY), Rural Housing, Sampoorna Gramin Rozgar Yojana (SGRY) and Swaranjayanti Gram Swarozgar Yojana (SGSY).

Department of Land Resources implements schemes to increase the bio-mass production by developing wastelands in the country. Department also provides the support services and other quality inputs such as land reforms, betterment of revenue system and land records. It also undertakes development of desert areas and drought prone areas in the country. The major programmes of the Department of Land Resources are Drought Prone Area Programme (DPAP) The Desert Development Programme (DDP) the Integrated Wasteland Development Programme (IWDP) and Land Reforms (LR). These aim at increasing the soil and moisture conservation and productivity of the wasteland of the degraded lands thereby increase the income of the people.

The provision of Drinking Water Supply and extension of sanitation facilities to the rural poor are the main components of the activities of the Department of Drinking Water Supply. The major programmes of the Drinking Water Supply Department are The *Swajaldhara*, the Accelerated Rural Water Supply Programme (ARWSP) and the Total Sanitation Programme (TSP).

State Level Organisation

Implementation of the rural development programme is the responsibility of the State governments. Generally, a Development Commissioner is in-charge of the CDP in every state. Some states have set up a body known as the State Development Committee consisting of the Chief Minister as the Chairman, the Ministers for Development Departments as members and the Development Commissioner as the secretary.

District and Block Level Organisation

At the district level, Zila Parishad is responsible for the coordination and implementation of the programme. At the block level, the Panchayat Samiti is responsible for the programme. The administrative personnel, consisting of a block development officer and eight extension officers who are experts in different fields such as agriculture, co-operation and animal husbandry, work under the direction of the Samiti. At the village level, while the Panchayat is in overall control of the programme helped by associate organisations, the Village Level Worker acts as a multi-purpose extension agent having about ten villages in his charge. However, grassroots bureaucracy failed to bring rural people's participation within the scope of development and implementation of the community development project. The objective of motivating, self-reliance and participation of the rural people could not be achieved as was expected. It was mainly due to the problems of co-ordination, lack of motivation of the rural bureaucracy and administrative weaknesses. It was also felt that unless the people were actively associated with the formulation and implementation of the CDP, it could not be a success and its main objectives could not be fulfilled. Even Jawaharlal Nehru who was enthusiastic about the programme in the initial years of community development observed that the programme has lost its clan, had faded away and become a pale shadow of its framers self.[63] Therefore, a study team on CDP and NES, headed by Balwant Rai Mehta, was appointed in 1957 to investigate the working of the CDP which recommended the establishment of Panchayati Raj Institutions.

IADP and IAAP

During the Third Five Year Plan (1961-66), greater emphasis was placed on agricultural production and introduction of scientific agricultural practices. The unexpected decrease in foodgrain production in 1960's led the policy shift from community development to a special focus on agriculture. The introduction of Intensive Agricultural Development Programme (IADP) and Intensive Agricultural Area Programme (IAAP) were significant approaches towards high investments in agricultural production and modern technological inputs and yield. These two programmes were mainly operated within the limitations set by the existing crop varieties which had a relatively low response to fertilizers. A major breakthrough was achieved with the introduction of the High Yielding Varieties (HYV). The Fourth Plan (1969-74) evolved a new agricultural strategy which focused on combining HYV seeds with a package of complementary inputs and concentrating these in selected areas with assured water. The strategy paid rich dividends in bringing large areas under HYV. However, the gain of increased production was primarily derived by large and progressive farmers.[64]

Anti-poverty Programmes

During 1951-60 efforts were made to create infrastructure that would facilitate increased agricultural production while during 1961-70 emphasis was shifted to a more intense development of agriculture. The Government of India felt the necessity of various ameliorative measures to avoid the socially volatile situation in the countryside. Accordingly in the 1970s and 1980s onwards, several programmes were designed and put into operation. The following deserves to be mentioned:[65]

(i) Area-specific programmes such as Command Area Development Programme (CADP), Desert Development Programme (DDP), Drought Prone Area Programme (DPAP), Integrated Area Development Programme (IADP), Whole Village Development Programme (WVDP), etc.

(ii) Target group-specific programmes like the Antyodaya, Integrated Rural Development Programme (IRDP), Integrated Tribal Development Programme (ITDP), Small Farmers Development Agency (SFDA), Marginal Farmers and Agricultural Labourers Development Agency (MFALDA), etc. The SFDA and MFAL schemes were later merged with the IRDP.

(iii) Employment programmes such as Crash Scheme for Rural Employment (CSRE), Food for Works Programme (FFWP), National Rural Employment Programme (NREP), Pilot Intensive Rural Employment Programme (PIREP), Training for Rural Youth for Self-Employment (TRYSEM), Rural Landless Employment Guarantee Programme (RLEGP), etc. The NREP and RLEGP were merged in April 1989 with the Jawahar Rozgar Yojana (JRY) which was meant to generate meaningful employment opportunities for unemployed and underemployed in rural areas.

(iv) Social welfare programmes such as Applied Nutrition Programme (ANP), Integrated Child Development Service Project (ICDSP), Mahila Mandals, Minimum Needs

Programme (MNP), National Adult Education Programme (NAEP), etc.

The rationale of the approaches was that all the aspects of rural life are inextricably interlinked with each other. Thus, agricultural development is not possible without spread of education and improved standards of health of the rural people.[66] The aim was to raise the standard of living, promoting social welfare, social justice, a cooperative way of life, community cohesion and building up the democratic organisations and institutions of the people. The problems as a whole and to converge on the totality of human development, destination of community development was, therefore, man.[67]

The Integrated Rural Development Approach (IRDP) which was extended to all development blocks in India, out of the above mentioned programmes, regarded by many as new deal of anti-poverty programme initiated to meet the deficiencies of earlier programmes. This approach stands for the development of the rural society in all its facets—social, economic, institutional and administrative. This new approach stands for 'integrated performance accomplishment of all the objectives stipulated'.[68] The IRDP emphasised the family rather than individual approach for identifying beneficiaries. It aims at lifting the beneficiary families above the poverty line by providing them with financial assistance (partly by way of loan and party by way of subsidy) to enable them to acquire productive and income-generating assets.[69] The main purpose of the strategy was to optimise the utilisation of local resources with a view to maximising production and employment. The focus of the strategy was on large-scale poverty elimination, lifting the poorest among the poor families in the rural areas above the poverty line on a lasting basis by providing them with productive assets and employment opportunities.

Beside these rural development approaches, a large number of other programmes comprise rural development strategies such as Supplementary Nutrition Programme (SNP), Midday Meal Programme (MDM), Dias Training Programme, National Family Welfare Programme, Leprosy Control Programme, National Social Assistance Programme such as National Old Age Pension Scheme (NOAPS), National Family Benefit Scheme, Rural Water Supply and Sanitation Programmes like the Central Sanitation Programme

(CRSP), Rajiv Gandhi National Drinking Water Mission (RGNDWM), etc.

During 1990 onwards creation of rural economic infrastructure and employment generation and housing were given prime importance.[70] These are Pradhan Mantri Gram Sadak Yojana (PMGSY), Rural Housing with two schemes—Indira Awaas Yojana (IAY) and Pradhan Mantri Gramodaya Yojana: Gramin Awaas (PMGY: GA), Rural Water Supply Programme (RWSP), Central Rural Sanitation Programme (CRSP), Jawahar Gram Samridhi Yojana (JGSY), National Social Assistance Programme (NSAP), National Family Benefit Scheme (NFBS), Annapurna, the Food for Work Programme, Employment Assurance Scheme (EAS), Swarnjayanti Gram Swarojgar Yojana (SGSY), Integrated Wasteland Development Programme (IWDP) and Drought Prone Areas Programme (DPAP) and Desert Development Programme (DDP) as a strategy to bring all round development of village infrastructure and elimination of poverty in the rural areas.

Recent Strategies of Rural Development in India

National Rural Employment Guarantee Act (NREGA): Wage employment programmes form an important part of the anti-poverty approach aimed at providing employment opportunities to rural poor. Therefore, the Government of India introduced a significant programme—the National Rural Employment Guarantee Act (NREGA), (now renamed as Mahatma Gandhi National Rural Employment Guarantee Act) enacted by legislation on August 25, 2005 and launched on February 2, 2006. It aims at enhancing the livelihood security of people in rural areas and provides a legal guarantee for one hundred days of employment in every financial year to adult members of any rural household willing to do public work-related unskilled manual work at the statutory minimum wage of Rs. 100 per day. This act was also introduced with an aim of improving the purchasing power of the rural people, primarily semi or un-skilled work to people living in rural India, whether or not they are below the poverty line. The on-going programmes of Sampoorna Grameen Rozgar Yojana (SGRY) and National Food for Work Programme (NFFWP) were subsumed within the NREGS in the 200 districts identified in the initial stage. All the districts in the country are covered under the scheme now. The main features of the scheme are:

- State Government to provide at least 100 days of guaranteed wage employment in every financial year to every household whose adult members volunteer to do unskilled manual work.
- Until such time as a wage rate is fixed by the Central Government, the minimum wage for agricultural labourers shall be applicable for the scheme.
- An applicant not provided employment within fifteen days, to be entitled to a daily unemployment allowance as specified by the state government subject to its economic capacity, provided such rate is not less than quarter of the wage rate for the first thirty days during the financial year and not less than a half of the wage.[71]

Bharat Nirman: Accepting the policy 'a step towards village', Union Government launched a new scheme, named 'Bharat Nirman Yojana' on December 16, 2005. This scheme aims at developing rural infrastructure. The duration of implementing this scheme has been determined for four years with the expected expenditure of Rs. 1,74,000 crore. The major six sectors and their targets for 2005 to 2009 are:

1. *Irrigation*: To ensure irrigation for additional one crore hectare of land by 2009.
2. *Roads*: To link all villages of 1,000 populations with roads and also to link all ST and hilly villages up to 500 populations with roads.
3. *Housing*: Construction of 60 lakh additional houses for the poor.
4. *Water Supply*: To ensure drinking water to all remaining 74,000 villages.
5. *Electrification*: To supply electricity to all remaining 1,25,000 villages and to provide electricity connection to 2.3 crore houses.
6. *Rural telecommunication*: To ensure that 66,822 revenue villages in the country, which have not yet been covered with Village Public Telepone, shall be covered.

While the agenda is not new, the effort here is to impart a sense of urgency to these goals, make the programme time-bound, transparent and accountable. Prime Minister of India Dr. Manmohan Singh said "Bharat Nirman will be a time-bound business plan for action in rural infrastructure for the next four years. Under Bharat Nirman, action is proposed in the areas of irrigation, road, rural housing, rural water supply, rural electrification and rural telecommunication connectivity. We have set specific targets to be achieved under each of these goals so that there is accountability in the progress of this initiative."[72] Probably the most significant rural development programmes that initiated by the Government of India in recent past and of the ongoing programmes, the Pradhan Mantri Gram Sadak Yojana (PMGSY), the National Rural Employment Guarantee Scheme (NREGS) and Bharat Nirman Yojana. PMGSY and NREGS, in particular, made a remarkable impact in creating all weather rural connectivity and in providing wage employment in rural areas, although a long way to go in achieving the desired goal. However, despite of all the above rural development programme introduced and implemented and the continuing efforts of the government, there is no substantial decline of percentage of rural households living below poverty line and rural unemployment. The number of poor continued to remain stable for a fairly long period, confirmed by the Planning Commission of India from time to time. According to the criterion used by the Planning Commission of India 27.5 per cent of the population was living below the poverty line in 2004-2005, down from 51.3 per cent in 1977-1978, and 36 per cent in 1993-1994. Some sort of headway is evident only during 1999-2000 when it is estimated that poverty has slumped to 27.09 per cent. Though it is also distressing that in 10 states well over 40 per cent rural population are poverty stricken Arunachal Pradesh, Assam, Bihar (44.30%), Manipur, Meghalaya, Mizoram, Nagaland, Orissa (48.01), Sikkim, and Tamil Nadu.[73] Although Indian economy has grown steadily over the last two decades, its growth has been uneven when comparing different social groups, economic groups, geographic regions, and rural and urban areas. The objectives of the successive Five Year Plans in reducing poverty and solving rural unemployment were not achieved. Critics opine that large number of programmes and sub-programmes with multiplicity of objectives causes monitoring and evaluation complicated and lead to misuse of resources and funds. Lack of knowledge of the rural people about the programmes implemented, lack of political will, inefficient bureaucracy, the structural, organisational and institutional constraints were also responsible for rural development being moving at a snail's pace. Therefore, while formulating rural development strategies in coming years, best utilisation of local physical resources for creating employment opportunities, rural connectivity and marketing arrangements, spreading of modern agricultural inputs, convergence of sub-programmes to a few exclusive themes with clear objectives and methodology, will need larger attention. Moreover, sincere commitment of the political parties, competent, dedicated and motivated bureaucracy and proper management and monitoring and involvement of voluntary organisations and democratic decentralisation are vital for the success of rural development programmes.

Rural Development: A Continuous Process

Rural development is a continuous process. It is "a process facilitation through policy changes and strategic interventions in rural areas to help the rural community perform 'field activities' for their gradual social, political and economical advancement'[74]. The need for progressive rural development was recognised by the Planning Commission in its draft outline of the First Five Year Plan in 1951. With the launching of the First Five Year Plan in 1950-51, India's development objective was 'balanced growth'. The First Five Year Plan Document stated: "Agriculture, including irrigation and power must ... have the topmost priority. But without a substantial improvement in the production of food and raw materials needed for industry, it would be impossible to sustain a higher tempo of industrial development. One cannot go without the other. The two are complementary.... In India with its varied resources, conditions are favourable for securing balanced pattern of development".[75] The Plan defined the central objective of planning as creations of conditions in which living standards are reasonably high and citizens have full and equal opportunities for growth and justice. Thus, India adopted innumerable strategies to uplift the rural masses which includes institutional as well as special agency and programme strategies.[76] A symbolic rural development strategies can be termed as one 'that achieves desired increase in farm output at minimum costs, makes possible widespread improvements in the welfare of rural population, contributes to the transformation of a predominant agrarian economy and facilitates a broader process of social modernisation'.[77] Therefore, rural development strategies are a set of requirements in advance in accelerating the process of rural development by increasing productivity and employment opportunities thereby increasing the income of every rural family especially the poor, developing the rural resources, providing social goods and services with the ultimate objective of welfare of rural poor which requires number of pre-requisites, which can be mentioned, but in their order of importance, they can be classified as,[78]

1. Proper coordination between different credit providing institutions, such as Nationalised Banks, Cooperative Banks and Regional Rural Banks.
2. Provision of subsidy for acquiring new assets for improving their existing assets to make the project bankable.
3. Ensuring supply for raw material or inputs at the doorstep of rural poor or at least at carting distance from the village.
4. Marketing arrangements for marketing of their products ensuring a fair price so that they may be able to repay loans and also get some money for consumption to improve their quality of life.
5. Arrangements for improving and upgrading of their existing skills.
6. Undertaking research and development on a continuous basis so that rural productivity increases in agriculture, animal husbandry and allied activities and rural industries by upgrading technology.
7. Provision of social infrastructure, especially: (i) drinking water, (ii) education facilities to inform artisans and vocational trades about the local needs, and (iii) adequate health care.
8. Provision of economic infrastructure in terms of: (i) roads which are at least cartable throughout the year connecting every village to the nearby market, and (ii) electricity and bus transport.

9. Organically linking voluntary agencies with the new rural development administrative structure.
10. Supplementing economic activities of the rural poor for several years to help raise his net income through providing employment in public works to those who are underemployed. It will have to be done by identifying: (i) periods of unemployment or under-employment in a year; (ii) areas or pockets in the district suitable for this purpose; and (iii) concrete public works project for creating double assets in such villages.
11. The designing recruitment and training of functionalities at different levels in such a way as to inculcate spirit of dedication to rural development among them and motivation among them to implement the programmes efficiently, honestly and economically. Good quality personnel should be recruited for rural development administration.
12. Continuous planning, monitoring and evaluation of rural development programmes to ensure that all the above-mentioned facets are properly integrated or coordinated. The effectiveness of achieving the objective depends upon the extent and efficiency of such integration/coordination.

Panchayati Raj as an Agency of Rural Development

In 1959, the Government of India decided to make the community development set up more democratic and to delegate the resources for planning and execution of development programmes for people's institution in accordance with the recommendations of the Balwant Rai Mehta Committee. The Committee recommended "devolution of power to a body which, when created.... will have the entire charge of all development work within its jurisdiction, the government...reserving to itself the functions of guidance, supervision and higher planning and where necessary, providing extra finance".[79] In pursuance of this decision, Panchayati Raj Institutions (PRIs) had been introduced with the objective of ensuring greater participation of people in the planning, decision-making and implementation process of community development programmes. The major recommendations of Balwant Rai Mehta Committee were:[80]

1. There should be a three-tier structure of local self-governing bodies from the village level to the district level, the bodies being organically linked up.
2. There should be a genuine transfer of power and responsibilities to them.
3. Adequate resources should be transferred to these bodies to enable them to discharge those responsibilities.
4. All welfare and development schemes and programmes at these levels should be channeled through these bodies alone.
5. Those bodies being charged with various duties and functions, no higher body should have an opportunity to do what a lower body can do itself.
6. The three-tier system should be such that it facilitates further devolution and dispersal of power and responsibility in future.

These recommendations were accepted by the National Development Council in 1958 and various states Rajasthan and Andhra Pradesh being the first, to implement the scheme followed by various other states. However, the PRI structure failed to increase the necessary democratic impetus and failed to provide to the needs of rural development. There are various reasons for its failure of which domination of people who were well-off, caste, factions, feudalism, political and bureaucratic confrontation to share power, lack of resources, lack of political will, etc. Therefore, to review the performance of PRIs, Government of India appointed various committees from time to time. In December 1977, the Janata Party government appointed Ashok Mehta Committee to examine and suggest measures to strengthen the PRIs. The main recommendations of the committee are:[81]

1. The district should be the first point of decentralisation, under popular supervision below the state level.
2. Below the district level, the people in development management can be best achieved, by grouping a number of villages to constitute Mandal Panchayats.
3. The performance of the Committee is for two-tiers—a district level Zila Parishad and a Mandal Panchayat.
4. Panchayati Raj elections should be conducted by the Chief

Election Officer of the state in consultation with the Chief Election Commissioner.

5. Participation of political parties in panchayat elections would ensure clearer orientation towards development programme and facilitate healthier linkages with higher level political process.
6. All the development functions relating to a district which are now being discharged by the state government would have to be placed under the Zila Parishads.
7. The functions of the Mandal Panchayats would have to be viewed from a new angle. They would be responsible for implementation of the schemes and projects assigned by the Zila Parishad.
8. All developmental staff with the Zila Parishad should be placed under an officer to be designated as the Chief Executive Officer of Zila Parishad.

The recommendations of the Ashok Mehta Committee were considered at the Chief Ministers Conference, in May 1979. In order to bring about model uniformity in the Panchayati Raj set up for the whole country, a model bill was prepared. However, the collapse of the Janata Government at the centre a few months later put a full stop to any further progress in this direction.[82]

The Union Government appointed two committees[83] in 1985 and 1986 to suggest ways and means for strengthening panchayati raj. One committee under the chairmanship of G.V.K. Rao in 1985, suggesting development must be taken in which PRIs must play a central role in handling people's problems. The main recommendations of the committee are:

1. PRIs have to be activated and provided with all the required support to become effective organisations.
2. PRIs at the district level and below should be assigned the work of planning, implementation and monitoring of rural development programmes, and
3. The block development office should be the spinal cord of the rural development process.

The other committee under the chairmanship of a

distinguished jurist L.M. Singhvi in 1986 studied Panchayati Raj and suggested that:

1. Local self-government should be constitutionally recognised, protected and preserved by the inclusion of new chapter in the Constitution.
2. Non-involvement of political parties in panchayat elections.

The findings and suggestions of these committees give the right momentum to amend the Constitution of India to provide PRIs under the justifiable part of the Constitution.

The New Panchayati Raj Institutions: The 73rd (Constitution Amendment) Act, 1992

With the intension of revitalising and making the panchayats effective units of self-governance, Government of India brought the historic Constitution (73rd) Amendment, which was passed by Parliament on 22nd December, 1992 and notified through Official Gazette on April 20, and came into force on April 24, 1993. This Act revolutionise the PRIs by giving constitutional status and more power to the people at the village level. It added a new part relating to PRIs in the Constitution of India under Article 243. The State Governments now required to take appropriate action under it. Some states have taken action in this respect and in other states as well statutory amendments have been made accordingly. Madhya Pradesh has become the first state in India by introducing new PRI on 20th August, 1994.[84]

Salient Features of the Constitution (73rd Amendment)

The main features of the 73rd Constitution Amendment Act may be summarised as follows:[85]

1. The Gram Sabha or Village Assembly as a deliberative body to decentralised governance has been envisaged as the foundation of the Panchayati Raj System.
2. A uniform three-tier structure of panchayats at village

Gram Panchayat (GP), intermediate Panchayat Samiti (PS) and district Zila Parishad (ZP) levels.

3. All the seats in a panchayat at every level are to be filled by elections from respective territorial constituencies.
4. Not less than one-third of the total seats for membership as well as office of chairpersons of each tier has to be reserved for women.
5. Reservation for weaker castes and tribes (SCs and STs) has to be provided at all levels in proportion to their population in the panchayats.
6. To supervise, direct and control the regular and smooth elections to panchayats, a State Election Commission has to be constituted in every State and Union Territory.
7. The Act has ensured Constitution of a State Finance Commission in every State/Union Territory, for every five years, to suggest measures to strengthen finances of PRIs.
8. To promote bottom-up-planning, the District Planning Committee in every district has been accorded constitutional status.
9. Panchayats will prepare plans for economic development, social justice and social welfare subjects enumerated in the Eleventh Schedule, which contains 29 items such as agriculture, rural housing, rural electrification, drinking water, roads, waterways, fisheries, soil conservation, education, health, etc.

Consequent upon the 73rd Constitution Amendment Act, 1992 significant reorganisation of the panchayats were made in almost all the states of India. At present, there are about 3 million elected representatives at all levels of the panchayat, one-third of which are women. These members represent more than 2.4 lakh Gram Panchayats, about 6,000 intermediate level tiers and more than 500 district panchayats. Spread over the length and breadth of the country, the new panchayats cover about 96 per cent of India's more than 5.8 lakh villages and nearly 99.6 per cent of rural population. This is the largest experiment in decentralisation of governance in the history of humanity. The Constitution of India visualises panchayats as institutions of self-governance. However, giving due consideration to the federal structure of our polity, most of the financial powers and authorities to be endowed on panchayats have been left at the discretion of concerned state legislatures. Consequently, the powers and functions vested in PRIs vary from state to state.[86]

However, inspite of the enormous progress over the past generation, more than 40 per cent of the people in developing countries, including India, still live in acute poverty and suffer grossly inadequate access to such resources as education, health services, infrastructure, land and credit. The primary obstacles to development are administrative rather than economic. Most administrators lack the administrative capability for implementing development plans and programmes.[87] Failure to incorporate folk wisdom and indigenous management practices in designing development projects, massive dislocations of rural populations to accommodate gigantic development projects, rural migration to urban areas and so forth the process of modernisation, in a real sense, fractured the society, with a handful of people concerning the benefits of development while a large majority remained excluded from achieving access to the same.[88] The distribution of wealth has been uneven, where the rich became richer and the poor became poorer. The agricultural sector, presenting 65 per cent of the country's population, contributes to just 20 per cent of National Gross Domestic Product (NGDP) clearly indicates the rampant poverty prevalent in rural areas of the country.[89] The new economic policy has also similar impact. According to Kh. Menjor Singh,[90] the social consequences of globalisation are more disappointing. A small majority of the upper and middle class people with higher skills would get gainful employment and, therefore, be able to consume more and more, while a vast majority of the middle and lower class people with less education and skills would be thrown out of employment. He further says how liberalisation of trade can expand agricultural exports in the absence of infrastructure facilities for export market. Even if it is taken for granted that exports are stepped up through promotion of agro-processing, the short-term effects on employment intensity of modern processing is less than the corresponding intensity of traditional industry.

According to Vasant Sathe[91], with the advent of an industrial society, both the life and self-supporting economy of the village was disturbed. A large chunk of the rural population dependent on their centuries old traditional occupations was deprived of the source of their livelihood and the emerging society did not provide them alternative employment in the rural area itself and were forced to become either landless labourers or to migrate to urban centres unwillingly in search of avocations to eke out a living.

Therefore, it is expected that the PRIs will be more development oriented now than democracy in realising the objectives of development. The present Panchayati Raj System after the 73rd Constitutional Amendment Act is a landmark towards decentralisation of power. The need is now to implement the system successfully. Adequate awareness among the rural people to participate in the development programmes, abolition of caste barriers and corruption, actual political willingness, a perfect coordination between bureaucracy and panchayati raj institutions are some of the key aspects to make the new panchayati raj system successful.

Notes and References

1. Basu, Rumki (200): *Public Administration*, Sterling Publishers Private Limited, New Delhi, p. 355.
2. http://en.wikipedia.org/wikipolitics, viewed on 10 September 2010.
3. Devis, K. Arthur (1949): Bureaucratic Patterns in the Navy Officer Corps, *Social Forces*, pp. 144-145.
4. Dey, Bata, K. (1978): *Bureaucracy Development and Public Management in India*, Uppal Publishing House, New Delhi, p. 1.
5. In Fadia, B.L. and Kuldeep Fadia (2007): *Public Administration*, Sahitya Bhawan Publications, Agra, pp. 419-420.
6. Dimock, E. Marshall, Bureaucracy Self-Examined in Sharma, Dr. MP and Sadana, Dr. B.L. (2008): *Public Administration in Theory and Practice*, Kitab Mahal, Allahabad, p. 325.
7. Pfiffner, M. John and Presthus V. Robert (1960): *Public Administration*, Ronald Press, New York, p. 40.
8. Avasthi, A. and Maheshwari, Shriram (1999): *Public Administration*, Lakshmi Narain Agarwal Educational Publishers, Agra, p. 223.
9. http://en.wikipedia.org/wikipolitics, viewed on 10 September 2010.
10. Sharma, M.P. and Sadana, B.L. (2008): *Public Administration in Theory and Practice*, *op. cit.* p. 341.
11. *Ibid.*, p. 342.
12. Bhattacharya, Mohit (2007); *Public Administration*, The World Press Private Limited, Kolkata, p. 66.
13. Merton, Robert K (1940): Bureaucratic Structure and Personality, Social Forces, in Fadia, B.L. and Fadia, Kuldeep, *Public Administration*, *op. cit.* p. 426.

14. Fadia, B.L. and Fadia, Kuldeep (2007): *Public Administration, op. cit.* p. 427.
15. Sharma M.P. and Sadana, B.L. (2008): *Public Administration in Theory and Practice, op. cit.* p. 348.
16. Fadia, B.L. and Kuldeep Fadia (2007): *Public Administration, op. cit.* p. 427.
17. Dwevedi, O.P. and Jain, R.B. (1985): *India's Administrative State*, Gitanjali Publishing House, New Delhi, p. 218.
18. Bhattacharya, Mohit (2007): *Public Administration, op. cit.* p. 71.
19. Naidu, S.P. (2004): *Public Administration*, New Age International Publishers, New Delhi, p. 86.
20. Sharma, M.P. and Sadana, B.L. (2008): *Public Administration in Theory and Practice, op. cit.* p. 377.
21. Sapru, R.K. (2002): *Development Administration*, Sterling Publishers Pvt. Limited, New Delhi, p. 311.
22. *Ibid.* p. 325.
23. Arora, K. Ramesh and Goyal, Rajni (1995): *Indian Public Administration*, Wishwa Prakashan, New Delhi, p. 626.
24. *International Encyclopedia of the Social Sciences*, Vol. 13, Macmillan Co. and Free Press, New York, 1968, p. 582.
25. http:// www. britannica.com/bps/rural, viewed on 8th October 20103.
26. http:// www.en.wikipedia.org/wiki/rural, viewed on 8th October 2010.
27. http:// www. webster's-online-dictionary/rural, viewed on 8th October 2010.
28. http:// www. ers.usda.gov/briefing/rurality, viewed on 8th October 2010.
29. http:// www. britannica.com/bps/development, viewed on 8th October 2010.
30. http:// www. webster's-online-dictionary/development, viewed on 8th October 2010.
31. http:// www. longmans dictionary/development, viewed on 8th October 2010.
32. http:// www. en.wikipedia.org/wiki/rural, viewed on 8th October 2010.
33. Sapru, R.K. (2003): *Development Administration*, Sterling Publishers Pvt. Ltd., New Delhi, p. 300.
34. http:// www. en.wikipedia.org/wiki/rd, viewed on 8th October 2010.
35. Rural Development Sector Policy Paper, World Bank, Washington D.C., 1975, p. 3.
36. Chamber, Robert. (1983): *Rural Development: Putting the Last First*, Longman Group Ltd., London, p. 147.
37. Copp, H. James. (1972): "Rural Sociology and Rural Development", *Rural Sociology* Vol. 37, No. 4, December pp. 515-523.
38. Ensminger, D. (1974): "Rural Development: What is it? Its contribution

in nation-building". Paper presented in East-West Center's Conference on Integrated Communication for Rural Development, Honolulu.
39. Lele, Uma (1975): *The Design of Rural Development: Lesson from America*", John Hopkins, Baltimore, p. 2.
40. Singh, Katar (1999): *Rural Development: Principles, Politics and Management*, Sage Publications India Pvt. Ltd. New Delhi, p. 21.
41. Shepherd, Andrew (1998): *Sustainable Rural Development*, Macmillan Press Ltd., London, p. 1.
42. Patel, A.R. (1985): "Rural Development: A Challenging Task for Voluntary Agencies", *Kurukshetra*, Vol. 34(1), New Delhi, October, pp. 24-28.
43. Reddy, Uday Bhaskar. (1987): "The Role of Voluntary Agencies in Rural Development". *The Indian Journal of Public Administration*. Vol. 33, No. 3, July-Sept. p. 547.
44. http://web.worldbank.org, viewed on 25th August 2010.
45. Choudry, Dr. D. Paul (1978): *New Partnership in Rural Development*, M.N. Publishers, New Delhi, p. 4.
46. Setty, E.D. (2002): *New Approaches to Rural Development*, Anmol Publications Private Limited, New Delhi, p. 18.
47. Seetharam, M. (1990): *Citizen Participation in Rural Development*, Mittal Publications, New Delhi, p. 8.
48. Choudry, D. Paul (1978): *New Partnership in Rural Development*, *op. cit.* p. 4.
49. *Ibid.*
50. Report of the *Royal Commission on Agriculture*, 1928, p. 672.
51. Patel, K.V. *et al.*, (1987): *Rural Economics*, Himalaya Publishing House, Bombay, p. 475.
52. Maheshwari, S.R. (2000): *State Government in India*, Macmillan India Ltd. Delhi, p. 267.
53. Planning Commission, First Five-Year Plan, Publications Division, Ministry of Information Govt. of India, New Delhi, 1952.
54. Government of India (1959): Community Development, Panchayati Raj and Cooperation, pp. 15-16.
55. Community Development Programmes: A Draft Outline—Introduction.
56. Seetharm, M. (1990): *Citizen Participation in Rural Development*, *op. cit.* p. 10.
57. Community Development, Publication Division, Government of India, 1958, p. 6.
58. Government of India (1953): The First Five-Year Plan: Planning Commission, p. 63.
59. Report of the Committee on Special Multipurpose Tribal Blocks, Ministry of Home Affairs (March, 1960): New Delhi, March, p. 5.
60. *Ibid.*
61. *Ibid.*

62. Avasthi, A.P. (2002): Indian Government and Politics, Lakshmi Narain Agarwal, Agra, pp. 518-519 Also see Profile; Ministry of Rural Development, Govt. of India, 2010.
63. Fadia, B.L. and Fadia, Kuldeep (2007) *Public Administration*, Sahitya Bhawan Publications, Agra, p. 917.
64. Sable, M.N. and G.B. Sondge, Rural Development in India: A case of Rural Area of Marathwada, Maharashtra State in C.R. Kothari (ed.) *Rural Development* (1991), Manak Publications (P) Ltd, New Delhi, p. 115.
65. Kothari, C.R. (1991): Rural Development in India: Retrospect and Prospect, in, Kothari, C.R. (ed.), *Strategy for Rural Development*, Vol. 1, Manak Publications (P) Ltd, New Delhi, p. 39.
66. Singh, Hoshiar (1985): *Rural Development in India*, Printwell; Jaipur.
67. Sharma, S.K. and Malhotra, S.L. (1977): "*Integrated Rural Development Approach, Strategy and Perspectives*", New Delhi, Abhinav, p. 21.
68. Chaturvedi, T.N. (1979): "Rural Development, the Elusive Horizons" *Administrative Change*, V. 1, July, 1978 June, p. 218.
69. S.B.I. Monthly Review (1985): Evaluation of the Impact of IRDP Assistance: A Study Conducted in Ten Lead Districts of SBI Vol. 24, No. 8, August.
70. Government of India, Ministry of Rural Development. (May 2001) "Gram Vikas Programmes at a Glance, New Delhi.
71. Government of India (2008): NREGA Operational Guidelines, Ministry of Rural Development, New Delhi.
72. Government of India (2005): Bharat Nirman, A Time-bound Plan.
73. Mandal, Amal (2003): Poverty Eradication in Rural India—Reflection on Methodology, *Kurukshetra*, Vol. 51, No. 10 August, p. 4.
74. Naithani, Pankaj (2000): 'Replicating an Established Rural Development Model, Kurukshetra, Vol. 49, October, New Delhi, p. 25.
75. Government of India, Planning Commission, the First Five-Year Plan, p. 44.
76. Singh, Hoshiar (1985): "*Rural Development in India*", *op. cit.* pp. 123-124.
77. Johnson, Bruce F., and Kilby Peter (1973): '*Agricultural Strategy*', Rural-Urban Interactions and the Expansions of Income Opportunities, Paris, OECD, p. 5.
78. Shah, M.G. (1984): "Restructuring of Rural Development Administration", *Indian Journal of Public Administration*, Vol. 30, No. 4, Oct-Dec, pp. 924-925.
79. Report of the Team for the Study of Community Projects and National Extension Service, vol. 1. New Delhi, Committee on Plan Projects; 1957. p. 7 (It is popularly known as the Balwant Rai Mehta Committee after the name of its Chairman).

80. Bhargava, B.S. (2009): "Balwant Rai Mehta and Balwant Rai Mehta Committee Report (1957)", Local Government Quarterly, July-September, Mumbai: All India Institute of Local Self Government, p. 76.
81. Fadia, B.L. and Fadia, Kuldeep (2007) *Public Administration, op. cit.* p. 922.
82. Avasthi, A.P. (2002): *Indian Government and Politics*, Lakshmi Narain Agarwal, Agra, p. 531.
83. http://en.wikipedia.org/wiki/History_of_panchayati_raj_in_India, viwed on 15.10.10.
84. Avasthi, A.P. (2002): Indian Government and Politics, *op. cit.* p. 532.
85. http://en.wikipedia.org/wiki/History_of_panchayati_raj_in_India, viewed on 15.10.10.
86. *Ibid.*
87. Sapru, R.K. (2002): *Development Administration, op. cit.* p. 302.
88. Sharma, Arvind K. (2004): *Bureaucracy and Decentralisation*, Mittal Publications, New Delhi, p. 28.
89. Rao, U.R., *Crisis in Agriculture, The Mizoram Post*, Aizawl, 9th September, 2006, p. 4.
90. Singh, Kh. Menjor (2001): *Economic Reforms in India: Problems and Prospects*, Mittal Publications, New Delhi, pp. 49-51.
91. Sethe, Vasant (1995): Relevance of Gandhian Economics Today, in Nanda, B.R. (edited), *Mahatma Gandhi 125 Years*, Indian Council For Cultural Relations, New Delhi, 1995 p. 252.

3
Democratic Decentralisation in Mizoram

This chapter is devoted to an analysis of democratic decentralisation—the organisation and functions of Panchayati Raj Institutions in India, the Village Councils and District Councils in Mizoram. Part-I deals with the organisation and functions of Panchayati Raj Institutions in India. Part-II covers the village administration before independence—the Chieftainship in Mizoram. Part-III covers the democratic decentralisation in Mizoram—the District Councils and Village Councils, its powers and functions.

INTRODUCTION

Democratic decentralisation is one of the fundamentals of governance. It is an important apparatus through which democracy becomes truly representative and real. Decentralisation ensures grassroots level people's participation in decision-making process. Supporters of decentralisation point out three basic virtues namely, participation, responsiveness and efficiency. The basic idea is to de-concentrate powers and make public governance closer to the people. The introduction of Panchayati Raj Institutions (PRI) and constitutional status to panchayats by the 73rd Constitutional Amendment Act is a momentous step in the direction of decentralisation in India. It makes the panchayats—the third tier of the Indian federal system—the union government, state governments and the panchayats at the village, block and district levels. While almost all the States and Union Territories have enacted their legislation following the enactment of the 73rd

Constellational Amendment Act, Mizoram has not introduced PRIs as local self-government. The State of Mizoram has been exempted from the 73rd Constitutional Amendment due to the existence of traditional local self-governing bodies—the Village Councils, created under the Lushai Hills District (Village Councils) Act 1953 and the Pawi-Lakher Autonomous Region (Village Councils) Act 1954 under sub clause (e) of Clause (3) of the Sixth Schedule of the Constitution of India. Now every village has its Village Council replacing chieftainship besides the three Autonomous District Councils for the Mara, Lai and Chakma communities. Before we analyse the powers and functioning of the District Councils and Village Councils in Mizoram, it is imperative to know the orgnisation and functioning of the panchayati raj bodies as local self-governing bodies in other states of India.

Organisation and Functions of Panchayati Raj Institutions[1]

In almost all the states of India, Panchayati Raj is three-tier system—village at the first level, block at the second level and at the district level. At the village level, three institutions—Gram Sabha, Gram Panchayat and Nyaya Panchayat are functioning under the Panchayati Raj Institutions—

(A) Gram Sabha (Village Level)

Gram Sabha is the general assembly at the village level. It consists of all the village people who are at least 18 years of age. The Gram Sabha elects the Gram Pradhan or the President. It is mandatory for it to hold at least two meetings in a year to perform certain functions.

The main functions assigned to the Gram Sabha are:

(i) to consider annual budget of Gram Panchayat;
(ii) to examine audit report of the Gram Panchayat;
(iii) to review report of Gram Panchayat;
(iv) to approve the income and the expenditure estimates for the year;
(v) to consider new taxes which the Gram Panchayat would like to levy; and

(vi) to select schemes, beneficiaries and locations, etc.

(B) Gram Panchayat

It is the executive committee of the Gram Sabha elected by the Gram Sabha for a term of 5 years. The number of members varies from state to state. In Rajasthan minimum is 5 and maximum 20 while in Uttar Pradesh it is 16 to 30. Seats are reserved for the Scheduled Castes and Schedule Tribes. One third of the total seats are reserved for women. Every Panchayat has a Sarpanch (Chairman) and Up-Sarpanch (Vice-Chairman) elected by the Gram Sabha.

The main functions of the Gram Panchayat can be divided into two categories–compulsory and optional.

The compulsory functions are: provision of safe drinking water, construction and repair of village roads, maintenance of public wells and tanks, public parks and playgrounds, registration of births and deaths, preparation of annual budgets and maintain its accounts, etc.

The optional functions are: to organise village sports, to run small scale industries, housing, electricity, non-conventional energy, poverty alleviation, etc.

Sources of Revenue: Grants from government, taxes on houses and buildings, professions, trades, vehicles, animals, fairs and melas, water, tea stalls and hotels, carts, rickshaws, registration fee on sale and purchase of land and cattle, etc.

(C) Nyaya Panchayat

Earlier Gram Panchayat used to perform *nyaya* (judicial) work. Now separation of power has been adopted in village level. In some states like Punjab, Himachal Pradesh, Panchayat itself acts as a court, in some other states like Bihar, Uttar Pradesh, West Bengal separate Nyaya Panchayats administer justice. It deals with minor criminal and civil cases, such as petty thefts, cheating and physical attack on a person. It can impose a fine upto Rs. 1000.00.

Nyaya Panchayat is a very useful institution where the villager's can get speedy justice without much expenditure. However, if any body fells dejected, with the judgement he or she can then go to a higher court.

(D) Panchayat Samiti (Block Level)

The Panchayat Samiti is the second or intermediate tier in the Panchayati Raj. The name of the body is not the same in all the states. In Assam it is Anchalik Panchayat, in Uttar Pradesh and Uttaranchal it is Kshetriaya Samitis, Block Panchayat in Kerala, in Madya Pradesh it is called Janpada Panchayat.

There is no uniformity in the composition of the Samiti in the states. Broadly speaking, a Panchayat Samiti consists of all the Sarpanchs of the Panchayats within the block, the MPs and MLAs of that area. Every Samiti must have seats reserved for women and also for Scheduled Castes and Schedule Tribes. The Samiti has a term of 5 years. The Pradhan or Chairman of this body is usually elected by the members of the Samiti. He convenes and presides over the meetings of the Samiti. He exercise control over the block development officer for the purpose of implementing resolutions of the Samiti or its standing committees.

The functions of the Panchayat Samiti extend to agriculture, animal husbandry, cottage and small scale industries, fisheries, health, communication, etc. and help the villagers in services of these sectors. The Samiti is to help the villagers in obtaining improved seeds and fertilizers and educated them about new and improved agricultural implements and use of pesticides, make aware the village people about family planning, immunization of children, establish small scale industries, to aware on the programmes initiated by the government, etc. For the performance of these functions, the Samiti is equipped with administrative machinery headed by the block development officer.

The main sources of income of the Samiti are grants and financial assistance from the government, income from the taxes levied by the Samiti on public ferries, fairs, etc. The budget of the Panchayat Samiti is sent to the Zila Parishad for approval. The Samitis have full freedom to frame their own budget and formulate their annual plans of development within the framework of state plan.

(E) Zila Parishad (District Level)

Zila Parishad is the highest tier of Panchayati Raj. It is also called

District Panchayat and Zila Panchayat. It coordinates the activities of the various Samitis under the district.

In most states it consists of ex-officio members, co-opted members and associated members.

Ex-officio members: All Pradhan of Panchayat Samitis, all MLAs and MPs of the district, District Development Officer.

Co-opted members: Two women and one person belonging to Scheduled Castes and Schedule Tribes.

Associated members: Chairman of the Central Cooperative Bank, Chairman of the District Cooperative Union.

Chairman and Vice-Chairman are elected by the members of the Parishad.

The main functions of the Zila Parishad are:

(i) to examine and approves the budget of Panchayat Samitis;
(ii) to supervise the activities of the Samiti;
(iii) to advise the state government on all matters relating to development activities of the district;
(iv) distributes funds allocated by the government to the Samitis;
(v) exercise such powers and functions as may be assigned to it by the State Government. The Zila Parishad functioning are through number of standing committees like—Planning and Finance, Production Programme, Social Amenities, Welfare of Weaker Sections of Society, etc.

The main sources of the Zila Parishad fund are grants from the state government, income from the property of the Zila Parishad, taxes, license fees, market fees, contribution from Panchayat Samitis, etc.

CHIEFTAINSHIP AND VILLAGE ADMINISTRATION

Prior to the advent of the British in late 19th century, each village was an independent unit of administration, under a chief called 'Lal', in the Lushai Hills (now Mizoram). The chief was the centre of authority in village administration. Theoretically, all that was in the village belonged to the chief. The Lal was the guardian of his people, head of the village, leader in wars, owner of the village land, protector and father of the subjects. In fact, he had the power of life and death. He was the secular head of the village. He had no religious functions, which were entrusted to a priest who was subject to the control of the Lal. He is the commander-in-chief of his army and the chief justice. He was responsible for the control of the village. He distributed land for cultivation among the villagers.[2] Thus; the chiefs were the supreme authority in the administration of the Mizo villages.

The exact record of the origin of the chieftainship institution in Lushai Hills cannot be mentioned but according to tradition, chieftainship originated in the 16th century[3] in the process of their migration. The institution of chieftainship emerged out of the collective need of the villagers. It originated out of the physical ability and intellectual power of an individual to provide safety to the tribal village life.[4] It was a necessity for migratory tribes where the population was unsettled and disorganised.[5] As such, a strong man was required to act as a guardian of the villagers. People had adopted the chief system so that they could be guided and governed in all activities of life.[6] chieftainship was originally not a hereditary one but voluntary to be a head of a clan.[7]

The Council of Elders

In the village administration, each chief was assisted by *Upas* or Council of Elders. The *Upas* were officials of his choice from amongst those who were rich, well informed, broad-minded and influential persons in the village.[8] One of the Upas was designated as Upa-Min, Chief of the Elders.[9] They were appointed by him and could dismiss them. In all matters of dispute and deliberations which concerned the welfare of the village or the lot of its people, the chief had, by custom to consult the Upas and could not normally ignore the consensus of opinion arrived at except at the risk of being disowned by his people.[10] The Upas help the chief in carrying on the administration of the village, in the administration of justice, to ensure that customary dues to the chief were paid in time by the villagers etc. and in return they were paid in kind for their services and also exempted from the payment of Fathang.[11]*

* Fathang means taxes to be paid to the chief.

The Officials other than Council of Elders

For smooth functioning of the village administration[12], some other officers were also appointed by the chiefs. The officials were entrusted with various responsibilities. *Zalen* were from the aristocrat groups required to help the chief in times of distress. They were appointed by the chiefs, to assist them, and were exempted from paying *Fathang* and entitled to select a plot of land for cultivation and house construction. Their privilege was due to the specific obligations to help the chief in time of distress and difficulties. *Ramhuals* were the jhuming experts who used to give advice to the chiefs in allotment of the land for *jhum* cultivation. They help the chief in the distribution of land to the villagers for cultivation and were allowed to have the first choice of jhum site. Because of the privilege they had, they were to pay heavier Fathang or paddy due to the chief. They were considered to be men of possession and to retain their prestige they never hesitated to pay a larger Fathang and they were to support the chief whenever needed.[13] Their position was similar to 'Patwary' in plain district of northern India.[14] The system of Ramhual and Zalen was entirely a local arrangement of the chief and their number varied from village to village.[15] *Tlangau* was the village crier who served the chiefs orders or any message to the villagers by going round the village. He was paid one tin paddy from each house for his services and exempted from Fathang. As the custom varied in different villages, the matter of remuneration was purely of local arrangement.[16] The *Thirdeng* was the village blacksmith. He helped the villagers in changing and repairing of the agricultural tools and other works connected the daily life of the villagers. He used to get a basket of paddy from each household and the spine and three ribs of any wild animal killed by the villagers, which is called "*Thirdengsa*". The *Puithiam* was the village priest. His duty was to perform all kinds of sacrifices for the villagers. He also gets a basket full of paddy annually for his services. *Sadawt* was the chief's special priest and *Thlahpawi* was his assistant. These two officers were concerned with the performance of sacrifices offered by the chief. They were paid in kind—paddy. But the remuneration system was varied from village to village.

Collection of Revenue

The chief being the head of the village administration had a regular collection of revenue[17] in terms of paddy as well as manual labour from each family under his jurisdiction. From each household, the chief was entitled to receive *Fathang* annually with the exception of Zalens. He is entitled to *Sachhiah*. Any villager who killed a wild animal must give its left foreleg failing which he was liable to be fined. Anybody who collected salt from a salt well or spring within his ram or land, must give a substantial quantity of it to the chief, which was known as *Chikhurchhiah*. The chief was also entitled to receive a portion of wild honey collected within his *ram* or land by the villagers, which was called *Khuaichhiah*. Besides the chief was entitled to share a fine of Rs. 5 or a pig for every case tried by him and his Upas called *Salam*. The chief also collected taxes from traders doing business within his jurisdiction.[18] The chiefs were also entitled for free labour. His house was constructed and repaired by the villagers free of cost and voluntarily. On completion of such construction, he must according to custom, provide feast to his villagers. This however, was optional on the chief's part and cannot be claimed by the villagers as a right.[19] The Lakher Chiefs were entitled to two days labour from each family every year for the cultivation of his lands and a basket full of cotton from each house annually.[20]

The Lushai Chief had also the prerogative to chose his successor and establish new villages for his sons and the right to keep *Bawis*.[21]* By custom, it was the chiefs duty to allot to each of his sons a tract of land and set him up with a village of his own as soon as he got married.[22]

Thus, the position of the chief was very much like a dictator. However, the chief was bound to help his villagers in their distress and difficulties, reward them in their achievements and punish them when they were found guilty of misdeeds. In practice his power was limited, and was certainly defined by custom and usage. The villagers in their turn were to obey him implicitly and help

---

* *Bawi* was a kind of slavery. The Chiefs house was a refuge to all who choose to enter it. They and their families became slaves to the Chief, and he in turn to provide for their wants. All orphans or widows with any relative go to the Chief become his slaves.

him in all possible ways.[23] The chief could not misuse his power and could not do so if he desired to retain his position as they could leave him and take shelter under another chief.[24] The chiefs were conscious of this indirect but very potent control over them. Consequently they were mild and lenient in their administration of the village.[25]

Institution of Zawlbuk

One of the most significant traditional institutions in Mizo village system was Zawlbuk[26] which is a bachelor's dormitory. Every village had one Zawlbuk made by villagers usually built near the chief's house. All the unmarried youths were required to sleep inside the Zawlbuk. The dwellers of Zawlbuk had one leader called 'Val Upa'. Among the Zawlbuk dwellers the most industrious person as a worker and an organiser as also the most courageous and efficient hunter who manage to establish himself as the undisputed leader was recognized by the Chief as the Val Upa or Superintendent.[27] He was assisted by Thingnawifawm Hotu or monitors appointed by him to carry out the daily routine work. Those who failed to perform the orders of the monitors were punished. The chief of the village was the supreme head of Zawlbuk who, however, did not interfere in its administration except on absolute necessity and the actual administration of the Zawlbuk was left in its internal organisation. No one dared to interfere and the village chief was the only person who could throw stones on the roof of the Zawlbuk with impunity to silence annoying chatter.[28] The adults who constituted the Zawlbuk group were called Tlangval, while those of the younger group were Thingnawifawm.[29]

The Zawlbuk institution occupied a central position in the organisation and administration of the Lushai village and functioned as the most potent institutional mechanism of social control.[30] It was a training ground for tribal warfare, discipline, defense of the village, hunting, dance, music and other cultural activities, and administration. The Zawlbuk institution served as an important reserved force to the chief and its successful maintenance denoted the ability of the chiefs to extent their hold over their villagers and command their authority.[31] The spirit of sacrifice for others 'Tlawmngaihna' originated from the Zawlbuk system of Mizo life.[32] Tlawmngaina has been the guiding principle and philosophy of Mizo social life till today.

Rights and Privileges of the Chiefs during British Rule

After the annexation of the Lushai Hills by the British, the powers of the chiefs were curtailed but allowed the chiefs to continue to exercise a number of rights and privileges.[33] The Lushai Chiefs were extinguished from the following traditional rights:[34]

1. Right to order capital punishment.
2. Right to seize all the property of a villager who was found to be disloyal and disobeying his orders or who wished to transfer his allegiance to another chief. This is known as Ram and it was perhaps the most severe punishment that could be inflicted on villagers by a chief and his council of elders.
3. Propriety rights over land, now arbitrarily reserved by the government. Traditionally, the land was owned by the chief in trust of the tribe. Now the government owned the land and approportioned out of the chiefs.
4. Right to tax foreign traders doing business within his jurisdiction.
5. Right to freedom of action to make his sons chiefs and to establish new villages for them. This was done as the process of fragmentation continued to erode not only the material possessions of the chiefs but also the viability of his position, and also due to the limitation of land.

However, the chiefs were allowed to receive their privileges of receiving Fathang, Chikhurchhia, Khuaichhiah, Sachhiah from their villagers and the right to keep Bawis. The right to appoint their officials such as Upas, Tlangaus, Ramhuals and Zalens were also remained. Lands were taken over by the government and redistributed among the chiefs. Hence, the chiefs gradually ceased to be the absolute owners of land and became only the settlement holders.[35]

DEMOCRATIC DECENTRALISATION IN MIZORAM: DISTRICT COUNCILS AND VILLAGE COUNCILS

Local self-government and political autonomy in Mizoram in true sense has been conceived with the abolition of chieftainship after independence following the creation of District Councils and the Village Councils established under the Sixth Schedule of the Constitution of India. The institution of the chieftainship was continued for some years even in the post-independent India till the formation of the Lushai Hills District Council and the Pawi-Lakher Regional Council which came into being in 1952 and 1953 respectively.[36] The Lushai Hills District Council enacted Chieftainship Abolition Act 1952, provided for the withdrawal of all powers and rights of the Chiefs from 1 January 1953.[37] The Government of Assam prepared a Bill which after obtaining consent from the Central Government, was passed by Assam Legislature as the Assam Lushai Hills District (Acquisition of Chiefs Rights) Act 1954.[38] The abolition of Chieftainship became effective from 1 April 1955 within the jurisdiction of the Lushai Hills District Council.[39] Under the same Act the chieftainship within the jurisdiction of the Pawi-Lakher Regional Council was also abolished with effect from April 15, 1956. By it, the Chief's land or ram was vested in the state and the District Council was entrusted to look after it.[40]

In pursuance of the provisions of the Sixth Schedule of the Constitution of India, the Government of Assam enacted the Assam Autonomous District (Constitution of the District Council) Act 1951.[41] The name of the district was changed from Lushai Hills District to Mizo District in 1954.[42]

Composition

The Autonomous District Council/Region is a local authority which has definite area of action in pursuance of Article 244(2) and 275(1) (a), (b) of the Indian Constitution.[43] The Council/Region consists of the members elected on the basis of adult franchise and nominated members, nominated by the Governor on the recommendation of the Chief Executive Member. The nominated members normally belong to the minority group. For the smooth conduct of the election, the Autonomous District/Region was divided into single member constituency on the basis of population and area.[44] The normal term of the Autonomous District/Region was five years but there is provision for extension of the term for one year.[45]

Till 1957, there were twenty-four members of the District Council, out of which two were reserved from Pawi-Lakher Region and other two for government's nominees.[46] Pawi-Lakher Regional Council consists of ten elected members, and two nominated members.[47] The District Council elects its Chairman and Deputy Chairman who presides over the Council in session and their offices were akin to the Speaker and Deputy Speaker of a legislature[48]. The Executive Committee is a miniature cabinet to carry out executive functions, of the District Council. It consists of one Chief Executive Member and two other members. The members of the District Council elect the Chief Executive Member. Besides two nominated members there is a Secretary who is appointed by the Chief Executive Member from outside.[49]

To be elected as a member of the District Council[50], he must be a citizen of India, has completed twenty five years of age and is entitled to vote in the election of the Council, must also belong to Schedule Tribe Community of the Council. Those who have attained the age of twenty-one years now 18 years are eligible for vote provided his name is registered in the electoral roll. He must also reside in the constituency at least for six months. In case of a non-tribal, he must be a permanent resident of the council areas and must have resided within its jurisdiction for not less than twelve years.

However, Mizo people were not satisfied with the self-government provided under the provisions of the Sixth Schedule due to various reasons. Therefore, the Government of India came out with a proposal to elevate the Mizo Hills District to the status of the Union Territory of Mizoram. The Mizo District Council, which worked for twenty years, was, abolished with the Pawi-Lakher Regional Council under the North-Eastern Areas (Re-Organisation) Act, 1971.[51] However, to safeguard the interest of minority tribes like Pawis, Lakhers and Chakmas, the Pawi-Lakher Regional Council was trifurcated into three Autonomous Regions or three Regional Councils and each one was upgraded to the District Council in 1972 under the Act of 1971.[52] On April 29,1972, the District Councils for the three Autonomous Districts of Pawi, Lakher and Chakmas came into existence with Headquarters at Lawngtlai, Saiha and Vaseitlang (now Kamalanagar). Regarding Acts, Regulations and Rules framed by the Pawi-Lakher Regional Council remained in force in all the three new District Councils till amended or repealed by them.[53] The Lieutenant Governor of Mizoram specified the number of members in each of these three Councils. The Pawi District Council is to have 14 numbers of whom 12 are elected and 2 are to be nominated. The Lakher District Council is to have a total of 10 numbers out of which 9 elected and 1 nominated and in the Chakma District Council, 9 members—8 elected and 1 nominated.[54] The names of the Pawi-District Council and the Lakher District Council has been changed as the Lai District Council and the Mara District Council in 1988.[55]

The Mizo District Council and Pawi-Lakher Regional Council now Lai District Council, Mara District Council and Chakma District Council have been given wide powers and functions—Legislative, Executive and Judicial and Financial under the provision of the Sixth Schedule of the Constitution of India.[56]

Powers and Functions

As regards the *Legislative Powers*, the District Councils had the power to make laws on allotment, occupation or use, or setting apart of land, management of any forest, other then reserved forests; use of any canal or waterways for agriculture regulation and practice of *jhum*, etc; establishment of village councils and town committees and their powers, public health and sanitation, inheritance of property, social customs, marriage, divorce, appointment or succession of chiefs or headman, inheritance of property; social customs, etc.

Under Para 10(i) and (ii) of the Sixth Schedule, it also exercises powers of enactment of laws and rules on regulation and control of money lending or trading within the jurisdiction of the Council by non-tribal. Under Para 2(vii a) of the Sixth Schedule, the District Councils can make laws on the formation of subordinate local councils or boards, procedure and conduct of business; matters relating to transaction of business pertaining to administration of the district. Under Para 4 of the Provision in the Sixth Schedule, the District Councils exercise the power of legislation on Constitution of Village Councils and Courts, appointment of members and presiding officers of Village Councils and Courts, and appointment of officers necessary for administration of laws made under Para 3 of the Sixth Schedule. The District Council or Courts constituted by it exercise powers of Courts of Appeal.

Para 8 of the Sixth Schedule also empowered the District Councils to levy and collect taxes on lands and buildings and tolls on persons, assessment and collection of revenues, levy taxes on professions, trades, callings, employment, animals, vehicles and boats, entry of goods into market for sale and taxes for maintenance of schools, dispensaries or roads.

All laws framed by the District Councils in respect to above mentioned matters put up before the Governor for his assent and after the Governors consent it becomes valid.[57] The Mizo District Council and Pawi-Lakher Regional Council had passed Acts Regulations and Rules on many subjects from time to time to meet the situation and time and amended the same.

The *Executive* function of the District Councils are performed by the Executive Committee who are the authorised body to administer the territorial jurisdiction as laid down in the Sixth Schedule of the Constitution of India and various Acts and Regulations enacted by the District Council. Under Para 4 (Sub-Para 6) of the Sixth Schedule, the District Council has the authority to establish, construct and manage primary schools, dispensaries, market, cattle pounds, ferries, fisheries, roads and paths and also to prescribe the language and manners of primary education in the Mizo District.

The District Council is provided with *judicial* powers. The District Council Court is the court of appeal in respect of all suits and cases. No other court except the High Court and the Supreme Court of India had jurisdiction over suits and case decided by the Council Courts.[58] Cases tried, heard and adjudicated by these Courts between tribal and tribal and were in accordance with the customary laws of the land but the District Magistrates were also empowered to try criminal and other case under Cr. PC under the provision of the Para 5 of the Sixth Schedule.[59]

As regards the *finance*, the District Councils are provided with exclusive power in respect of assessment and collection of land revenue and also imposition of taxes on lands within their respective jurisdiction under Para 8 of the Sixth schedule.

There is also provision for a District Fund for each Autonomous District and Regional Fund for each Autonomous Region to which shall be credited all funds received respectively by the District

Council and the Regional Council in course of administration of such district or region.[60] The District Councils also empowered to levy taxes on buildings, shops, entry of goods into market and tolls on persons, residents, and forests within their respective jurisdictions. In case of taxes on motor vehicles, it is assigned to and collected by the state government on behalf of the District Council.[61] The Councils also derive their income from grants-in-aid, loans and advances etc. from the State Government for their administration and certain purpose, such as the development of the roads and communications, rural health and sanitation, maintenance of forest, tribal culture, rural water supply, regeneration of forest, etc.

The Village Councils

The Administration of Lushai (Mizo) village by a hereditary Chief has been replaced by the Village Councils. The Lushai Hills District Council, (Village Councils) Act 1953 was passed under the Lushai Hills Act. of 1953 on the 1st December, 1953, which received the assent of the Governor of Assam on the 29 November, 1953 published in the Assam Gazette on the 9th December, 1953. Similarly, the Pawi-Lakher Regional Council (Village Council) Act was passed in September, 1954 to streamline village administration in the Pawi-Lakher region.[62] By the Lushai Hills Autonomous District (Administration and Justice) Rules 1953, the District Council Court was established and Pawi-Lakher Autonomous Region (Administration of Justice) Rules, 1954, the Village Council Courts were constituted in the Pawi-Lakher Region.[63] Thus, with establishment of the Village Councils/Courts, the power and rights of the chiefs were abolished and people elected their representatives on the basis of adult franchise for the first time in village administration in Mizoram.

Composition

As per the Village Council Act, the Village Council for each village or a group of villages consists of 4 to 10 Members according to the number of houses in a village.[64]

The District Council decides the numbers constituting Village Council. President and Vice-President are elected by the members of the Council from among themselves. The District Council would be empowered to take steps for filling up the post of Village Council President lying vacant owing to death or resignation of the person.[65]

If not dissolved earlier, the term of the Village Councils or Courts is for three years from the date appointed for its first meeting, provided that the term of a Village Council may be extended or reduced for a period not exceeding six months by the orders of the administrator and the District Council.[66]

The executive functions of the Village Councils are discharges through the executive, which consists of the President, the Vice-President and Secretary. The Secretary is appointed by the administrator of the District Council. The President and the Vice-President are elected by the members of the Village Council. The President who presides over the meeting, summons the meeting of the Village Council. The President may resign any time from the Executive Committee. However, the Village Council has no power to remove the President.[67]

To become an elected member of the Village Council, a person: must be a member of Scheduled Tribe, must attain 25 years of age with sound mind, must be a voter where he seeks election, must not be a party to any other Village Council and should not have been convicted of an offence under the Lushai Hills Autonomous District (Administration of Justice) Rules, 1953.

A member of the Village Councils including the President, the Vice-President and Secretary shall be entitled to receive such remuneration and privileges as determined by the Government.

The President is the chief functionary at village administration. He issues notices, instructions for prevention of dangers such as out break of fire, epidemic, etc. in the respective village. He carries out all orders/notification issued either by the Deputy Commissioner or the District Councils. The President presides over the meetings of the Village Councils and summons it whenever necessary. The President can report in writing the conduct of a member to the administrator or executive committee, when failed to carry out the direction of the President. Accordingly, the administrator/executive committee may suspend the member for any period.[68] The Vice-President performs all the duties of the President in his absence. The President is assisted by the Secretary who records all proceedings of Village Council and Village Council Court, which are signed by the President. The president can examine the registers, books kept by the secretary. The President is also the chief custodian of the Village Council fund.[69] The president is also act in compliance with the orders and notification from the Deputy Commissioner, Local Administration Department, Rural Development Department, block development officer and other line departments of the Government of Mizoram.

The Tlangau or village crier is also a member of the staff of the Village Council who has the responsibility to bring all the orders and notification received from the government and the Council to the public, all development activities taken up by the Council and carry summons of the Village Council Court to all parties and other persons to attend the court meeting as also the Presidents notice to all members of the council to attend meetings. He is appointed by the Village Council and can be dismissed by it under intimation to the District Council/government. He is exempted from Hnatlang or voluntary services and entitled to receive such remuneration as determined by the government.

Powers and Functions

The functions of the Village Council may broadly be divided into two—Executive and Judicial.[70]

The executive or administrative functions includes–(i) the distribution of jhum lands within their jurisdiction in accordance with the laws framed by the District Council[71], (ii) The Village Council has the power to enforce Hnatlang wherein all the able bodied villagers which the residents of the village are to render their services for the welfare of the village whenever occasion so demands, (iii) Any person not complying with Hnatlang order shall be liable to pay fine in kind or cash which may extend to Rs. 4 (now Rs. 50) per Hnatlang day unless he has been exempted[72], (iv) The Village Council can also exempt any person by recording the reasons for exemption in writing and people below 15 years of age and person of the 60 years or above are not forced to work, and (v) It shall be responsible for ensuring sanitation in the village. It may form a sanitation committee. It can evict a person having unauthorized occupation of land and can also order for vacation within seven days.

The Village Council is also the main agent of the Government from which the Government gets vital statistics, serious incidents occurring in the village, out break of fire incidents etc. The Village

Council also reports to the government the basic needs of the village like infrastructure facilities, inter village paths, to take remedial measures in case of poor harvest, etc.

It also assists the rural development department in the selection of beneficiaries under various anti poverty programmes. The village council also can pass orders under Mizo Hnam Dan—the Mizo customary law, to run the village administration smoothly. Thus, the administrative duties, some are provided for in the acts, rules and regulations, while others are based on convention, usage, practice and custom of the Mizo people.[73]

The Village Council Court is the lowest court comprises of three members, elected by the Council from among its elected members with a three-year term in office.[74] The judicial functions of the Village Council are based on Lushai Hills Autonomous District (Administration of Justice) Rules, 1953. The Village Council Court is the lowest court in Mizoram. The court deals with both civil and criminal cases of petty offences of theft, pilferage, mischief and trespass, assault and hurt, etc. It has no power to decide inheritance cases and cases for which imprisonment is obligatory under the Indian Penal Code.[75]

When Mizoram became a Union Territory in February 1972, Mizoram Legislative Assembly was installed in place of the Mizo District Council with Council of Ministers and other officials to run the state. Thereafter, the Village Councils, now looked after by the Mizoram Legislative Assembly. The three newly formed District Council Lai, Mara, Chakma looks after the Village Councils in their respect jurisdiction.

Thus, village administration in Mizoram is a two-tier system where there is no District Council and three-tire system where there is District Council. The Village Council forms village level administration and the Mizoram Legislative Assembly forms the state level administration. Therefore, there are no intermediate bodies between villages. The Local Administration Department of the Government of Mizoram is supervising the working of the Village Councils.[76]

However, the present position of the Village Councils in Mizoram may be compared with the Panchayats of Indian states before the Constitution (73rd Amendment) Act 1992. Socio-economic development is beyond the scope of the Councils due to lack of financial and political power. The main deficiency of the

Village Council is its financial handicap. Although there is a provision for village fund, no permanent source of income is mentioned. It is empowered to collect very nominal amount of animal tax out of which fifty per cent goes to state exchequer and the rest remains in the village fund. Apart from this, another source of revenue is occasional fines collected by way of punishment. Moreover, people cannot take part in the discussions of Village Council meetings. They cannot decide on any issue pertaining to them in the Village Council. Failure to observe this rule is subject to punishment. Under Lushai Hills District (Village Councils) Act, 1953 (amended up to date), Sub-section (3) of Section 13 reads, "No person other than a member of the Village Council shall vote nor shall speak or take part in its deliberation and any person contravening this provision shall be punishable with fine not exceeding Rs. 50 by the Village Courts. The Sub-section (1) of section 25 of the Act provides, "The Governor, by public notification, order the dissolution of a Village Council if in its opinion, the Village Council is too inefficient or is not able to carry on the village administration or is acting in the manner prejudicial to the interest of the state or for any other reasons sufficient for such dissolution." Thus, autonomy of the Village Councils as the local self-government in Mizoram is highly restricted by the governmental interference and without financial power; the Village Councils seem to be irrelevant local self-institutions.[77] Although Village Councils are being involved in the process of rural development, it is not as synchronised as it is under the PRIs. Bureaucracy can easily override the Village Councils. Lalzawnga[78] made some comparison between PRIs and Village Councils in Mizoram. Some of them are mentioned below:

1. The PRIs has root in the Constitution of India whereas Village Councils has no such (PRIs now constitutional bodies).
2. Unlike two or three-tiers of PRIs there is only one tier in Village Council.
3. Absence of seat reservation for women.
4. While the duration of Panchayat is 5 years, Village Councils term is only 3 years.
5. Election to the panchayats is vested in the hands of State Election Commissions whereas the elections of the Village

Councils are conducted by the State Local Administration Department.

6. Gram Sabha provides a platform for public grievances and exchange of ideas whereas, public participation in Village Councils are restricted.
7. Power, authority and responsibilities of Panchayats to prepare plan for economic development and social justice and the implementation of such schemes (including the matters listed in the Eleventh Schedule) are not comparable to Village Councils.
8. The representation of different level of panchayats from local to district level is not comparable with Village Councils in Mizoram.

As there is no provision of reservation of women, they are rarely represented in the Village Councils of Mizoram. In the 2009 election, for 555 Village Councils, there were 5258 candidates. Out of the 2071 elected candidates in 555 village councils, only 31 women managed to get elected, against 2040 men, which is comparatively very less. In Aizawl district, 22 women were elected, in Lunglei district 6, in Serchhip, Kolasib and Mamit districts 1 each and Champhai district no women were elected. Thus the Village Councils have been dominated by male. It is time now for Mizoram to involve more women in decision making especially at the village administration in ensuring the goal of women's empowerment. Reservation of seats in the Village Councils through legislation or introduction of Panchayati Raj is the only alternative in male bastion grassroots democracy in Mizoram. While the establishment of the new democratic institutions marked the participation of women in the decision making bodies, which was traditionally the exclusive domain of men, the traditional value of gender inequality operating as a political norm in Mizo society seems to have prevented participation of women in larger number in politics.[79] Moreover, legally constituted Village Councils are increasingly losing its power and authority to the ethnic based organizations such as the Young Mizo Association (YMA), Mizo Upa Pawl (MUP) and Mizo Hmeichhe Insuihkhawm Pawl (MHIP), etc. The Village Council, which is expected to uphold the traditional customs and practices of the Mizo, is often ineffective on certain accounts thereby rendering the rule of law meaningless. The three constitutional bodies and other associations often function as rivals and not as partners. The fact that works are carried out in a climate of tension and rivalry between the District Administration and the District Councils has led to slow and inefficient implementation. The problem is not only of development but is also political. The people of Mizoram are interested in sustaining the modern political institutions but they do not seem to have internalised democratic values. The values of democratic institutions are yet to be firmly entrenched in the Mizo society.[80] Therefore, it is essential for streamlining the grassroots democratic bodies in the state. The existing local self-government in Mizoram was introduced by the Lushai Hills District Council; (Village Councils) Act 1953 which need to be reviewed as 50 years has passed since then, if panchayati raj institutions as par with 73rd Amendment Act, are not to be introduced. The existing term, the decision-making power, and financial powers of the Village Councils need to be increased.[81]

Notes and References

1. Sharma M.P. and Sadana, B.L. (2008): Public Administration in Theory and Practice, *op. cit.* pp. 867-887 Also see Avasthi, A.P. (2002): *Indian Government and Politics, Lakshmi Narain Agarwal, Agra* 522-535 and Lalzawnga, R. (2010): *Panchayati Raj in India*, in Laskar, Baharul Islam (ed.) *Mizoram—the Emerging Issues of Development*, DVS Publishers, Guwahati, pp. 247226-231.
2. Rao, V. Venkata, Thansanga, H., Hazarika, Niru. (1987): *A Century of Government and Politics in North-East India*, Volume III, Mizoram, S. Chand and Company (Pvt.) LTD., New Delhi, p. 65 also see Malsawma, H.L. (2002): *Sociology of The Mizos*, Spectrum Publications, Guwahati, Guwahati: Delhi, p. 14.
3. *Ibid.*, p. 62. Zahmuaka being a brave and strong man was the first chief during the migration period. He had six sons equally brave and strong viz. Zadenga, Paliana, Thangluaha, Thangura, Rivunga and Rokhuma became Chiefs subsequently of different villages. Thangura, one of the six sons of Zahmuaka had two sons namely Chawnglula and Thangmanga. Thangmanga had only one son, Sailova. Sailova had three sons from which Sailos traced their origin. The Sailo Chiefs established their domination throughout the Lushai Hills except in Pawi-Lakher region.
4. Zorema, J. (2002): *The Bureaucracy, The Chiefs and Indirect Rule in*

the Lushai Hills of Assam, 1898-1952, A Thesis submitted for Doctor of Philosophy to North Eastern Hill University, Shillong, p. 22.

5. Singh, S.N. (2002): *Mizoram*, Mittal Publications, New Delhi, 1994, p. 135.
6. Malsawma, H.L. (2002): *Sociology of The Mizos*, Spectrum Publications, Guwahati: Delhi, p. 14.
7. *Ibid.*
8. V. Venkata Rao, H. Thansanga, Niru Hazarika. (1987): *A Century of Government and Politics in North-East India*, Volume III, Mizoram, *op. cit.* p. 67.
9. *Ibid.*
10. Chatterjee, N. (1975): *The Mizo Chief and His Administration*, Aizawl, p. 15 (here in after the Mizo Chiefs).
11. Rao, V. Venkata, Thansanga, H., Hazarika, Niru. (1987): *A Century of Government and Politics in North-East India*, Volume III, Mizoram, *op. cit.* p. 67.
12. Lewin, T.H., n. 4, p. 100. Quoted in Singh, S.N. Mizoram, *(2002) op. cit.* p. 136.
13. Zorema, J. (2002): *The Bureaucracy.*, *op. cit.*, p. 25.
14. Singh, S.N. (2002): *Mizoram*, *op. cit.*, p. 137.
15. Zorema, J. (2002): *The Bureaucracy.*, *op. cit.* p. 26.
16. *Ibid* p. 24.
17. *Ibid* p. 26.
18. V. Venkata Rao, H. Thansanga, Niru, Hazarika. (1987): *A Century of Government and Politics in North-East India*, Volume III, Mizoram, *op. cit.* p. 66.
19. Parry, N.E. (Reprint 1976): A Monograph on Lushai Customs and Ceremonies, Shillong, 1928, p. 12, (herein after, A Monograph).
20. V. Venkata Rao, H. Thansanga, Niru, Hazarika. (1987): *A Century of Government and Politics in North-East India*, Volume III, Mizoram, *op. cit.* p. 67.
21. Zorema, J. (2002): *The Bureaucracy*, *op. cit.* p. 28.
22. Parry, N.E. *A Monograph*, *op. cit.*, p. 3, By tradition when a chiefs son attained maturity and got married, the chief would setup a separate village for his son to rule and a few household were transferred to the new village. The son was not supposed to pay any tribute to his father chief but left to himself to set up his position as a chief through his personal ability.
23. Zorema, J. (2002): *The Bureaucracy.*, *op. cit.* p. 23.
24. Shakespear, J. *op. cit.* p. 43. By custom a villager could transfer his allegiance to another chief at will, hence it happens that a chief's village becomes large or small according to the happiness of the people within his rule.
25. Zorema, J. (2002): *The Bureaucracy.*, *op. cit.* p. 25.

26. Venkata Rao, V. Thansanga, H. Niru, Hazarika. (1987): *A Century of Government and Politics in North-East India*, Volume III, Mizoram, *op. cit.* p. 77.
27. Chatterjee, N. (1975): *Zawlbuk As a Social Institution in the Mizo Society*, Tribal Research Institute, Aizawl, Mizoram, p. 13.
28. Hminga, C.L. (Serkawn, 1987): *The Life and Witness of the Churches in Mizoram*, p. 29.
29. Chatterjee, N. (1975): Zawlbuk, *op. cit.* p. 15, The young boy of between six and fourteen years of age were to keep up the supply of firewood for the Zawlbuk. Each boy was assigned a number of bundles to supply each day and failure to do so was severely punished.
30. Zorema, J. (2002): *The Bureaucracy op. cit.* p. 29.
31. *Ibid.*
32. Siama, V.L. (1961): *History of Mizoram*, Zoram Printing Press, Aizawl, p. 24. Quoted in Lalkima, C. (1997): *Social Welfare Administration in a Tribal State—A Case Study of Mizoram*, Spectrum Publications, Guwahati; Delhi, p. 17.
33. Ray, Animesh. (1982): *Mizoram Dynamics of Change*, Pearl Publishers, Calcutta, pp. 33-34.
34. Zorema, J. (2002): *The Bureaucracy*., *op. cit.* pp. 88-89.
35. Ray, Animesh. (1982): *Mizoram Dynamics of Change*, *op. cit.* p. 34.
36. Singh, S.N. (2002): *Mizoram*, *op. cit.*, p. 145.
37. Zorema, J. (2002): *The Bureaucracy*., *op. cit.* p. 236.
38. Zorema, J. (2002): *The Bureaucracy*., *op. cit.* p. 241.
39. Prasad, R.N. and Agarwal, A.K. (1991): *Political and Economic Development of Mizoram*, Mittal Publications, New Delhi, p. 116.
40. *Ibid.*
41. Singh, S.N. (2002): *Mizoram*, *op. cit.*, p. 145.
42. *Ibid.*
43. *Ibid.* p. 146.
44. *Ibid.*
45. *Ibid.*
46. Mizoram District Gazetteers, Department of Art and Culture, Government of Mizoram, Aizawl, 1989, p. 287.
47. Singh, S.N. (2002): *Mizoram*, *op. cit.* p. 146.
48. Mizoram District Gazetteers op. cit, p. 287.
49. Singh, S.N. (2002): *Mizoram*, *op. cit.* p. 147.
50. *Ibid.*
51. North East Area (Reorganisation) Act, 1971.
52. North East Area (Reorganisation) Act, 1971. The leader of three tribes submitted several memoranda to the Government of India at the time of formation of Union Territory of Mizoram, demanding creation of the separate Union Territory for their areas. Finally the Government of India agreed to the creation of District Councils.

53. Ray, Animesh. (1982): *Mizoram Dynamics of Change, op. cit.* p. 116.
54. *Ibid*: The name of the District was changed from Lushai Hills District to Mizo District in 1954 by the Lushai Hills (Change of Name) Act, 1954. Consequently the name "Mizo Hills" has been used for all references to "Lushai Hills" in its sequence after the change of the name in 1954.
55. Sixth Schedule of the Constitution of India (Amendment) Act, 1988.
56. Sixth Schedule of the Constitution of India Article (2), 275.
57. *Mizoram District Gazetteers, op.* cit., p. 290.
58. Prasad, R.N. (1987): *Government and Politics in Mizoram 1947-1986* Northern Book Center, New Delhi, p. 133.
59. Nag, Chitta Ranjan (1999,): *Post-Colonial Mizo Politics, 1947-1998*, Vikas Publication Pvt. Ltd, New Delhi, pp. 35-36.
60. Singh, S.N. (2002): *Mizoram, op. cit.* p. 149.
61. *Ibid.*
62. Collection of District Council Acts, Rules and Regulations. p. 1. Mizoram District Gazetteers, (1989): *op. cit.*, p. 1.
63. Broachers of Mizo District Council and Pawi-Lakher Regional Council. Quoted in Singh, S.N. (2002): *Mizoram, op. cit.* p. 149.
64. Nag, Chitta Ranjan (1999): *Post-Colonial Mizo Politics, 1947-1998, op. cit.* p. 38.

    For villages not exceeding 100 houses—4 Members

For villages between	101	and	200 houses	-	5 Members
"	"	"	201	" 300	" - 6 "
"	"	"	301	" 400	" - 7 "
"	"	"	401	" 500	" - 8 "
"	"	"	501	" 600	" - 9 "

    for villages exceeding 600 houses there shall be 10 Members. But one third of the members or nearest to one third would be nominated by the Executive Council and the rest on election.
65. *Mizoram District Gazetteers*, (1989): *op. cit.*, p. 293.
66. Prasad, R.N. and Agarwal, A.K. (1991): *Political and Economic Development of Mizoram*, Mittal Publications, New Delhi, p. 117.
67. Singh, S.N. (2002): *Mizoram, op. cit.* p. 150.
68. Prasad, R.N. and Agarwal, AK (1991) *Political and Economic Development of Mizoram, op. cit.* p. 118.
69. Singh, S.N. (2002): *Mizoram, op. cit.* p. 150.
70. *Ibid* p. 150.
71. As per Provision of Forest Act, 1955 and the Jhuming Regulation Act, 1954 the Village Council is allowed to distribute lands for Jhuming purpose.
72. Prasad, R.N. and Agarwal, A.K. (1991): *Political and Economic Development of Mizoram, op cit.* p. 119.
73. *Ibid.*, p. 120.

74. *Ibid.*
75. Satpathy, R.K. (1995), Local Government in Mizoram: Some Observations, in Prasad, R.N. and A.K. Agarwal (ed.) *Landmarks: A Study of Public Administration in Mizoram* IIPA, Aizawl Local Branch, Mizoram, p. 357.
76. Malswama, H.L., (2002): *Sociology., op. cit.* pp. 27-28.
77. Satpathy, R.K. (1995): *Local Government in Mizoram: Some Observations, op. cit.* pp. 358-362.
78. Lalzawnga, R. (2010): Panchayati Raj in India, in Laskar, Baharul Islam (ed.) *Mizoram: The Emerging Issues of Development*, DVS Publishers, Guwahati, p. 247.
79. Haokip, T.T. (2009): "Traditional Self-governing Institutions and Democratic Governance in NE India", *Local Government Quarterly*, July-September, All India Institute of Local Self Government, Mumbai, p. 43.
80. *Ibid*, pp. 34-35.
81. Sinha, Harendra (2010) : Block Administration without Panchayati Raj Institutions—An Assessment in Lunglei District of Mizoram, Kurukshetra, New Delhi.

4
Bureaucracy and Rural Development in Mizoram

This chapter makes a study on bureaucratic structure and rural development in Mizoram. Section I traces the evolution of rural development and the bureaucratic organisation in Mizoram. Section II sketches the state and centrally sponsored rural development programmes implemented in the state.

INTRODUCTION

Mizoram is a socio-economically backward state. The state economy is mainly agrarian, about 70 per cent of the population is directly or indirectly dependent on agriculture. Agriculture still remains under-developed and the primitive method of shifting cultivation known as *'jhum'* predominates. The state is not self-sufficient in foodgrain production where about 75 per cent of rice alone comes from outside the state. Mizoram imports a large quantity of food staff, fruits, vegetables, fish and livestock like pig, cattle, goat, poultry essentially required for the over all food supply of the people. Such items are presently imported from other states particularly neighbouring states of Assam, Tripura and Manipur. Some quantity is also imported through informal boarder trade from Myanmar. As per the Trade and Commerce Department, Mizoram, the value of import of Agriculture, Horticulture and Livestock's items etc. during 2008-2009 was Rs. 40.50 crores. Therefore, development strategies of the Government of Mizoram, after independence, has been mainly towards agricultural development for economic self-sufficiency and to protect the land from degradation, to protect burning of forests for jhuming, encouraging permanent cultivation in achieving sustainable development in eco-friendly manner vis-à-vis to find out alternative way of livelihood for the jhumia families. Economic development in Mizoram depends on rural development. Development of agriculture and allied sector and small-scale industries are important for increasing the income of rural people as well as for overall economic development. In planning and implementation of all the development programmes of the government, bureaucracy plays an important role in the state. Bureaucracy is the dependable machinery of the government for the successful implementation of all the rural development programmes which is typically responsible, in the absence of viable local self-governing institutions like panchayati raj bodies in Mizoram. In Mizoram, the Directorate of Rural Development, Government of Mizoram, heads the administration at the state level. At the district level, the Deputy Commissioners are the controlling officers of the rural development. The programme drawn up by the directorate is implemented at block level by the respective block development officers under the supervision of the controlling officers. The block development officer implements both state and centrally sponsored rural development schemes in Mizoram.

Rural Development before Independence in Mizoram

Before independence, in Lushai Hills, the means of livelihood was largely through agriculture. Rural Development was primarily meant for development of agriculture. Jhum cultivation was the main occupation of the rural people due to absence of flat land, rugged mountainous terrains in the Lushai Hills. No systematic effort was made for the development of agriculture although a focus on agricultural development was started when the British Missionaries encouraged agricultural experiments in different kind of cash crops and cereals, potato cultivation, rubber cultivation and terraced cultivation was experimented.[1] However, these efforts were not successful due to lack of financial support, administrative coordination and technical guidance.[2] As a result, jhum cultivation was continued as a dominant feature of Mizo rural economy and rural activities remained confined to basket weaving, animal rearing and collecting things from the jungle.[3]

The British administration felt that until the Lushai abandon their migratory habits little improvement could be hoped for. It was, however, in the interest of the chiefs to perpetuate the migratory habits as with permanent cultivation the tendency would have been for the existing large communities to split up, which would have diminished the authority of the chiefs over their people.[4] The migratory habit had an adverse effect on the economic stability of the people.[5] The Administrative Report of 1895-96,[6] recounts:

Owing to the improvidence of the Lushai as a result of their migratory habits, and the impossibility of carrying about with them large stock of grain there is never a surplus share of rice in any village, and the failure of a single harvest breaks it up, the inhabitants dispersing to the villages of chiefs more fortunately situated.

The government was keen to introduce permanent cultivation primarily to facilitate law and order enforcement because it was difficult to contain migratory tribes to peaceful behaviour. Because of the terrain it was, however, difficult to introduce permanent cultivation anywhere. But some suitable areas were found where long stretches of flat lands were available. A lot of interest was generated in agricultural experiments, reclamation of valley lands were taken up. Experimental cultivation of many new crops was being undertaken. Potatoes were doing well. Small quantities of wheat were also successfully raised. Experiment in rubber cultivation was started. Terraced cultivation was introduced, as this was the only scientific way of agriculture in the steep hills. As terracing was a good success in the Naga Hills, a party of Lushai chiefs was taken by the Superintendent to the Naga Hills to show them the benefits of terracing.[7] However, these programmes were not successful and taken up in a half-hearted way, with no financial support and technical guidance.[8] It was observed in the Administrative Report, 1933-34,[9] that the progress of agricultural work in the district was very slow mainly because of water scarcity in the district and also due to the fact that with the exception of a few places there were no arable lands, no available places for making water canal irrigation, nor were there suitable places for cattle grazing. The British administration further felt that as the people migrated in search of jhum lands, new crops which would serve as staple crops of permanent nature suitable in the locality could be carried out without jhuming, should be tried. It was hoped that "fruit cultivation will not only encourage the people to be permanent, to dig and plough, to sow and plant and harvest, to feed and milk the cows and to rear all kinds of domestic stock, but it will also open the way for various related industries that are dependent on agriculture.[10]

The British administration was thus alive to the problems in agriculture and general economic conditions in the Lushai Hills (Mizoram), but there was no concerted effort and wide-based move from the government to tackle the problems.[11]

In 1940's, A.G. McCall, Superintendent of Lushai Hills introduced certain economic and welfare measures[12]. To raise the economic status, he drew up a plan of all round economic development in which the lead was to be provided by the administration. McCall suggested the adoption of cottage industries and he took steps to start the first cottage industries in the area. For the welfare and economic well being of the Lushai villages, he organised a Village Welfare Committee operated under the guidance of the District Red Cross Committee at Aizawl. The objective was to improve public health and living conditions in the villages, under the technical guidance of the civil surgeon. However, Village Welfare Communities could not do much due to lack of financial support.

The 1961 Census reveals the poor and primitive agriculture in the overall backward economy of Mizoram where there was no agro-based industries and other manufacturing agencies and 90 per cent of the people depended on primitive method of agriculture.[13] While it was one of the districts of Assam, it contributed only 1.5 per cent of the states income, being the lowest among all the districts of Assam.[14]

Rural Development after Independence: Community Development and Bureaucratic Organisation

After independence, agriculture was given top priority of all the development plans in the Mizo Hills. It took a new turn with the inauguration of Community Development Project (CDP) in Mizoram on the first April 1953.[15] The first CDP was opened at Aizawl and later more CD blocks were opened at Lunglei in 1956,

Kolosib in 1958 and Mamit in 1959.[16] Before 1972, there were nine CD blocks with the inauguration of Hnahthial, Lawngtlai, Saitual, Champhai and Serchhip blocks. Aizawl, Kolosib, Mamit, Serchhip, Saitual and Champhai in the Aizawl Sub-Division and Lunglei, Lawngtlai and Hnahthial were in Lunglei Sub-Division.[17] Each blocks were headed by a Project Executive Officer.

The CD blocks in the tribal areas were gradually converted into the Special Multi-purpose Tribal Blocks organised under a special scheme initiated by Ministry of Home Affairs in 1956 for the development of the tribal areas.[18] The essence of these Tribal blocks were to bring about rapid improvement in the economic and social standards of the tribal people by selecting specially underdeveloped but compact areas for multi-sided development. The object was to make their programme of development more intensive in character than that undertaken in the normal community development blocks.

The Ministry of Home Affairs, Government of India provided a sum of Rs. 6,45,00,000 under the Second Five Year Plan for the establishment of 43-Special Multipurpose Tribal blocks.[19] Lunglei block[20] was one of the first to be covered into a Tribal Development Block which was converted during the second plan period and it served as a model for conversion of other blocks in Mizoram. The purpose of this scheme was to utilise the blocks for determining the development process suitable for tribal life.[21] One of the objectives was to wean away the tribal people from the practice of shifting cultivation to take a settled agriculture and therefore, special attention was given to terracing, irrigation, agriculture, horticulture, drinking water facilities, public health, medical facilities, communications, education, arts and crafts, social education, cooperation, rural housing.[22]

During the early period of the introduction of the CDP, it was the largest scheme in Mizoram which undertaken various developmental works through various developmental groups under it.[23] There were agriculture group, medical group, education group, rural communication and building group.

The agriculture group includes developmental works of animal husbandry and veterinary, fisheries development, soil and water conservation. This group has undertaken 75 per cent of the developmental works for rural development. During the Second Five Year Plans (1951-61) attention was mostly concentrated on the development of agriculture in Mizoram with special emphasis on irrigation, soil conservation, wet paddy cultivation, land reclamation, fisheries and community projects. Land reclamation work was executed by the Agriculture Department whereas other development work was taken up through the CD blocks in the district.[24]

The medical group was involved in health care. Various health centres, medical sub-centres were initiated with health workers posted under this group.

The education group was involved in social education programmes like health awareness for woman and children, sports and cultural development, etc. was undertaken by this group. Social Education Organizers both male and female were appointed for the same.

The rural communication and building group undertaken the communication development works. It undertakes construction of roads and bridges, construction of halls, office buildings for which number of Civil Engineers and Overseers were appointed for the same.

In each CD block, ten Gram Sevaks and two Gram Sevika's were appointed for multi-purpose rural development works, as per the guidelines of community development scheme.[25]

During the Third Five Year Plan 1961-66, emphasis was mainly laid on the development of means of communication, agriculture development and marketing of agricultural products. A three years special development plan for the development of the state was undertaken in 1963-64 with the following provisions:[26]

1.	District Development Board	:	Rs. 1.50 lakhs
2.	Major Roads	:	Rs. 34.00 lakhs
3.	Rural Roads	:	Rs. 30.00 lakhs
4.	Education	:	Rs. 20.00 lakhs
5.	Medical	:	Rs. 20.87 lakhs
6.	Air trip	:	Rs. 12.00 lakhs
7.	Rural Water Supply	:	Rs. 6.90 lakhs
8.	Soil Conservation	:	Rs. 8.58 lakhs
9.	Agriculture and Marketing	:	Rs. 5.18 lakhs
10.	Power Electricity	:	Rs. 6.10 lakhs
11.	Inland Water Transport	:	Rs. 3.88 lakhs
12.	Publicity	:	Rs. 0.15 lakhs
	Total	:	Rs. 150.00 lakhs.

For the implementation of the plan a District Development Board was established at Aizawl with Deputy Commissioner as Chairman.

The Fourth Five Year Plan 1969-74 also laid emphasis on agriculture and allied activities including cooperation and community development to make the hill areas self sufficient in food production. Emphasis has also been made to create a base for industrial development and social service sector including education, water supply etc. However, the Fourth Five Year Plan has suffered serious setback in Mizoram due to large-scale disturbances, which had started in 1966.[27] Many block officials were also attached to Administrative Officer's Office.[28] About 2000 families have been uprooted and regrouped into new villages for security reasons. As a result, the cultivators and common man had to depend on supplies of food-grains from outside Mizoram.[29]

When Mizo Hills District was upgraded to the Union Territory status in 1972, for smooth functioning of developmental operations, the entire structure of the Community Development Blocks was re-organised into twenty blocks in 1973.[30] They are:(1) Tlangnuam (2) Thingdawl (3) Thingsulthliah (4) Reiek (5) Aibawk (6) Phaileng 'W' (7) Zawlnuam (8) Serchhip (9) Khawzawl (10) Darlawn (11) Ngopa (12) Lungdar 'E' (13) Lunglei (14) Lungsen (15) Bunghmun (16) Sangau (17) Hnahthial (18) Lawngtlai (19) Tuipang (20) Chawngte. Many developments were also started functioning such as Agriculture and Animal Husbandry, Forest and Soil conservation, Public Works Department, etc.

However, the Community Development Project was not involved in such sectors as agriculture and animal husbandry, soil conservation, medical, etc. which were taken up by development departments such as Agriculture and Animal Husbandry, Forest and Soil conservation, Public Works Department, etc.[31] As a result, the activities of the CDP was reduced to nothing worth mentioning, with a office only under Deputy Commissioner with a Mizoram Civil Service Officer as its head till 1974.[32]

In 1974, a significant development was made with the establishment of the Directorate of Community Development separating from the Deputy Commissioners control and in 1983-84, the nomenclature of Community Development was changed to Rural Development.[33] The Directorate, is headed by a Director, Assistant Director, Finance and Accounts Officer and a Special Officer, Nutrition. At the district level the Deputy Commissioners are the Controlling Officer of the CD block and the block development officers (BDO) within their respective blocks except budget allotment and work programmes, which are exclusively in the hands of the Directorate of Community Development. The Deputy Commissioner further entrust the Sub-Divisional Officer to supervise the execution of the Block Development Committee in their respective Sub-Divisions. The programme drawn by the Directorate of Rural Development is implemented at block level by the respective BDOs under the supervision of the controlling officers.[34]

The Directorate of Rural Development started functioning with special focus on alleviation of rural poverty. The blocks functions[35] with special emphasis to uplift the day to day living standard of the backward communities in the rural areas, to popularize improved breeds of live-stock and poultry at domestic level by selling better breeds to villagers at subsidized rate, and taken up social education, health and rural sanitation, communication and housing.

The objective of social education is to give effective moral and physical education at the village levels by providing them with play grounds, community assets community halls, village wells, water points, urinal sheds and prizes for cleanliness. The programme under communication includes construction of jeep roads, inter-village paths, suspension bridges, masonry steps and culverts and housing programmes includes construction of office buildings and quarters for BDO were proposed.[36]

The Fifth Five Year Plan 1974-79 laid emphasis on agriculture and community development. Under agriculture sector, it proposes to bring 20,000 hectares of land under permanent cultivation of paddy and seasonal crops and 10,000 hectares of land under plantation.

The objective[37] was largely to minimize shifting cultivation and to preserve natural forest wealth by restoring to permanent cultivation to step up food production for self-sufficiency. Emphasis was also laid on the improvement of rural health services by bringing up more new primary health centres and sub-centres, upgradation of primary health centres to rural hospitals. For this purpose, the Government of India evolved several new programmes as centrally sponsored schemes. Three of the important programmes are: (1) Multipurpose Workers Scheme (2) Community Health Workers Scheme, and (3) Indigenous Dhai Training Schemes which were launched and implemented with substantial success.[38] The Sixth Five Year Plan 1980-85 laid top priority on the achievement of economic and technological self-reliance, reduction in the incidence of poverty and unemployment, a speedy development of the indigenous sources of energy, promoting the involvement of all sections of people in the process of development.[39] The rural development blocks were also entrusted to implement the Integrated Rural Development Programme (IRDP). Besides IRDP, Development of Women and Children in Rural Areas (DWCRA), National Rural Employment Programme (NREP), Rural Landless Employment Guarantee Scheme (RLEGP) were launched in 1981 and 1983-84 as centrally sponsored schemes. The District Rural Development Agency, an autonomous body created under the Societies of Registration Act, 1860 which was also inaugurated in the year 1980, to administer centrally sponsored schemes. In Mizoram, the District Rural Development Agency was inaugurated in 1982 at Aizawl, Lunglei and Saiha[40].

The Seventh Five Year Plan 1985-90 lay down 'Food, Work and Productivity as the basic objectives. It emphasises on accelerating food production, increase in employment opportunities and raise productivity.[41] The planning process, in true sense, in Mizoram started only with effect from the Seventh Five Year Plan, when the region launched her development programme for the first time under conditions of peace.[42] Till 1972, Mizoram was one of the autonomous districts of Assam. Since Assam had four other autonomous districts, the share of Mizo district was but meagre.[43] Then from 1966, insurgency broke out which was lasted two long decades, which severely slowed down the developmental plans and developmental strategies in true sense in Mizoram, started following the Peace Accord signed on 30.06.1986 and when Mizoram was conferred statehood on February, 1987.[44]

New Land Use Policy and Re-organisation of Bureaucracy

With the introduction of New Land Use Policy (NLUP), which had commenced with effect from the year 1990-91, the Directorate of Rural Development of the Government of Mizoram was entrusted to operate and supervise all activities of the NLUP. For the smooth functioning of the NLUP, a major reorganisation of the Rural Development Department was effected in 1989.[45] The directorate was redesigned as the Commissionerate of Rural Development. To implement the NLUP effectively, a Minister of State was placed, as its political head and a Commissioner IAS, Super Time Scale, became the administrative head of the Commissionerate. The supporting staffs from nine development departments were taken in this enlarged bureaucratic structure for its effective implementation.[46] They were from Agriculture, Soil and Water Conservation, Animal Husbandry, Sericulture, Forest, Fisheries, Finance and Accounts, Industry and Information and Public Relations.

The reorganisation was needed as the NLUP schemes were spread over various fields, which required experienced and expert personnel in each discipline. The NLUP scheme was divided into three sectors agriculture and allied sector, animal husbandry, veterinary and industry and each sector was placed under the charge of a Deputy Commissioner (DC) drawn from the concerned departments on deputation. In addition to these three Deputy Commissioners, there is one Deputy Commissioner, who was in charge of the overall administration of the department. The Technical Commissioners (TC) had their own staff. There is Information and Public Relations (I&PR) section headed by a joint director with his staff was also attached.[47] The following chart 4.1 presents the organisation of Commissionerate.

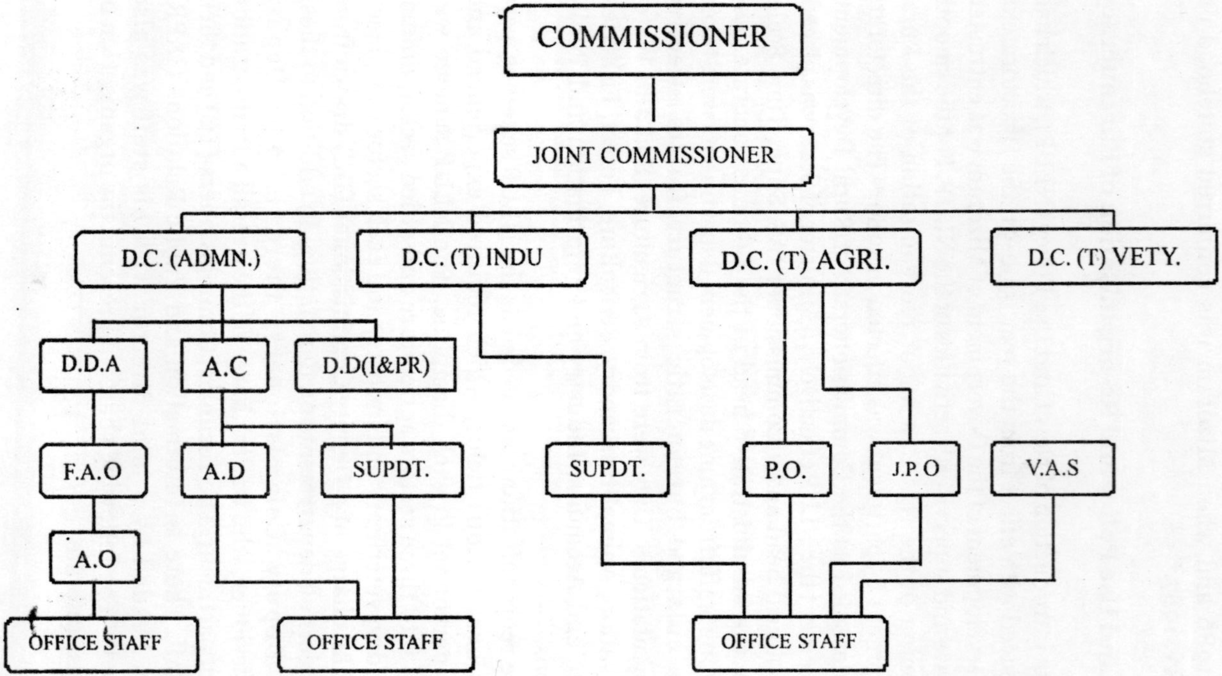

Chart 4.1: The Organisational Chart of Commissionerate of Rural Development (As in 1991)

Source: Commissionerate of Rural Development, Government of Mizoram, Aizwal.

However, the Commissionerate again converted into the Directorate of Rural Development and re-designate the existing posts[48] and the NLUP scheme was discontinued from the year 2001-2002.

Sl. No.	*Present Posts*	*Re-designated Posts*
1.	Joint Commissioner, Rural Development Department	Director, Rural Development Department
2.	Deputy Commissioner (T), Veterinary Department	Joint Director, Rural Development Department
3.	Deputy Commissioner (T), Industry	Joint Director, Rural Development Department
4.	Assistant Commissioner	Deputy Director.

Source: Rural Development Department, Government of Mizoram.

Present Organisational Structure of Rural Development Department

The present administrative set up of the Department of Rural Development, Government of Mizoram, has a state level directorate. A director heads the directorate. The director is assisted by one joint director, three deputy directors, one project officer, one assistant director, two superintendents, one rural planning officer. Besides, a number of technical officers are also assisting the director in respect of the different schemes of development work. These are one joint director (horticulture), one junior project officer (horticulture), five horticulture extension officers, and one veterinary assistant surgeon and an engineering cell with one executive rural engineer and two assistant rural engineers. The directorate is looking after the general administration, preparation of all allocation of funds, frame policy and plans. It also co-ordinate with respective District Rural Development Agencies (DRDA), blocks and the Government of India for general matters and fund release. At the district level, a DRDA office exists in all the districts for administration, implementation and monitoring of all development activities. The DRDA has a Project Director for the administration of the DRDA and control of the blocks within the district. The Deputy Commissioners, officiate as "Chairman DRDAs" in the context of the rural development and is the administrative head of the DRDAs. The Project Director submits all proposals, reports and returns, submits the shelf of projects under various schemes; maintain beneficiary list and records and co-ordinates with the directorate and the blocks on all implementation process. The present organisational structure of Rural Development Department is presented in the Chart 4.2.

At the block level, there are 23 rural development blocks headed by the block development officers. The BDO, through personal contact and direct involvement ensures proper progress, coordination and monitoring activities of the Village Councils, help in the selection of priority based, needful schemes by the Village Councils and actual ground implementation of all schemes and issue of completion certificates after personal verification and submit the same to the director/chairman for fund release.

The monitoring of the schemes are undertaken by the District/State Vigilance and Monitoring Committees as constituted by the Government of Mizoram and Ministry of Rural Development Department as the case may be, wherein the Members of Parliament, Lok Sabha and Rajya Sabha are the concerned chairperson and members. The State Institute of Rural Development was established in 2000 which is now located at Kolasib, and an Extension Training Centre at Lunglei in 2003 in order to provide policy guidance and to ensure efficient implementation, monitoring, supervision and evaluation of rural development training programmes and to impart training to senior and junior officers of rural bureaucrats.

RURAL DEVELOPMENT PROGRAMMES IN MIZORAM

State Sponsored Programmes

With the objective of eradicating rural poverty, attainment of self-sufficiency in food production, to create durable assets and rural housing and communication, etc., the Government of Mizoram over the years has been operating a number of rural development programmes. Some of the major programmes initiated by the Government of Mizoram in recent years are discussed under the following heads:[49]

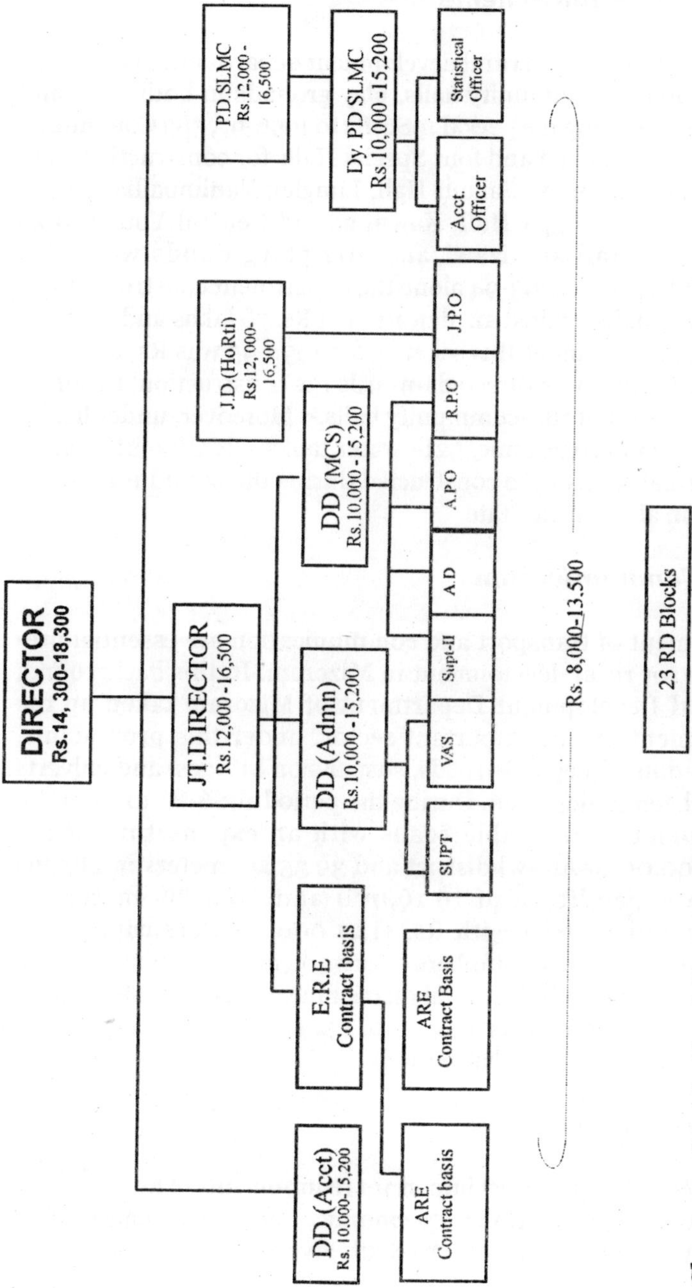

Chart 4.2: Organisational Structure of Rural Development Department (As on October 2005)

Source: Directorate of Rural Development, Government of Mizoram.

Social Education Scheme

Under this scheme, the rural development department takes up the construction of community halls, play grounds in both rural and urban areas. During the period 1986-87 to 1996-97, 583 Community Halls were completed and four Special Halls for construction were undertaken. These are Saikuti Hall, Lunglei; Vanhnuailiana Hall, Champhai, Aithangpa Hall, Kawnpui and Central Young Mizo Association Hall at Aizawl, and 202 playgrounds were also completed. During 1993-94 alone the department constructed 236 community halls against an allocation of Rs. 76 lakhs and the total outlay approved under this scheme, for 1994-95 was Rs. 86 lakhs. This expenditure was directed towards the construction, repairing and completion of 182-community halls.[50] Moreover, under health and sanitation programme, 521—water tanks—RCC/points and 42 public urinal sheds were constructed during the period 1986-87 to 1996-97 in all over the state.

Rural Communication

Development of transport and communication are essential pre-requisite for rural development in Mizoram. In this background, the Rural Development Department of Mizoram taken up the development of this important sector, under this programme, construction of jeep able roads, suspension bridges, and culverts etc. has been undertaken. During the period 1986-87 to 1996-98, 148 kilometers jeep able roads with an expenditure of Rs. 68,90,000.00 in Aizawl district and 39.35 kilometers in Lunglei with an expenditure of 16,16,000 and 30.4 kilometers in Chhimtuipui District with Rs. 11,21,000.00 were completed. During this period, 46 numbers of culverts in Aizawl district, 21 in Lunglei and 11 in Chhimtuipui district have been completed with a total expenditure of Rs. 6,01,000. 152 suspension bridges were also completed during that period.

Rural Housing

Housing is one of the most important requirements of human being for survival, which provides economic, and social security and better quality of life. During the Sixth Five Year Plan 1980-85 and

Seventh Five Year Plan 1985-90, the Government of Mizoram laid special emphasis on rural housing. Under the rural housing programme, rural development department provided GCI sheets, four bundles each, free of cost to the rural families. During 1993-94, the department incurred an expenditure of Rs. 100 lakhs for the purchase of 6624 bundles of GCI sheets which were distributed to 1656 families.[51] During the year 1998-99, 6770 families were assisted with an expenditure of Rs. 492 lakhs that incurred and during 1999-2000, 770 families assisted with Rs. 492 lakhs incurred expenditure.[52]

Housing for Project Staff

This programme initiated to provide office and staff quarters at various block headquarters. Under this programme, during 1994-98, 36 numbers of buildings were constructed in Aizawl district, 9 in Lunglei district and 11 in Chhimtuipui district with a total expenditure of Rs. 66,00,000.00.

New Land Use Policy[53]

In the year 1990, the Government of Mizoram launched a major initiative under the label of New Land Use Policy (NLUP) which aims at eradicating the practice of jhuming and to provide alternative means of livelihood to the jhumia families who depend upon jhuming for their livelihood. The objectives of NLUP was to augment the afforestation drive, to provide marketing facilities for produce obtained from the NLUP programme, to encourage to take up wet rice cultivation in the potential flat lands for self-sufficiency in food production.

The NLUP scheme provides three sectors of agriculture and allied sectors, animal husbandry and veterinary and industries sectors available to choose by the beneficiaries. Each family given two hectares of land and each beneficiary get an amount of Rs. 30,000 in installments over a period of three years.

The block development officers were the implementing agency, which submits monthly and annual reports on its progress to rural development directorate. The BDO assigned specific territorial units—circles to the field functionaries—his assisting team of functionaries—extension officers and village level workers to verify and inspect the beneficiaries within their respective circles. Then they report it to the BDOs; the BDO submit these reports to the directorate. In 11 blocks in Aizawl district, 48,005 families and 6,927 families in Lunglei district were selected in three blocks with a total assistance of Rs. 1,51,36,01,025.[53]

With the change in government, NLUP was discontinued from the year 2001-02 with subsequent introduction of another major project known as Mizoram Intodelhna Project during 2002-2003 under MNF Ministry under Zoramthanga.[54]

Revival of New Land Use Policy

Coming to power after 10 years in 2008, the Congress Ministry headed by Lal Thanhawla, revived NLUP as a flagship programme for all-round development in Mizoram in pursuance to election manifesto with its basic aims and objectives intact.[55]

Project Management: Considering lack of coordination between various development departments in its earlier decade period of implementation as one of the major causes for its failure, it is decided to implement NLUP under one apex body—the NLUP Apex Board. The project management system comprises of 4-tier system viz. (i) NLUP Apex Board (Chairman Lal Thanhawla, and Vice-Chairman R. Selthuama, MLA), (ii) NLUP Implementing Board (Chairman R. Selthuama), (iii) District Level Implementing Committee (headed by Deputy Commissioner), (iv) Village Level Implementing Committee (headed by Village Council President). The main functions of this Apex Board are to consider the projects and schemes made by the Implementing Board, disbursing of funds to the implementing departments, etc. The Implementing Board is the executive wing of the Apex Board which will prepare projects and schemes and submit to the Apex Board for consideration, to conduct independent assessment and monitoring of project implementations by the line departments from time to time to ensure the success of the policy, etc. The District Level Implementing Committee is the key executing agency in the district, also entrusted for setting up of village level implementing committee and to look after it etc. The Village Level Implementing Committee is the implementing agency at the village level.

The procedure this time has been extended to 52 trades to be implemented by various development departments such as Industries Department (29 trades), Horticulture Department (9 trades), Veterinary Department (5 trades), Agriculture Department (4 trades), Soil and Water Conservation Department (3 trades), Fisheries, Sericulture and Environment and Forest Departments (1 trade each) under the umbrella of NLUP Implementing Board.

The number of households to be covered in next five years is 1.2 lakh with an average annual coverage of 24 thousands and the quantum of assistance this time is Rs. 1.10 lakh (average). A base-line survey has been made and the number of eligible families for NLUP assistance is 1.60 lakh out of total number of 2.8 lakh families surveyed. A detailed action plan of the NLUP project (both physical and financial) was made and the total funding of the project is Rs. 2907.90 crore to be approved and financed by the Government of India and Planning Commission of India finalised annual plan of 2010-11 for Mizoram at Rs. 1500 crore and Additional Central Assistance of Rs. 70 crore for projects of special interest.

A comprehensive Monitoring and Social Audit System was designed for NLUP. A separate cell has been created to each level of administration viz. village, district and state level for transparency, social audit and evaluation of the project. As one of the objectives of the project is to create marketing outlets for products from the NLUP schemes, a Marketing Cell has also been created for marketing plan of the products. Detail programmes on training, model schemes/plans for various departments and publicity has also been finalised.

Penalty for Misuse of Assistance:

1. Beneficiary will be barred from receiving NLUP installments further.
2. No further assistance from the government in future.
3. The value of assistance already given, calculated on the basis of the prevailing market rate, will be recovered in full and with 5 per cent interest in case of cash money.
4. In case recovery is not feasible, the Mizoram Public Demand Recovery Act 2001 shall be applied by the government.

The Prospects

(a) *Jhum Control and Livelihood Opportunities*: It is expected that NLUP Programme as designed will progressively wean away farmers to alternative livelihood activities. Moreover, the farming community with the benefit of plan intervention will be able to increase their income substantially in view of increased productivity, economics of scale and availability of markets. The project envisages creating sustained livelihood activities to an estimate 1,20,000 households over next 5 years. Projected impact on income is shown in Table 4.1.

Table 4.1: Projected Impacts on Income from NLUP

Sl. No.	*Land Use System*	*Annual Income (Rs.)*	*Return to Labour Rs./day*
1.	Initial Situation	5,626	23
2.	Jhum—Agro-forestry mixed G. (0.5 ha)	27,000	68
3.	Jhum—passion fruit/turmeric (0.5 ha)	19,340	56
4.	Jhum—lowland irrigated crops (0.2 ha)	13,190	37
5.	Jhum—orange/broom grass (0.5 ha)	28,280	85

Source: Executive Summary of NLUP, 2010.

(b) *Food Security and Self-Sufficiency*: NLUP programme focused on increased production of essential items like paddy, pulses, oil seeds, vegetables fruits, livestock, fisheries, etc. for food security and progressively attaining self-sufficiency for many items which have potentials for local propagation and production. Successful implementation of NLUP programmes will augment the state revenue by dispensing with the need of importing such items valued Rs. 40.50 crores annually.

(c) *Afforestation*: Programmes being eco-friendly and attuned to soil and water conservation would encourage of forestation on a large scale with the benefit of environmental protection and over a period time opening up scope for carbon economy.

(d) *Introduction of Commercial Agriculture*: NLUP is aiming at commercial production of agri-horticultural produces on commercial scale for which Mizoram has a great potential. Sustained efforts in this direction are bound to yield results.

(e) *Employment Generation*: Apart from generating livelihood opportunities in rural areas, NLUP will also promise Micro Enterprises in cottage and small scale industries would generate employment opportunities in non-farm sector. Commutative impact of such micro enterprises is expected to generate employment for 6500 families.

(f) *Promotion of Agro-based Industries*: Increase production in agro-horticultural crops and spices like ginger, turmeric etc. could facilitate agro-based industries generating income and employment and thereby heralding economic development. The existing processing unit at Chhingchhip may operate full time with increased availability of raw materials and setting up of more such processing units the near future.

(g) *Impact on Overall Economy*: With community participation, and farmers' active involvement, defined role of implementing agencies and mechanism of monitoring/social audit as built into the programmes, the agrarian sector is expected to get a major boost for development. Sustained efforts as envisaged in the NLUP programmes with focus on target realization has the potential of a catalytic impact of transforming Mizoram economy.

If the NLUP is successfully implemented and the proposed trades under the above sectors so develop, will usher a new era of hope and development among rural masses. If it fails as it was in 1990's, the overall economic development in the most peaceful state in the North East, would halt and the objective of economic self-sufficiency will remain a distant dream.

Mizoram Intodelhna Project

The Government of Mizoram launched another Project known as Mizoram Intodelhna Project (MIP) during 2002-2003, funded by the Government of India for its effective implementation.[56] The main purpose of MIP is the upliftment of the rural poor especially the shifting cultivators. Its main concern is attainment of self-sufficiency, food security and better livelihood for the cultivator as a whole. On consideration of the above background, the Government of Mizoram has introduced a project known as MIP, which may be translated as a "Project for Self-Sufficiency in Mizoram". Directorate of Agriculture, Mizoram is the Nodal Department of MIP for this project.

The objective of the Project is to develop in low land areas and terraces in the upland areas and to develop piggery for diversification on farming system. The Rural Development Department was the Nodal Department of this project in the beginning 2002-2003. During 2003-2004, it has been transferred to the Agriculture Department.

Supervision of field works had been taken up by the Project Officers of MIP and Assistant Project Officers covering all selected villages under overall control of Deputy Commissioner who is also the Chairman of District Level Monitoring Cell (DLMC) and District Level Project Committee (DLPC).

Funds were released to the Project Officer (MIP)/Assistant Project Officer (MIP) for deposit in Bank Accounts of Village Farmer's Association. All payments to the beneficiaries were made with due approval of the Chairman, DLPC concerned.

A comprehensive monitoring system has been designed for MIP. A separate cell has been created to each level of administration namely village, district and state level and their working modalities spelt out.

Village Level Monitoring Cell (VLMC)

The members of the VLMC are:

1. *Convener*: Assistant Project Officer
2. *Member (Two)*: One member from any of the following organisation which a member of the committee of the Farmer's Association.
   - (i) Village Council
   - (ii) Young Mizo Association
   - (iii) Mizo Upa Pawl
   - (iv) Mizo Hmeichhe Insuihkhawm Pawl

The Farmers Committee will propose the composition of members of the VLMC to the DLMC for approval.

District Level Monitoring Cell (DLMC)

There is a separate body called District Level Monitoring Cell at the District Headquarters. The members are as follows:

1. *Chairman*: Deputy Commissioner
2. *Member Secretary*: Head of one of the Line Department in the District.
3. *Members*: Two members from outside the government, each of whom is having a good reputation and known to be honest trusted by General Public and preferably no responsible position in political parties.

The Deputy Commissioner may appoint an officer of his choice for the post of Member Secretary and submit four or five names for the membership of DLMC to the State Level Monitoring Cell (SLMC) for necessary action and approval.

State Level Monitoring Cell (SLMC)

MIP Executive Authority has constituted a State Level Monitoring Cell at Aizawl, the State Headquarters of Mizoram for effective implementation of MIP.

The MIP targets the rural poor especially the shifting cultivators in selected villages only covering all the rural development blocks in Mizoram.

Centrally Sponsored Schemes of Rural Development

The following centrally sponsored schemes of rural development are worth mentioning out of the many schemes (due to its multi-faceted objectives) that were implemented and under implementation in Mizoram.

Integrated Rural Development Programme

Integrated Rural Development Programme (IRDP) was being

implemented in Mizoram since its inception in 1978-79 on a limited basis. Only three blocks were covered during 1978-79 and extended to five blocks in 1979-80. From 1980-81, the programme was extended to all the blocks of the state.[57] IRDP aims to provide means of income generation to the poorest of the poor to enable them to cross the poverty line through a package of assistance, including subsidy and institutional credit. The programme targets the small and marginal farmers, agriculture labourers, rural artisans, scheduled castes and scheduled tribes and other disadvantaged group, like rural women, funded by the Central and the State Governments on 50:50 basis. It was implemented through District Rural Development Agencies (DRDA's). From 1988-99 only sharing of the same was made when Mizoram got statehood in 1987. Before that, it was entirely provided by the centre. But linkage of credit with the subsidy could not be introduced till Seventh Five Year Plan (1985-90), because of several constraints like the poor infrastructure and communications, poor coverage of blocks by bank branches, etc.[58]

The number of families assisted under IRDP during the period 1978-79 to 1994-95 was 57821 at an expenditure of Rs. 2718.988 lakhs.[59] During the year 1998-99, 3080 beneficiaries with a total expenditure of 184.80 lakhs in all rural development blocks in Mizoram.[60]

Training of Rural Youth for Self-Employment[61]

Training of Rural Youth for Self-Employment (TRYSEM) was started at the National level on 15th August 1979. The main objective of Training of Rural Youth for Self-Employment was to provide technical and managerial skills to the rural youth in the age group of 18-35 from families living below the poverty line to enable them to take up self-employment ventures in the fields of agriculture and allied activities, industries, service and business. In Mizoram, Training of Rural Youth for Self-Employment was started in the year 1982. The scheme was implemented through District Rural Development Agencies and the expenditure shared 50:50 by the Centre and the State. During the period, 1982-83 to 1997-98, the numbers of youth trained under this programme in Aizawl District were 4,983, in Lunglei District 1,896 and 1,451 in Chhimtuipui District with a total of 8,330 in Mizoram.[62]

During the year 1998-99, 401 numbers of youth were trained with total expenditure of Rs. 14,78225 lakhs covering all the rural development blocks.[63]

Development of Women and Children in Rural Areas

Development of Women and Children in Rural Areas (DWCRA) was started in the year 1982-83 to provide the rural poor women with suitable avenues of income generation according to their skills and local conditions which correlates nutritional and educational status of the family and building up of positive change in the attitudes of the women. Under this programme, financial assistance was meant for 'group' of women and an amount of Rs. 15,000 was given to each group of 15-20 Women.[64] DWCRA was launched in the Aizawl District in the year 1985-1986 and extended to Lunglei and Chhimtuipui District in the year 1991-92 and 1992-93 respectively.[65] The programme was implemented through DRDA. From the period 1989-1990 to 1997-1998, 703 groups were assisted under this programme throughout Mizoram with 331 groups in Aizawl, 209 groups in Lunglei and 163 groups in Chhimtuipui district having 15-20 women in each group and Rs. 15,000 was paid in each group.[66] During the year 1998-99, 60 groups were benefited with a total expenditure of Rs. 15.088 lakhs.[67]

National Rural Employment Programme

National Rural Employment Programme (NREP) was launched in October 1980 to generate additional employment opportunities, to create durable community assets and to improve the quality of life of rural masses. In Mizoram, under the Sixth Five Year Plan 1980-85 and Seventh Five Year Plan 1985-90, lakhs and 4.642 lakhs man days of employment were respectively generated under NREP in the state and during the year 1983-89, 2396 hectares of social forestry, 2075 kilometers of construction and widening of rural roads, 226 school buildings and 52 pavilions have been completed in Mizoram.[68] This programme was also implemented through District Rural Development Agencies, and expenditure shared on 50:50 basis by the centre and the state.

Rural Landless Employment Guarantee Programme

Rural Landless Employment Guarantee Programme (RLEGP) wholly funded by the Centre was launched on 15th August 1983 to generate gainful employment for the rural landless labourers by creating productive assets for overall quality of life in the rural areas. This programme was implemented through DRDA. In Mizoram this programme was started from 1984-85. During 1984-89 period 957.51 kilometers of roads were constructed, improved and 17.204 lakhs man-days were generated under this programme.[69]

Jawahar Rojgar Yojana

Jawahar Rojgar Yojana (JRY) was launched by merging NREP and RLEGP from the year 1989, to generate additional gainful employment for the un-employed persons both man and women in the rural areas. The programme started during 1990-91 in Mizoram. Under this scheme in Mizoram, construction of roads, drinking water sources, school and community buildings, sanitary latrines were taken up, to give working and earning opportunities at the same time. During the period 1989-90 to 1997, 955 kilometers of rural roads, 154 numbers of drinking water sources, 155 numbers of school buildings, 519 numbers of community halls, etc. 43 numbers of sanitary latrines and 145 houses were constructed.[70]

Million Wells Scheme

Million Wells Scheme (MWS) was started in 1990. As Mizoram is a hilly area, this scheme was implemented in minor irrigation and land development. The scheme was provided to individual beneficiaries. During the period 1990-91 to 1997-98, 4299 people were benefited under this programme in Aizawl 2958, in Lunglei 586 and 755 in Chhimtuipui district.[71]

Indira Awaas Yojana

Indira Awaas Yojana (IAY) was launched during 1985-86 as a sub-scheme of RLEGP, IAY thereafter continued as a sub-scheme of

Jawahar Rozgar Yojana (JRY) since its launching in April 1989 and 6 per cent of the total JRY funds were allocated for implementation of IAY to provide houses to the poor in the rural areas. The main objective of the scheme is primarily to help construction/up gradation of dwelling units of members of scheduled castes/schedules tribes, frees bonded labourers and other below the poverty line non-scheduled castes/schedules tribes rural house holds by providing them a lump sum financial assistance. IAY was delinked from JRY and made an independent scheme with effect from 1st January 1996.

IAY is a centrally sponsored scheme funded on cost-sharing basis in the ratio of 75:25 between the centre and the states. The DRDAs are implementing the programme through BDO in Mizoram.

In Mizoram, the scheme was started during the year 1985-86. During the period 1985-86 to 1997-98, 3530 below poverty line rural households were constructed/upgraded. In the year 1998-99, 519 numbers of beneficiaries with a total expenditure of Rs. 114.04 lakhs and in 1999-2000, 1,798 households were benefited with a total expenditure of Rs. 320.80 lakhs. Out of the total fund available for new construction in the year 2000-2001, of IAY fund, Rs. 337.66 lakhs was the expenditure out of Rs. 344.667 total fund available and 1533 houses were constructed. During this year 757 houses were upgraded with an expenditure of Rs. 75.70 lakhs out of the fund Rs. 78.855 lakhs available.[72]

Employment Assurance Scheme (EAS)

People in rural areas are still largely dependent on agriculture for wage employment. But this sector is not able to provide sustained employment to all persons who are in need of employment. The Government of India thus launched a scheme 'Employment Assurance Scheme' (EAS) to provide employment to persons below the poverty line during periods of acute shortage of employment such as a lean agricultural season or drought, etc. The scheme is open to all rural poor who are in need of wage employment in the form of manual work to the rural poor living below the poverty line. 70 per cent of the funds are earmarked to the intermediate (block) panchayats while 30 per cent is intended to be used by the Zila Parishad in blocks having difficult seasonal conditions.[73] The scheme is being implemented by DRDAs in Mizoram. During the period from 1993 to 1997, 1,22,389 persons below poverty line were engaged in wage employment. During the year 2001-2002, 5,773 lakhs maydays with an expenditure of Rs. 475.535 lakhs out of the total fund available of Rs. 576.109 lakhs.[74]

Border Area Development Programme

Border Area Development Programme (BADP) was started with the objective of balanced development through the provision of infrastructure facilities to promote a sense of security among the local populations of international border and sensitive areas. The programme was started in the Seventh Plan and funds for the BADP are met fully by the Government of India. BADP covered the North Eastern States, covering Assam, Meghalaya, Mizoram, and Tripura during Eighth Plan (1992-97). The Government of Mizoram is implementing this programme with an aim of developing the remote, inaccessible areas situated near the international border. Under this programme, 95 kilometers of jeep able road and 35 kilometers of truck able roads had been completed by the year 1995-96 in Mizoram.[75]

Swarnajayanti Gram Swarozgar Yojana

Swarnajayanti Gram Swarozgar Yojana (SGSY) is the major on going programme for self-employment generation for the marginalised sections of rural communities. This programme came into being on 1st April, 1999 after merging the erstwhile IRDP, TRYSEM, DWCRA, Supply of Improved Toolkits to Rural Artisans (SITRA), Ganga Kalyan Yojana (GKY) and Million Wells Scheme (MWS). SGSY is a holistic progamme covering all aspects of self-employment such as organisation of the poor into Self-Help Groups (SHGs), training, credit, technology, infrastructure and marketing. The objective of the SGSY is to bring the assisted poor families (*swarojgaris*) above the poverty line by ensuring appreciable increase in incomes over a period of time. This objective is to be achieved by inter-alias organising the rural poor into SHGs through a process of social mobilisation, capacity building and provision of income-generating assets through a mix of bank and government subsidy.[76] In Mizoram the DRDA is implementing this progamme. During 2002-2003in Lunglei district, 12 SHGs, 120 Swarozgaris and 44 individual beneficiaries has been benefited with a total expenditure of Rs. 10.60 lakhs.[77]

A Special Project on Integrated Piggery Development at Lunglei District of Mizoram under Special Swarnajayanti Gram Swarozgar Yojana (SGSY) had been submitted to the Government of India. This project implemented in the district to cover 75 number of SHGs and 1500 beneficiaries for a period of two years with effect from financial year 2004-05 to 2006-07. The Project cost is Rs. 718.72 lakhs with 568.72 lakhs government share and Rs. 150.00 lakhs institutional credit. The DRDA, Lunglei was the nodal agency for implementing this project with the help of the Veterinary and Animal Husbandry Department. The primary objective of this project is to generate self employment opportunity, poverty alleviation, enabling BPL families above the poverty line through piggery farming, to introduce recommended method of piggery farming, to adopt innovative marketing strategies to ensure guaranteed sale of surplus pork meat for fetching reasonable prices to the farmers, to enhance the awareness level of the farmers about scientific piggery farming, etc.[78]

Pradhan Mantri Gramodaya Yojana; Gramin Awaas Yojana (PMGY; GAY)

This scheme is in operation for the rural poor for those whose name is in the list of BPL families. They are provided assistance for the construction of a house at Rs. 20,000 per beneficiary in the hill/ difficult areas. Houses are to be constructed by the beneficiary himself.[79] This scheme is generally based on the pattern of the IAY in the sphere of rural housing, but considering the magnitude of the task it has been felt to be imperative to supplement the efforts being made in this direction through the introduction of comprehensive scheme which aims at reducing the shortage of houses for BPL families in the rural areas.[80] This scheme is being implemented with the provisions of new construction and up gradation of houses. During 2001-2002, 2,098 houses, newly constructed with an expenditure of Rs. 4,61,56,000 and 1,149 upgradation with an expenditure of Rs. 1,14,90,000 has been spend under this scheme in Mizoram.[81] In the Lunglei district, during

2002-2003, 434 houses newly constructed and 256 houses upgraded with an expenditure of Rs.121.08 lakhs.[82]

Sampoorna Grameen Rozgar Yojana (SGRY)

The SGRY was launched on 25th September 2001 by merging the on-going schemes of Jawahar Gram Samridhi Yojana (JGSY) and Employment Assurance Scheme (EAS). The objective[83] of the scheme is to provide additional wages employment in all rural areas and thereby provide food security and provide nutritional levels and the creation of durable community, social and economic assets and infrastructural development in rural areas. The funds are shared between the Centre and the States in ratio of 75:25. Food-grains should be given as part of wages under the SGRY to the rural poor at the rate of 5 kilogram per man-day. Should a state government wish to give more than 5 kilogram; it may do so within the existing state allocation subject to a minimum of 25 per cent of the wages to be paid in cash. While providing wage employment, preference shall be given to agricultural wage earners, non-agricultural unskilled wage earners marginal farmers, women, members of SC/ST and parents of child labour withdrawn, parents of handicapped childern.[84] In Mizoram, during 1998-1999 to 2002-2003, a total of Rs. 29,57,15,500 has been spend and 40100 quintals of foodgrains (rice) distributed.

The latest centrally sponsored rural development programmes implemented and some are under implementation by the Department of Rural Development, Government of Mizoram other than Bharat Nirman and MGNREGS, are IAY, SGSY, SGRY, Special SGSY, BADP, PMGY and Bamboo Flowering and Famine Combat Scheme (BAFFACOS).[85]

Bamboo Flowering and Famine Combat Scheme

Bamboo Flowering and Famine Combat Scheme (BAFFACOS) is a new famine combat scheme in Mizoram. Famine visits Mizoram at regular intervals of about 50 years. Known in the Mizo dialect as Mautam is a situation marked by large flowering of bamboos (Botanical name—*Melocanna baccifera*) and massive multiplication of rats and other rodent population which devour hectares of standing crops overnight, leading to famine. Bamboos started flowering in Mizoram in 2007-08 and the last occurrence was in 1958-59. Therefore, the Government of Mizoram has formulated a comprehensive progamme of BAFFACOS, with an aim to reduce poverty among farmers during famine period. This programme would be achieved through adoption of intensified and diversified cropping system, mechanisation of agriculture, connectivity for market linkage and Rodent Control Programmes for which total outlay of Rs. 3,300.00 was approved during 2005-2006.[86]

Thus, various rural development programmes both state and centrally sponsored, has been undertaken in Mizoram since the inception of the CDP and many are under implementation with the administrative structure build for its effective implementation especially after Mizoram got Union Territory. The state, no doubt, is marching ahead with the implementation of these programmes, yet a long way to go towards achieving economic self-sufficiency, eradication of poverty, solving rural unemployment, development of infrastructure and communication, etc. The achievements on various rural development programmes are mainly enclose on the aggregate physical and financial targets which does not include any record of the impact of the programmes undertaken for economic self-sufficiency and general economic condition of the rural people in Mizoram.[87] Understanding of the technical factors involved by the block administration, timely supply of appropriate inputs, flow of assistance, marketing of outputs, strict and continuous monitoring of the programmes and dedicated bureaucracy are essential for the effectual implementation of rural development programmes.

Notes and References

1. Das, Kalpana (2004): *Rural Development in Mizoram*, Mittal Publication, New Delhi, p. 35.
2. Lianzela (1994): *Economic Development of Mizoram*, Spectrum Publications, Guwahati, p. 113.
3. Das, Kalpana (2004): *Rural Development in Mizoram op. cit.*, p. 35.
4. Ray, Animesh. (1982): *Mizoram Dynamics of Change*, Pearl Publishers, Calcutta, p. 189.
5. *Ibid.*
6. Administrative Report of the North Lushai Hills for the year 1895-96,

Government of Assam, Shillong, 1896, p. 1 in Ray Animesh (1982): Mizoram...*op. cit.* p. 189.

7. Administrative Report of the Lushai Hills for the year 1907-1908, Government of Assam, Shillong, 1908, p. 18-19.
8. Ray, Animesh (1982): *Mizoram, op. cit.* p. 190.
9. Administration Report of the Lushai Hills for the year 1933-34, Government of Assam, Shillong, 1934, p. 26-32.
10. Report on the administration of the Mizo Hills for the year 1935-36, Government of Assam, Shillong, 1936, p. 34.
11. Ray, Animesh (1982): *Mizoram, Dynamics of Change, op. cit.* p. 191.
12. McCall, A.G. (1949): *Lushai Chrysalis*, Luzac & Co. London 1, p. 283-285.
13. Mizoram District Gazetteers, *op. cit.* pp. 208-209.
14. *Ibid.*
15. Das, Kalpana (2004): *Rural Development in Mizoram, op. cit.* p. 35.
16. Mizoram District Gazetteers, Department of Art and Culture, Government of Mizoram, Aizawl, 1989, p. 228.
17. Ray, Animesh (1982): *Mizoram Dynamics of Change, op. cit.* p. 191.
18. Report of the Committee on Special Multipurpose Tribal Blocks, Ministry of Home Affairs, Government of India, New Delhi, March 1960, p. 5.
19. *Ibid.*
20. Ray, Animesh (1982): *Mizoram Dynamics of Change, op. cit.* p. 324. It was the first block to be covered into a Tribal Development Block which was converted during the Second Plan period and it served as a model for conversion of other blocks in the area.
21. Ray, Animesh (1982): *Mizoram Dynamics of Change, op. cit.* p. 209.
22. *Ibid.*
23. Fambawl, Lalsiama (1998): Mizoram a Rural Development Department In Kum 50 chhung a Hnathawh Tlangpui, '*NLUP Sekibuhchhuak*': A Bulletin of Commisionerate of RD, Government of Mizoram, October-December, p. 27-29. also see Issue No. 4, 1997, pp. 11-12.
24. Lianzela (1994): *Economic Development of Mizoram*, Guwahati, Spectrum Publications, p. 113.
25. Mizo District Gazetteers, (1989): *op. cit.* pp. 224-25.
26. *Ibid.* pp. 224-25.
27. *Ibid.* pp. 25-26.
28. Fambawl, Lalsiama, (1998): *Mizorama* a... *op. cit.* p. 29: The Protective and Progressive Villages (regrouped villages were called) was placed under an Administrative Officer. Sub-Deputy Collectors (ACS) and Block Development Officers were appointed as Administrative Officers.
29. Mizoram District Gazetteers, *(1989): op. cit.*, p. 226.
30. Ray, Animesh (1982): *Mizoram, op. cit.* p. 325.
31. Fambawl, Lalsiama (1998): *Mizoram*: a.... *op. cit.*, p. 29.

32. *Ibid.*
33. *Ibid.*
34. Mizoram District Gazetteers (1989): *op. cit.*, pp. 277-278.
35. Das, Kalpana (2004): *Rural Development in Mizoram op. cit*, p. 37.
36. Mizoram District Gazetteers (1989): *op. cit.* p. 278.
37. *Ibid* p. 226.
38. *Ibid* p. 227.
39. Lianzela (1995): *Four Decades of Planning in Mizoram*, Khuangthangi, Aizawl, p. 6.
40. Fambawl, Lalsiama (1998): *Mizoram* a.... *op. cit.*, p. 30.
41. Lianzela (1995): Four Decades of Planning in Mizoram, *op. cit.*, p. 6.
42. Lianzela (1994): *Economic Development of Mizoram, op. cit.*, p. 52.
43. Das, Kalpana (2004): *Rural Development in Mizoram, op. cit*, p. 38.
44. Mizo Accord 30th June 1986, Memorandum of Settlement Constitution of India (53rd) Amendment Bill and the State of Mizoram Bill was passed simultaneously and the declaration of 'Disturbed Area' was withdrawn. Mizoram was conferred statehood on 20th February 1987 and became the 23rd State of the Indian Union.
45. Das, Kalpana (2004): *Rural Development in Mizoram, op. cit*, p. 38.
46. Government of Mizoram, Department of Rural Development; Project Report on New Land Use Policy, Aizawl, 1990.
47. Das, Kalpana (2004): *Rural Development in Mizoram, op. cit*, p. 39.
48. Notification No. B/16011/1/86-RD/Pt, Government of Mizoram, Rural Development Department, Aizawl, November 3, 2000.
49. Fambawl, Lalsiama (1997): *Mizoram* a.... *op. cit.* p. 13.
50. Das, Kalpana (2004): *Rural Development in Mizoram, op. cit,* p. 42.
51. *Ibid* p. 42.
52. Statistical Handbook Mizoram 2000, Economics and Statistics, Government of Mizoram, Aizawl, 2000.
53 Project Report on New Land Use Policy, Rural Development, Government of Mizoram, Aizawl, September 1993.
54. Fambawl, Lalsiama (1997): *Mizoram* a.... *op. cit.* p. 30.
55. NLUP Manual, Detailed Action Plan and Summary 2009.
56. Government of Mizoram (2002): Statistical Abstract, Department of Agriculture and Minor Irrigation, Mizoram, Aizawl 2002-2003, p. 85. On 26th March and subsequent Detailed Project Report was submitted to the Planning Commission, Government of India, for approval and release of funds for its effective implementation. Subsequently, Planning Commission has agreed to release Rs. 15.00 crore as Additional Central Assistance to the Government of Mizoram vide Letter No. PC (P) 1/10/03-2000 (Mizo) Vol. II, dt. 24.10.2003. Further, Government of India, Ministry of Finance has conveyed the sanction of the President of India amounting to Rs. 15.00 crore vide Letter No.-F.44 (1) PFI/2002-242, dt.10.2.2003 and accordingly he

Government of Mizoram has sanctioned the same vide Letter No. G.28914/6/2002-AGR/Pt dt.27.3.2003.

57. Department of Rural Development Report in Achievements of Poverty Alleviation Programmes, Centrally Sponsored Schemes, Mizoram, Aizawl, 1992-93.
58. Potential Linked Rural Credit Plan of Lunglei District Mizoram, National Bank for Agriculture and Rural Development, Regional Office, Guwahati, 1990-91 to 1994-95, p. 72.
59. Das, Kalpana (2004): *Rural Development in Mizoram, op. cit*, p. 51.
60. Statistical Handbook of Mizoram, 2000, *op. cit.* p. 115.
61. Das, Kalpana (2004): *Rural Development in Mizoram, op. cit*, p. 51.
62. Fambawl, Lalsiama (1998): *Mizoram: a.... op. cit.*, p. 33.
63. Statistical Handbook of Mizoram, 2000, *op. cit.* p. 116.
64. Das, Kalpana (2004): *Rural Development in Mizoram, op. cit*, p. 53.
65. *Ibid.*
66. Fambawl, Lalsiama (1998): *Mizoram a..... op. cit.*, p. 33.
67. Statistical Handbook of Mizoram, 2000, *op. cit.* p. 199.
68. Das, Kalpana (2004): *Rural Development in Mizoram, op. cit*, p. 52.
69. *Ibid.*
70. Fambawl, Lalsiama (1998): *Mizoram* a..... *op. cit.*, p. 34.
71. *Ibid* p. 33.
72. Statistical Handbook of Mizoram, 2002, *op. cit.* p. 73.
73. Gram Vikas: Programmes at a Glance, Ministry of Rural Development, Government of India, 2001, p. 16.
74. Fambawl, Lalsiama (1997): *Mizoram* a.... *op. cit.*, p. 14.
75. Das, Kalpana (2004): *Rural Development in Mizoram, op. cit*, p. 54.
76. SGSY Guidelines, Ministry of Rural Development, Government of India, New Delhi, June, p. 1.
77. Statistical Handbook, Lunglei District, 2003, p. 48.
78. Project for Special Report on Integrated Piggery Development at Lunglei District of Mizoram under Special SGSY, Submitted to Ministry of Rural Development, Krishi Bhawan, New Delhi, 2004-2005.
79. SGRY Guidelines, Government of India, Ministry of Rural Development, Department of Rural Development, Krishi Bhawan, New Delhi, (Effective from 01,04,02) pp. 1-3.
80. A brief note on Schemes being taken up by Rural Development Department, Government of Mizoram, Aizawl, October 2005, p. 1.
81. Rural Development Department Hmalakna in Kum LI Chhunga Zokhaw Hmasawnna, Directorate of Rural Development, Government of Mizoram, August 2003, pp. 9-10.
82. Statistical Handbook, Lunglei District, 2003, p. 48.
83. A brief note on Schemes being taken up by Rural Development Department, Government of Mizoram, Aizawl, October 2005.
84. SGRY Guidelines, Government of India, Ministry of Rural

Development, Department of Rural Development, Krishi Bhawan, New Delhi, (Effective from 01, 04, 02), pp. 1-3.

85. A brief note on Schemes being taken up by Rural Development Department, Government of Mizoram, Aizawl, October 2005, p. 1.
86. Government of Mizoram, Department of Agriculture, Crop Husbandry and Minor Irrigation, Revised Annual Plan, 2005-2006, p. 14.
87. Sinha, Harendra, "NLUP towards Economic Self-sufficiency in Mizoram", A seminar paper presented in UGC Sponsored State Level Seminar organised by Govt. J. Buana College, Lunglei, Mizoram. 22-23rd September, 2010.

5

Problems and Prospects of Rural Development in Mizoram

This chapter is focused on the problems and prospects of rural development in Mizoram with special reference to Lunglei district. In Part-I an attempt was made to identify the problems and prospects of rural development and initiatives undertaken by the development departments in the district. Part-II looks at the major crops and potentials in the district.

INTRODUCTION

Mizoram is a poor under developed state. The geographical location, poor condition of road networks, remoteness of the market, poor infrastructural facilities, no broad gauge rail road and waterways to transport goods to outside world, slow growth of alternative employment avenues, lack of industries, deficiency in natural resource management, inappropriate programmes and policies initiated and poor implementation of development programmes are some of the evils towards development in Mizoram. Despite its abundant natural forest resources, favourable climate and a fertile land, the state remains backward. It has been stated that, "during the sixty years of planned development, India have made impressive progress in developing Agriculture and Industry, Science and Technology, Health and Education and the infrastructure for a wide range of services". But it is sad to note that this statement has no relevance so far as Mizoram is concerned. Mizoram is still virtually where it was at the time of attainment of Union Territory. No doubt, the rest of the country has made impressive progress, but Mizoram is still far behind even in building up the requisite infrastructure.[1] Still today about 3 lakh work force in Mizoram are engaged in low productivity jhum practices and it is estimated that an average area of 2 lakhs acres of forest cover are annually destroyed by slashing and burning of trees for jhum land in Mizoram.[2] It indicates that jhuming continues unabated and posing threat to the main objectives of the rural development programmes. As per report of the Environment and Forest Department, Government of Mizoram, 17046.33 hectares of hilly land had burnt and eight people died in jhum fire from January 2010 to April 2010 causing environmental problems too in the State.[3] The total requirements of rice for one year for human consumption only as on 31st March 2003 is 14,61,335. The total annual requirement of rice including miscellaneous consumption such as pigs, dogs, cattle and floating people is 1871960 quintals. But the total production of rice by farmers of Mizoram during 2002-2003 is 744430 quintals, which was 40.80 per cent of the total annual requirement. The total area for cultivation of paddy during 2002-2003 is 57067 hectares with an average production of 1.3 quintals per hectares. For self-sufficiency in food production 85194 hectares of more land is required to produce another 1107530 quintals. The deficiency of production is 59 per cent.[4] The region is at an infantile stage in the field of industry. Whatever industry, it may be called; at present is only small-scale industry, fed by indigenous agricultural produce, covering only a small market zones.[5] The situation in respect of allied sectors is in no way better. The potential in animal husbandry, a common subsidiary activity, is grossly under utilised. Meat, eggs, fish come from out side the state.[6] Infrastructural facilities for economic growth are at their nominal level, mainly due to isolation and nature of terrain and population quality as well.[7]

In this background, the development of infrastructures like road transport, waterways, education, irrigation, power, etc. are the basic necessities for rural development. The increase of productivity of agriculture, horticulture, livestock, small-scale industries, fishery, sericulture, etc. is vital which will lead to increase in income of rural population leading to economic development of the State.

Potentials and Problems of Rural Development in Lunglei District

Lunglei is a backward district and most of the population is engaged in agricultural activities. The percentage of total population of workers in 1991 was 50.19 and in 2001, 52.33. The main workers were 42.51 and in 2001, it was 44.42. The total non-workers in 1991 was 7.68 and in 2001, 7.90. Table 5.1 reveals the percentage of total workers, marginal workers and non-workers to total population by residence and sex of Lunglei District in 1991 and 2001.[8]

Table 5.1: Percentage of Total Workers and Main Workers, Marginal Workers and Non-Workers to Total Population by Residence and Sex of Lunglei District—1991 and 2001

Total Rural-Urban	*Persons Male-Female*	*Total Workers*		*Main Workers*		*Marginal Workers*		*Non-Workers*	
		1991	*2001*	*1991*	*2001*	*1991*	*2001*	*1991*	*2001*
1	2	3	4	5	6	7	8	9	10
T	P	50.19	52.33	42.51	44.42	7.68	7.90	49.81	47.67
	M	55.61	57.32	50.72	52.14	4.89	5.18	44.39	42.68
	F	44.25	46.91	33.38	36.06	10.76	10.85	55.76	53.09
R	P	57.25	57.57	45.85	49.42	5.39	8.14	48.75	42.43
	M	55.62	60.05	51.70	55.27	3.93	4.78	44.38	39.93
	F	46.54	54.88	39.56	43.09	6.79	11.78	53.46	45.12
U	P	48.60	45.21	37.48	37.63	11.12	7.58	51.40	54.79
	M	55.59	53.62	49.30	47.98	6.29	5.73	44.41	46.38
	F	40.69	36.08	24.11	26.49	16.58	9.59	59.31	63.12

Source: Statistical Handbook, Lunglei District 2003, Mizoram, p. 7.

The cultivators constituted 64.38 per cent of total workers—main and marginal in 2001 and 3.87 were agricultural labourers, 0.78 workers in household industry and 30.97 were other workers out of 71770 persons. Table 5.2 reveal the percentage of workers by category of workers by sex in state and Lunglei district.[9]

Table 5.2: Percentage Distribution of Total Workers (Main and Marginal) by Category of Workers by Sex in State and Lunglei District 2001

	Persons Male/ Female	*Total Workers (Main and Marginal)*	*Percentage of Total Workers (Main and Marginal)*			
			Culti-vators	*Agri-cultural Labourers*	*Workers in House-hold Industry*	*Other Workers*
1	2	3	4	5	6	7
	P	469597	53.91	5.85	1.40	38.83
Mizoram	M	264162	48.77	4.93	1.20	45.11
	F	205435	60.52	7.05	1.66	30.77
	P	71770	64.38	3.87	0.78	30.97
Lunglei District	M	40899	57.33	3.15	0.74	38.76
	F	30871	73.70	4.83	0.81	20.66

Source: Statistical Handbook, Lunglei District 2003, p. 13.

The percentage of cultivators is higher than the State percentage of total cultivators of 53.91. Out of the total number of household of 24,332, total number of cultivator's families is 14655 in the district as on April 2003. Table 5.3 reveals that 60.22 per cent of the total households are engaged in cultivation of the total of 160 villages.[10]

Table 5.3: Abstract of Village Level Statistics as on 1st April 2003

Sl. No	*Name of District*	*No. of Village*	*Total No. of Household*	*Total No. of Cultivators Families*	*Percentage*
1.	D.A.O., Aizawl	177	59747	22873	38.28
2.	Aizawl Mamit	59	10003	7070	70.67
3.	Kolasib	24	12619	9388	74.39
4.	Lunglei	160	24332	14655	60.22
5.	Saiha	232	28264	13219	46.76
6.	Champhai	89	20481	17103	83.50
	Total	**702**	**1,43,240**	**71,658**	**50.02**

Source: Statistical Abstract, Department of Agriculture and Minor Irrigation, Government of Mizoram, Aizawl, 2002-2003, p. 14.

The percentage of female cultivators is 73.70 (Table 5.4), which is more than males 57.33 of total cultivators in the district, which is even higher than the state percentage of 60.52.[11]

Table 5.4: Percentage Distribution of Total Workers (Main and Marginal) as Cultivators, Agricultural Labourers, Workers in Household Industry and other Workers in State and Lunglei District by residence and sex 2001

	Persons Males-Female	*Total Workers (Main and Marginal)*	*Category of Workers (Main and Marginal)*			
			Cultivators	*Agricultural Labourers*	*Workers in Household*	*Other Workers*
1	2	3	4	5	6	7
Mizoram	P	469597	53.91	5.85	1.40	38.84
	M	246162	48.77	4.93	1.20	45.11
	F	205435	60.52	7.05	1.66	30.97
Lunglei	P	71770	64.38	3.87	0.78	30.97
	M	40899	57.33	3.15	0.74	38.76
	F	30871	73.70	4.83	0.81	20.66

Source: Statistical Handbook, Lunglei District 2003, p. 17.

The female work participation also increases to 44.39 in 1991 to 49.91 in 2001 and the male work participation in the district is 57.31 in 2001 when in 1991 it was 54.01 per cent[12].

The percentage of non-workers decreases in rural area to 48.75 in 1991 to 42.43 per cent in 2001 and in urban areas it is increased to 51.40 in 1991 to 54.79 per cent in 2001.[13]

Out of the total geographical area of states 2108.700 hectares, Lunglei district covered an area of 455,600 hectares, and with 19,406 hectares Net Sown Area; 38,402 hectares fallow land and 164,399 hectares of land are not available for cultivation.[14]

Table 5.5, shows the total area of land utilisation in Mizoram.[15]

Table 5.5: Land Utilisation in Mizoram 2006-07

Sl. No.	*Area under*	*In '000 Hectare*	*Percentage of Total*
1.	Forest	1593.700	75.57
2 .	Not available for cultivation	134.040	6.37
3.	Other cultivated land	79.230	3.76
4.	Fallow land	207.543	9.84
5.	Net shown area	94.187	4.46
	Total	**2108.7**	**100**

Source: Directorate of Agriculture and Minor Irrigation, Government of Mizoram, Aizawl.

The total geographical area of the State is 21,08,700 hectare in which 9.84 per cent is under fallow land and only 4.46 per cent is under net shown area (Table 5.5).

In 2002-2003, the paddy-cultivated area has been 7,794.00 hectares only with a total production of 2,12,540.00 quintals. The main crops of the area are paddy, maize, pulses, oilseeds and sugarcane. The major crops cultivated in the Lunglei District along with production for the year 2002-2003 are given below in Table 5.6[16].

Table 5.6: Major crops cultivated in the Lunglei District along with production for the year 2005-2006 in Lunglei District

Name of the Crop	*Area Cultivated in Hectares*	*Production in Quintals*	*Productivity*	*State Average*
Paddy	7,794	212,540	2.72	0.91
Maize	948	18,400	1.94	1.98
Pulses	1,469	7,060	0.48	1.06
Soil Seeds	865	8,620	1	0.74
Sugarcane	82	4,400	5.36	5.43

Source: Potential Linked Credit Plan, Lunglei District, NABARD Mizoram, 2005-2006.

However, the productivity of these above-mentioned crops is much below the state level average.

Jhuming is predominantly practiced in the Lunglei district. The major constraints to agriculture production are lack of water in dry season, which restricts double cropping. To increase double cropped area and increase production, it is essential to cover more and more area under irrigation. The area of wet rice cultivation by seasonal rain is 681 hectares and the area of wet rice cultivation by minor irrigation was 86 hectares only.[17]

As on May 2003, 107 minor irrigation projects with a total command area of 4,527 hectares has been completed in the state and in Lunglei district under Lunglei Irrigation Division, 20 numbers of minor irrigation projects were completed with a total command area of 582.[18]

The Lunglei Irrigation Division is headed by Divisional Agriculture Engineer, Irrigation Complex, Hrangchalkawn, Lunglei. The division covers the areas under Lunglei, Saiha and Lawngtlai Administrative Districts. There are three sub-divisions under Lunglei Irrigation Division: Lunglei Irrigation Sub-Division, Saiha Irrigation Sub-Division and Chawngte Irrigation Sub-Division.

Lunglei Irrigation Division was established in May 29, 1987 at Lunglei. At present, there are 51 Irrigation Department personnel's workings for the irrigation development in the district under the division. The division at present started nine Minor Irrigation Project for Lunglei Division, seven in Chhimtuipui District.[19] The division looks after the Minor Irrigation Projects/works and command area development project. The development under Minor Irrigation Scheme provides irrigation potential areas by concrete channel, G.I. pipes, pump sets, aluminum pipes and sprinkler irrigation for maximum production of crops in rural areas.

Under Rural Infrastructure Development Fund (RIDF), National Bank for Agriculture and Rural Development (NABARD)[20] had sanctioned Rs. 237.17 lakhs to Government of Mizoram for completion of 21 Minor Irrigation Projects and it is estimated that as a result of the projects, irrigation potential has been created to the tune of 756 hectares, non-recurring employment to the extent of 24760 man days and under RIDF V, sanction amounting to Rs. 364.42 lakhs has been accorded for a further 20 Minor Irrigation Projects. The irrigation potential expected to be created is 290 hectares and all the projects are slated to be completed by 31 March 2004.[21] The NABARD has prepared banking plan for On-Farm Water Management (OFWM) scheme for increasing crop production in eastern region of the country and all the districts of Mizoram are covered under the scheme. The scheme provides financing of low lift points with 30 per cent subsidy from the Government of India. In Lunglei district 97 units have been allocated during 2003-04 with a bank loan assistance of Rs. 12.11 lakhs and subsidy component of Rs. 7.29 lakhs.[22] Policy of NABARD for Minor Irrigation Development in the District, Projection for the year 2005-06 are as follows in Table 5.7.

Thus, in spite of the physical constraints for irrigation, there has been a steady progress in putting the land under irrigation despite the fact that a large area of cultivation is yet to be covered.

Table 5.7: Block-wise/Activity-wise Projection for the Year 2005-06 in Lunglei District

Activity	*Unit Cost*	*Unit Size*		*Lung-lei*	*Hnah-thial*	*Lung-sen*	*Bungh-mun*	*Total*
Minor Irrigation								
	0.25	Nos.	Physical	8	8	8	6	30
Pump Sets								
			Bank Loan	1.8	1.8	1.8	1.35	6.75
	0.25	No	Physical	5	5	5	5	20
L1 Points								
			Bank Loan	2.925	1.125	1.125	1.125	4.5
Minor Irrigation Total			Bank Loan	2.925	2.925	2.925	2.475	11.25

Source: Potential Linked Credit Plan, Lunglei District, NABARD Mizoram, 2005-2006.

To explore and create potential areas for crop production and to increase yield potential per unit area by adopting new technologies, replacement of low yield local varieties of crops with high yield, construction of irrigation facilities for maximum production per unit area covering all the districts of Mizoram, the following works are being taken up by the Agriculture and Minor Irrigation Department of the Government of Mizoram during 2002-2003:[23]

1. *Foodgrain Development*: Under this scheme fresh flat lands as well as land improvement are done by dozer, tractor, power tiller or manual labour, certified seeds of paddy, oil seeds, maize, pulses, etc. are introduced and made available to the farmers for sale at subsidised rate.
2. *Fertility Management*: Organic farming was introduced in the state as a result of which use of chemical fertilizers was discouraged by discontinuing the subsidy available with the Government of Mizoram. However, private dealers were encouraged to sell the fertilizers at the rate fixed by the government. The sale of fertilisers by the private dealers was monitored by the Department of Agriculture.

The Soil Testing Laboratory of the Directorate of

Agriculture at Aizawl has been maintained and 2200 numbers of soil samples collected from different parts of the state were analysed against the target fixed of 8,000 numbers in the year 2002-2003 with a total outlay of Rs. 6.00 lakhs. The establishment of a new Soil Testing Laboratory at Lunglei is in progress to cater the southern part of Mizoram.

Bio-fertilizers production unit set up at Neihbawi Farm on 30.8.2001 is taken up Rhizobium, Azotobacter, Azospirillum and Phosphotica. The bio-fertilizers are distributed to the farmers free of cost in order to encourage the farmers in its uses.

3. *Plant Protection*: Plant protection chemicals are made available to the farmers at subsidised rate with Mautam or famine occurred during 2007-08 which occurred in fifty year cycle.
4. *Extension and Farming Training*: The scheme is meant to impart technical know how and skill to the farmers through trainings, seminars, tours, audio-visual, etc. Under this scheme "*Zoram Loneitu*" a periodical magazine, leaflets, booklets, etc. are published and distributed to the farmers free of cost. Under the department there are Integrated Training Centre at Hnahthial in Lunglei district and Krishi Vighyan Kendra at Kolasib.
5. *Commercial Crop Development*: This scheme has been implemented for large-scale production of commercial crops like sugarcane, chilies, cotton, etc.
6. *Agriculture Research and Education*: Under this scheme various crop trials/demonstration are carried out to find out the suitability of different crops under various climatic conditions in the departmental farms.
7. *Farm Power and Machinery*: Under this scheme farm power and machineries, power tiller, tractor, pump sets, etc. are given to the farmers at subsidized rate. Besides these, Agro Processing Unit—Oil Expeller with Rice-Mill etc. are installed at 34 villages for the farmers. During the period 2000-2003, 43 tractors and 17 numbers of power tillers were sold on subsidy.

8. *Agriculture Extension*: Under extension services, there is a Training Van equipped with complete Audio-Visual aids with electricity generator as extension aid. There is also a Video-Studio at the Directorate, which telecast farmer's success stories, department's achievements through Doordharshan and Local Television. Over 100 documentary films so far produced from the studio and established one Farmer's Library at the Directorate of Agriculture.
9. *Control of Shifting Cultivation*: Under development component, total area of 213 hectares of potential area has been developed for wet rice cultivation and 144 hectares of hillside slope, 132 hectares land improvements has also been developed for terraced cultivation. Moreover, a total length of 63 kilometers of Potential Area Connectivity has been constructed at different locations wherever necessary. 450 numbers of families were also assisted under the component (scheme) of Household Production System.

However, the most immediate needs are rural road to connect population areas of perishable items with truck able roads, a market area and primary Agro-Processing Unit, which can provide value addition and at the same time reduces the transportation costs.[24]

Reclamation of Land and Soil Conservation

Reclamation of land for permanent cultivation plays an important role to boost up the economy. The quality of soil is an important factor in crop-yield. It provides nourishment and water to the plant life. It consists of minerals, organic matter, water, air, etc. all of which determine its characteristics, fertility, depth, texture and structure and thus govern the type and quality of plants and crop that can be grown in any region of the country.[25]

Land reclamation activities are not emphasised in the pre-union territory days. In fact, land reclamation work has started, practically from the year 1974-75. During the period from 1974-75 to 1977-78 the area measuring 8,672 hectares in 378 villages benefiting 17,011 families have been reclaimed in Mizoram. In 1978-79 about 2500 hectares of land in 243 villages were under reclamation which benefited 1300 families.[26] The broad targets for land reclamation and development in Mizoram in the 8th Plan (1992-97) was 8400 hectares with a financial outlay of Rs. 400.00 lakhs.[27]

The main objective of the Soil Conservation Department which started in April 1959 have been to do away with the age old practice of shifting cultivation in Mizoram.[28] When Mizoram became Union Territory, the Soil Conservation Department was tagged with the Forest Department and again transferred to Agriculture Department in 1977 and in 1986 it became a full-fledged Department as Soil and Water Conservation Department.[29]

In Lunglei district, Soil Conservation Range was established on September 28, 1968. Now the Soil and Water Conservation Department, Lunglei Division has been working which includes stream bank erosion control, construction of water harvesting tank and road, terracing, contour bunding, conservation by cash crop plantation like coffee, rubber, tea, areca nut (kuva) and large cardamom (alaichi big).[30]

During 1990-91,[31] the Soil and Water Conservation Department, Lunglei District, undertaken terracing scheme under which irrigable terrace (9.5 ha.), rainfall terrace (5 ha.), contour bunding/ditches (17 ha.), renovation of terrace (10 ha.) and conservation of terrace catchments by fruit tree plantation of grass planting (18 ha.) with a total physical achievement of 59.5 hectares under the scheme. During this period, soil conservation engineering practice measures were undertaken—which were as follows in Table 5.8.

Under demonstration scheme, coffee 121 ha, tea 2 ha, rubber 64 ha, with a total of 187 hectares were achieved along with cash crop, nursery coffee 4 hectares, rubber 100 hectares, tea 80 hectares, clove/cinamom with a total of 180 beds and 4 hectares. At present the department has undertaken.[32]

(a) Coffee plantation under non-lapsable fund for 150 hectares,
(b) Areca nut expansion scheme under the state fund 10 families,

Table 5.8: Soil Conservation Engineering Practice Measures, Lunglei District 1992

1. Gully Plugging/Control	
(a) Vegetative Check Dam	20.5 ha
(b) Rock Fill gabion box type check dam	13 ha
(c) Tree and Deep rolling grass planting	45 ha
(d) Earthen Check Dam	14 ha
2. River Training Works	
(a) Bed digging	40 ha
(b) Construction of embankment	—
(c) Stream Course Straightening	26 ha
3. Conservation of Land Fertility	
(a) Tree or Grass Planting	7 ha
(b) Construction of Silt dentations dam	9.5 ha
4. Stream Bank Erosion Control	
(a) Vegetative Spur	36 ha
(b) Gab ionic Spur	19.5 ha
(c) Live Vegetative Spur	25 ha
Total	**225.5 ha**

Source: Statistical Handbook, Economics and Statistics Department, Lunglei, 1992.

(c) Rubber expansion scheme under state fund 10 hectares,
(d) Large cardamom (*Alaichi*) Expansion Scheme 3 hectares,
(e) Construction of link road Haulawng to Tlawng Project 8 kilometers,
(f) Catchments area for treatment for Kau Tlabung Hydel Project.

The Soil Conservation Department has decided to give priority for terrace conservation under run-off scheme for creating farms. The terracing above 5 to 25 per cent slope as it is the safest for conservation of soil and moisture. The Department also proposes to implement soil conservation engineering works.[33]

Horticulture

Development of horticulture, perhaps, the most feasible project to boom agriculture produce in Mizoram considered from a geographical purview.[34] The geographical location and climate of Mizoram offers excellent scope for growing different types of horticultural crops such as fruits, vegetables, species etc.[35] Out of the total area of horticulture crops of 32,187,45 hectares in Mizoram,[36] Lunglei district has 5115 hectares with a total production of 16066.9 metric tones.[37] The major horticulture items in the district are orange, assam lemon, banana, hatkora, passion fruit, pineapple, pumpkin, betel vine, etc. Chilly plantation occupies the largest area followed by ginger, banana and pineapple. The principal horticulture crops production in Lunglei district with areas of major crops for the year 2002-03[38] are in Table 5.9.

Table 5.9: Horticulture Production in Lunglei District for the Year 2002-03

S. No.	*Name of Crops*	*Area in Ha*	*Production (Qtls)*
1.	Mandarin Orange	715	6,930
2.	Assam Lemon	54	900
3.	Passion Fruit	60	450
4.	Hatkora	125	148
5.	Banana	350	9,620
6.	Mango	115	2,800
7.	Areca nut	65	920
8.	Betel vine	125	1,956
9.	Coconut	56	156
10.	Ginger	587	7,650
11.	Chilies	2,760	514
12.	Cola cassia	45	1,125
13.	Cabbage	25	1,022
14.	F. Mustard	52	1,779
15.	L. Mustard	265	1,160
16.	Pumpkin	270	8,535
17.	Capsicum	15	250
18.	French Bean	35	1,230
19.	Samtawk (Solanum spp)	35	525

Source: District Horticulture Officer, Lunglei District.

Mizoram falls under Sub-Region No (111) of Eastern Himalayan Zone II.[39] The soil is very fertile and fruits and other plantation crops can be taken up in a big way in areas having assured irrigation.[40] However, the main problem in development of this sector is lack of storage unit particularly cold storage to preserve the fruits and vegetables and transport system has not been fully developed to cope up with the emerging needs.[41]

The Horticulture Directorate in Mizoram, Aizawl, has been separated from the parent Department of Agriculture since July 1993[42] working in boosting horticultural productions in the state.

Under the Directorate, Five Sub-Divisions and 38 Horticulture Circles under the divisions are functioning in the state for horticulture development activities.[43]

Horticulture Department, Lunglei Division was established in 21st July 1994.[44] At present, the department has one sub-division at Hnahthial and 8 Circles. The Circle Horticulture Offices in the district are:

1. Lunglei Circle
2. Thingfal Circle
3. Haulawng Circle
4. Lungsen Circle
5. Tlabung Circle
6. Hnahthial Circle
7. S. Vanlaiphai Circle
8. Thingsai Circle

Lunglei Division is at present working for the development of vegetables, floriculture, plantation of various crops, mushroom development and development of horticulture link roads for its marketing links. It also supplies organic manure, plant protection material, equipment like budding knife, kodali, vegetable seeds, and plantation crop, mushroom spawns to the farmers on subsidy. The department also provides extension and training to the farmers and organise seminar, awareness campaign, farmers tour, exhibition and publish booklets, etc. Under Integrated Waste Land Development Projects (IWDP) scheme,[45] taken up by the National Wasteland Development Board in 1989, aimed at developing wastelands on watershed basis. An area of 24,775 hectares is to be developed for agricultural purposes. Under the scheme, the Lunglei Project-II, is implemented by the District Rural Development Agency, Lunglei through Horticulture Department. The total cost of the Project is Rs. 742.50 lakhs with an area of 12,375 hectares.

Besides, Watershed Development Project in Shifting Cultivation Areas (WDPSCA) and National Watershed Development Project (NWDP) are under implementation. The WDPSCA scheme was launched in 1994-95 in the Seventh North Eastern States and continues during 9th and 10th Plan with an objective to protect and develop the hill slopes of jhum areas through soil and water conservation measures on Watershed basis, to mitigate all effects of shifting cultivation by introducing appropriate land use etc. A total of 3,808,00 hectares has already completed in the district covering 8 projects as on September 2003 during Tenth Plan.[46] The selected WDPSCA Micro Watershed Project for Tenth Plan in Lunglei District are in Table 5.10.

Table 5.10: WDPSCA Micro Watershed Projection for the Tenth Plan in Lunglei District 2002-03

S. No.	*Name of Project*	*Area (in Ha)*	*Location Village*	*R.D. Block*	*Amount (in Lakh)*
1.	Ruangte Lui	500	Runtung	Lunglei	50.00
2.	Upper Ngengrual	500	Thingfal, Mamte	Lunglei	50.00
3.	Lungpher Lui	490	Theiriat, Phaizawl	Lunglei	59.00
4.	Saphak Lui	480	Pangzawl	Hnahthial	48.00
5.	Zaupui	470	S. Vanlaiphai	Hnahthial	47.00
6.	Tuiphai	460	Tarpho	Hnahthial	45.00
7.	Saang	458	Hnahthial	Hnahthial	45.00
8.	Zalrenglui	450	Kauchhuah	Lungsen	45.00

Source: Statistical Abstract, Agriculture and Minor Irrigation Department, Government of Mizoram, 2002-03.

The National Watershed Development Projects (NWDP) scheme was launched in 1990-91 by the Government of India and continues during the Ninth and Tenth Plan with an objective of conservation, development and sustainable management of natural resources, enhancement of agricultural productivity, restoration of ecological balance and creation of sustained employment opportunities for the rural community including the landless.

In Mizoram, the NWDP has been implemented since its inception. A total of 20 and 36 numbers of project with an area of 17,666 hectares and 44,475 respectively has been treated with a total expenditure of Rs. 3,236 lakhs during Eighth and Ninth Plan period. During Tenth Plan an area of 9416 hectares has already been treated as on October 2003 and 50723 hectares to be developed in the following years.

The list of Watersheds of NWDP identified for implementation during Tenth Plan 2002-03 to 2006-07 in Lunglei district are as follows in the Table 5.11.

Table 5.11: List of Watershed of NWDP, Identified for Implementation during Tenth Plan 2002-03 to 2006-07

(Area in Hectares)

S. No.	*Name of Watershed*	*Name of Village*	*Name of R.D. Block*	*Area to be Developed*	*Cost (in lakh)*
1.	Tuisen-I	Zote	Lunglei	600	36.00
2.	Tuisen-II	Zote	Lunglei	550	33.00
3.	Thingva-I	Ramlaitui	Lunglei	540	32.40
4.	Thingva-II	Ramlaitui	Lunglei	583	34.98
5.	Thuhruk-I	Haulawng	Lunglei	595	35.70
6.	Thuhruk-II	Haulawng	Lunglei	580	34.80
7.	Dibuk-I	Zobawk	Lunglei	595	35.70
8.	Dibuk-II	Zobawk	Lunglei	590	35.40
9.	Tuichawng-I	Hnahthial	Hnahthial	595	35.70
10.	Tuichawng-II	Pangzawl	Hnahthial	590	35.40
11.	Middle Tuipui-I	Tuipui-'D'	Hnahthial	580	34.80
12.	Middle Tuipui-II	Tuipui-'D'	Hnahthial	585	35.10
13.	Saithah-I	Zawlpui	Lungsen	600	36.00
14.	Saithah-II	Zawlpui	Lungsen	590	35.70
15.	Tuidam-I	Dengsur	Bunghmun	570	34.20
16.	Tuidam-II	Dengsur	Bunghmun	560	33.60
17.	Tuithurlui	Buarpui	Bunghmun	600	36.00
18.	Tuithurlui-II	Buarpui	Bunghmun	590	35.40
	Total			**7,615**	**595.48**

Source: Statistical Abstract, Department of Agriculture and Minor Irrigation, Government of Mizoram, Aizawl, 2002-2003, p. 52.

With the implementation of NWDP and WDPSCA schemes, the potential for horticulture, spices, vegetables and fodder will increase to a substantial extent. The state government has provided seven community water tanks in the district for supply of water for cultivation of vegetables. Attempt has also been made to grow off-season vegetables. Now a Food Park is being developed at Chhingchhip Village in Aizawl with the help of Government of India assistance. The proposed Food Park will provide infrastructure facility to 20 small units of food processing.[47]

MAJOR CROPS IN MIZORAM

Like other parts of India, agriculture in Mizoram is crop oriented and emphasis is on food crops.[48] There are two principal cropping seasons in Mizoram. Kharif (Fur) and Rabi (Thal). The Kharif season starts from the beginning of the pre-monsoon rain in the month of March and sowing is done by the end of May. The Wet Rice Cultivation (WRC) is done in late June or July. The WRC transplantation is done in late June or early July. Weeding starts only in late May which lasts till September followed by the harvest of the Kharif crops from August to December. The rabi season starts from the early part of September and sowing is completed by the end of October. During the rabi season beans, cabbage and mustard seeds are grown in the same plot of land.[49]

The major crops cultivated in the Lunglei district are paddy, maize, pulses, oilseeds, sugarcane, cotton, ginger, pumpkins, etc.

Rice: Rice is the staple food crop in Mizoram. Throughout Mizoram, two varieties of rice grown. The early[50] paddy or autumn rice is sown in the month of March/April and harvest in the month of August/September. The late paddy or winter rice is sown in May (in jhums) and in June/July in wet cultivation and harvest in November/December. The crops in the district mainly depend on seasonal rain except a few irrigated fields. The annual production of rice during 2002-2003 was 2,12,540.00 quintals, which is not sufficient for the entire district. The rest of rice comes from outside the state. During 2002-2003, 1,1,7711.04 quintals of SF/Rice and 5672.66 quintals of C/Rice have been imported under Food and Civil Supplies Department.[51]

Maize: Maize is an important food crop next to paddy in Mizoram. It is grown in the Jhum fields along with paddy and also in the subsidiary jhum fields called Leipui.[52] The production in 1985-86 were 642 metric tonnes occupying only 568 hectares of land. With the increase of area 948 hectares by 2002-2003, the production was raised to 18,400.00 quintals. Maize is also used for feeding poultry. It is also grown within a short time and stands in a good stead.[53]

Under technology mission, Government of Mizoram is implementing Accelerated Maize Development Programme (AMDP) to improve the level of production of these crops.

Pulses: Pulses are also growing extensively in Lunglei district. The production of pulses in the district in 1985-86 is 268 metric tonnes in an area of 329.2 hectares and with the increase of its area to 1,469.00 quintals in 2002-2003.

Sugarcane: Sugarcane is a tropical crop required high

temperature and high rainfall mainly grown on hill slopes below 3,000 feet.[54] Area under sugarcane was about 49 hectares in 1991-92 and its production was 132 metric tonnes in terms of *gur* (molasses). The area and production in 2002-2003 stands at 82 hectares and 4,400 quintals in Lunglei district. Under Technology Mission, the Government of Mizoram is implementing Sustainable Development of Sugarcane Based Cropping System (SUBACS) to increase the production of sugarcane through field demonstration, incentive for purchase of implements such as *gur* boiling pan, bullock drawn cane crusher, power operated cane crusher. Lunglei district is self-sufficient in *gur* production, which is found in the local markets. But, there is no production of sugar, which led to import of 8701.65 quintals in the year 2002-2003 from outside the state.[55]

Oilseeds: Oilseeds are also cultivated in the district. Oilseeds cultivation has drawn a good number of peasants. In 1990-91, area of oilseeds in the district was 581 and its production was 171 metric tonnes. In the year 2002-2003, the area and production grows to 865 hectares and 8,620.00 quintals. Til (sesamum) also grows in the loamy or clayey loamy soil in Tlabung area under Lungsen block. Oilseed Production Programmes (OPP) has been implemented as Centrally Sponsored Programmes under the umbrella of Technology Mission on Oilseeds, Pulses and Maize in Mizoram since 1999-2000 to harness best of its production.

Ginger: The geographical location and climate of Mizoram is helpful for the cultivation of ginger. Ginger cultivation has been taken up in a larger scale. The production of ginger was 130 natric tonnes in 93 hectares in 1990-91. The production rose to 7.650 quintals in area of 587 in the district. It is one of the crops exported to outside Mizoram. Being a perishable commodity the delay in its export cause worry to the cultivators due to communication constraints.

Chilly: The agro-climatic condition of the district offers excellent scope for production of chilies. The areas and production of chilies in 2002-2003 were 2,760 hectares with productions of 514 quintals. Chilies are also one of the crops that exported outside Mizoram. But, there is no regulated market for its export from the district.

Though the bulk of the population of the Lunglei district is engaged in agriculture the district is far from self-sufficiency in foodgrain production. The district as a whole with little exception to some of few villages, depends on imported foodgrains.

The Government of Mizoram is implementing various schemes for development of crops and continues supplying organic manure, equipment, vegetable seeds, fertilizers, and irrigation facilities for accelerated growth in crops production.

Dairy Development

The agro-climatic condition of the district is helpful for undertaking dairy farming.[56] According to the Livestock and Poultry Census of Mizoram, 1997, the population of cattle and buffaloes in the district were 2955 and adult buffaloes were 85. A chilling plant of the government had been completed at Lunglei with a capacity of 5,000 liters. Approximately 9979 liters of milk was produced in the district during 2002-03. But there is no private chilling plant in the state and milk cooperatives not developed in the state as a whole.[57]

The main problem of dairy development is lack of cross bred cows, lack of grazing lands since the region is hilly, availability of quality fodder which has to be procured from outside the state which adds to high cost.[58]

There is one hospital, 5 dispensaries and 22 Rural Animal Health Centres in Lunglei district. There is a school of Veterinary Science in Lunglei to provide knowledge and also to protect the livestock resources. Two Animal Husbandry and Veterinary rest houses in the Lunglei district. There is a Disease Investigation Laboratory and a Central Medicine and Vaccine depot at Aizawl covering the entire state. Lunglei district is covered under Integrated Dairy Development Programme (IDDP) and under the scheme subsidy is available for purchasing cows, feed and transportation. The animal husbandry and veterinary department procured 378 cows from outside and planning to purchase 940[59] cows for dairy sector to increase the milk production besides capacity building of fertilizers.

Poultry Development

As per the 1997 Livestock Census there were 61,000 desi and 95,000 improved poultry birds in the state. The total egg production in the state during 2001-2002 stood at 288 lakhs. The per capita availability of eggs in the state was estimated at 32 per year.[60] During 2002-2003, the number of poultry unit sold in

Lunglei district is 1627 with 2,502 of quantity.[61] During this year egg production in the district was 5,804.

To meet the poultry requirements of the district, there is a poultry farm at Lunglei. The poultry farm make available of parent stock for layers as well as broiler chicks. The Rural Animal Health Centres looks after its vaccination required in rural areas. But, there is no infrastructure developed in the district in terms of collection, storage, processing, packing and marketing of eggs and boilers.[62] People in the villages are not much exposed to rearing poultry birds in a scientific way as an economic activity.

Piggery Development

Pig is an important domestic animal in Mizoram and pork forms a very important part of the diet of the people. As per the Livestock Census of 1997, the population of pig was estimated at 168.8 thousand, goats at 16.04 thousand and sheep at just 0.70 thousand. Thus, it indicates that piggery is the most popular activity of the people. Almost every household rears at least two pigs.[63] In January to December 2000, 1973 cattle/buffalo were slaughtered and 2748 pigs slaughtered in Lunglei town.[64] Out of the 9 pigs breeding farms in Mizoram, one has been established in Lunglei for production of exotic breed of pigs and other in Hnahthial. To increase the availability of meat and pork, the Government of Mizoram is implementing Development of Sustainable Base for Pig Production (DESBAPP) and under this programme one model piggery village has been set up in the districts and two farms has been established. The Government of Mizoram is encouraging piggery as an alternative source of livelihood for the jhum cultivators in particular. Under New Land Use Policy, Mizoram Intodelhna Project, and other State and Centrally sponsored schemes implemented by District Rural Development Agencies, like Swarnajayanti Gram Swarozgar Yojana (SGSY), and Special SGSY, the Government is encouraging piggery as an alternative source of livelihood under which supply of good quality pigs are supplied to the farmers.[65]

Fisheries Development

Though the terrain of Mizoram is mostly hilly and landlocked, there are some plain stretches, which is being utilized for fish farming. In

Mizoram, there are 24,000 hectares of potential fisheries resources in the culture sector out of which 2,000 hectares have been developed under pond culture and brought under fish farming.[66] The total water area brought under composite fish culture in the Lunglei district is 4.4 acres and total water area brought under all fish farms is 15 hectares as on 2000.[67] There are eight government fish ponds and 720 private fish ponds as on April 2004 in Lunglei district.[68] The total number of fish farmers in the district is only 750, as on 2001 and one fish seed farm and two demonstration farms.[69]

The Fisheries Department, Government of Mizoram is giving technical support and guidance to the fish farmers for its development in the state. The department is imparting training, development of fish farms, distribution of feed, seed, fertilizers. Total number of fish seeds distributed among private farmers at 50 per cent subsidized rate during 2000-2001 in Lunglei district is 4,50,000 and 52 persons trained under Paddy-cum-Fish Culture at Fishery Department, Lunglei District.[70]

The department is maintaining 5 units of Fish Farmers Development Agency in the State. However, there is no cold storage cum ice plants in the district. Fish production in the state is very poor. During the year 2002-2003 fish production in the state was 32,500 quintals only and fish imported was 6226 quintals from outside the state.[71] Although the river Karnaphuli and Chhimtuipui (Kolodyne)[72] provide abundant fish during the period covering February to May, there is no refrigerated vans for its transportation to outside market.

Local fish are not available in the Lunglei district and about 99 per cent of the fish found in the markets in the district are brought from outside Mizoram. Fish farming as an economic activity is yet to generate employment to a sizeable section of the rural people of this district.

Industrial Potential in the District

Industrially, this district is very backward. In fact, industrial development is still at an infantile stage in the state. Mizoram is one of the most industrially backward state of the Indian Union and is defined as "Non-Industries District" under category 'A'.[73] The extreme location, hilly terrain, poor infrastructure facilities like road network, power, water, markets, lack of trained man-power, etc. are the main reasons for the poor industrial development. Small enterprises like vehicle repairing, carpentry, quilt making, handloom etc. are prominent in the district.[74]

Road Network

The existing mode of transport system in the district is road transport and waterways. The agency of road-network development in the district is Border Road Task Force (BRTF) and State Public Works Department (PWD). Lunglei District is connected with the National Highway No. 54. This highway connects Silchar (Assam) with Tuipang in the southern corner of the state through Aizawl and Lunglei. The total length is 572 kilometers, but Mizoram portion is 521.70 kilometrs.[75] Other then the Highway No-54, there is State Highway of all weathered, truck able metalled roads like Lunglei to Tlabung (97 kilometers), Chawngte (101 kilometers) and numerous other district roads Lunglei to Aizawl via Thenzawl.[76] Almost all parts of the district and growth centres of industries are linked with the network of motor able roads. But the position of all weathered road, metalled road in the district are still to be developed. The Public Works Department, road description during the year 2002-03 to 2003-04 under Lunglei Division is presented in Table 5.12.

Table 5.12: Road Description during the year 2002-03 to 2003-04 under Lunglei Division

Sl. No.	*Description*	*Unit in km*	*2002-2003*	*2003-2004*
1.	Villages connected with roads	km	22	24
2.	Motorable road	km	169.58	169.58
3.	Jeepable road	km	100.75	116.75
4.	Less than jeepable road	km	122.25	122.25
5.	Total road length excluding NH	km	381.54	397.58
6.	Out of total road Total Surface road	km	381.54	397.58
7.	Out of total road Length total metal road	km	270.30	286.30
8.	Out of total road Total kutcha road	km	111.28	111.28
	Total Road Density Per 100 sq.km.	km	14.80	14.80

Source: Executive Engineer, PWD Road, Lunglei.

Power

The most serious bottleneck for the development of industry in Mizoram is the inadequate supply of power and the state is still to have a good network of power line and source of supply.[77] Efforts were being made to harness the abundant hydro-power potential in the region and a few project at Serlui 'A' (1.0 MW), Khawiva (1.05 MW) and Tuirivang (0.30 MW) been completed.[78] Power coming to Lunglei is through Aizawl, Serchhip to Khawiva from Khawiva to Lunglei, Theiriat, Lungsen, Lawngtlai and Saiha. Power supply to Lunglei town is through Lunglei Powerhouse. The Lunglei Power house has seven 250 KW DC Set. DG Set has been installed in Lungsen, Tlabung, Chawngte, Mualthuam, Tawipui, Lawngtlai, Saiha, Buarpui, Hnahthial, etc. Hydel Projects taken up and almost under operation are Kau Tlabung and Tuipang Project under Power and Electricity Department, Lunglei.[79]

Water

Supply of water is essential for some type of agro-based, forest based and chemical industries and its scarcity in Mizoram is another problem for the healthy growth of industry. Till 1957, there was no water supply system for Lunglei. However, post 1972, supply of water in the district has improved.[80] With the formulation of Greater Water Supply Scheme that finally formulated and sanctioned in March 1989 for a population of 66,000,[81] the problem of water supply in urban areas of the district solved to a great extent. The types of water supply scheme executed in rural areas are piped water scheme, rain water harvesting tanks, hand pump tube well, improvement of spring sources, etc. During 2002-2003, 13 villages covered under pipe water supply. Altogether 122 villages are covered under this scheme in the Lunglei district, 37 villages with Rain Water Harvesting Scheme, 53 villages provided IVSS and 27 villages with hand pump tube well.[82]

Agricultural Resources

Lunglei district is having good potential to grow agro-based industries. Sugarcane, Ginger, Mandarin Orange, Banana, Pineapple, etc. are grows in plenty which can be used as raw materials.

Fruit Processing Industries for squash, jam and jelly from orange and pineapple, canning of pineapple, etc. may be undertaken.[83]

Chilly Processing Industries can be developed as the district produces large quantity. Its marketing after packing will have a good export market. Besides, oil mill, maize and rice mill, dal mills, leaf plat making, broom making, are other agro-based potential of the district, which can be undertaken. Sugarcane based industries may be developed. Apart from extracting for preparing *gur*, a mini-sugar mill can be developed in the district as income generation.

Ginger Processing Industries may be undertaken as the district has plenty of ginger and extradition of oleo-resins and oil from raw ginger are having excellent export market outside.[84]

Extraction of Fibre (Decortications) from Pineapple Leaves and Banana Stems:[85] This type of fibre industry can be developed in the district in the rural areas. Some good fancy household articles like different types of bags, mats, etc. can be made from the fibre. Very fine clothes also can be waved from the fibre.

Bamboo Based Industries

Bamboo is the most important forest produce of Mizoram in terms of revenue collection and it is the only resource which can support the future forest-based industries.[86] The district has protected reserved forest of 145.80 square kilometers, reverine reserved forest of 436.96 square kilometers and safety and supply reserved forests of 283.00 square kilometers with a total of 865.75 square kilometers[87] In terms of forest cover, it is next to Aizawl but in terms of bamboo forest it tops the list.[88]

Bamboo is a major forest resource used as raw material for handicrafts, village industries. It is used for making carry basket, bamboo mat ply, tent poles, agarbati stick, hanger, head cap, flower vessel, temporary wall of the house, support system for vegetable crippers, storage articles, decorative pieces, etc.[89]

Sericulture

Topographic feature and climatic conditions of Mizoram are highly favourable for sericulture practices.[90] Sericulture is an important activity giving employment to the rural people. The Government of Mizoram is encouraging the activity by way of distributing the Mulberry Saplings to the people, collecting the cocoons from the cocoon growers and the Department of Sericulture is the only purchasing agency of cocoons and also gives farmers training through the Training Institute of Sericulture, Zemabawk, Aizawl.

In the Lunglei district, District Sericulture Officer is looking after its development. The district has one Cocoons Collection Centre, Government Mulberry Seed Farm, Farm Veng, with 9 acres, Government Eri Seed Farm, Thingfal (20.6 bighas), Mulberry Extension Centre, Hnahthial (20 acres), Mulberry Extension Centre, Haulawng (5 acres), Silk Processing Centre, Zobawk (1 acre) and Extension Officer's Office now at Hnahthial Sub-Division, Hnahthial (1 acre).[91] The District has necessary potential to develop sericulture as employment generation for the rural people. The department fixed the rate of cocoon and purchases the same. The present rate of Eri cut Cocoon is Rs. 200 per kilogram and Rs. 60 to Rs. 120 Mulberry Reeling Cocoon.

The Department of Industries at the state level and the District Industries Centre at the district level are working for industrial development in the State. Due to hilly terrain and lack of availability of flat land for setting up large and medium industry is ruled out in the district, efforts have been made to promote cottage, village and tiny industries under small-scale industries sector. The total number of registered units in Mizoram at the end of March 2002 was 4828 of which 2252 units were in Lunglei district.[92] The units are mostly tailoring, knitting, wooden furniture, vehicles repairing, food processing that is bakery units, handloom, pillow quilt making, handicrafts, poultry, etc. The department is also providing grant-in-aid and training and conducts exhibition for rural artisans. The State Government has set up Mizoram Khadi and Village Industries Board to purchase handicraft products and an Emporium is also at Lunglei. The district has a branch of Zoram Industrial Development Corporation (ZIDCO) to meet the credit requirements and to provide marketing assistance to the entrepreneurs. An Integrated Infrastructure Development Centre has also been set up at Pukpui, Lunglei to provide all basic requirements for the promotion of small-scale industries. The Zoram Electronics Industries Corporation (ZENICS) was established to promote Information Technology in the State.

Government of Mizoram is providing training to the unemployed educated youth for entrepreneurship development. National Bank for Agriculture and Rural Development (NABARD) has also provided financial assistance for conducting three Rural Entrepreneurship Development Programmes during 2004-2005 on tailoring, broom making and leaf plate making for 90 participants.[93] The District Industries Centre, Lunglei is the implementing agency of Prime Minister Rojgar Yojana (PMRY) under which subsidy and bank loans are available. During the year 1999-2000, 520 persons were trained in Knitting and Tailoring Centre at Lunglei and working capital grant was paid to 73-persons to Handloom Weavers in this period.[94] The District Industries Centre also provide Electronics and Computer Learning under the Government of India assistance. The Mizoram Polytechnic College, Lunglei, imparts training in civil and mechanical engineering, which produces technical manpower for the promotion of non-farm activities. The Zoram Handloom and Handicraft Development Corporation (ZOHANDCO) are working for the development of handloom and handicrafts in the state and to provide marketing facilities. The District Industries Centre continued to provide grant in aid to rural artisans. The proposed outlay for industries and minerals development in village and small industries, sericulture and industries other than village and small industries, mines and minerals is Rs. 1,860.00 lakh.[95] The main responsibility of the government is to create an environment that is conducive to faster growth of business and industry and should undertake a study in depth to investigate into the reasons of high sickness and slow growth of industries.[96]

The major problems rural people facing in Mizoram are lack of adequate road transport facility, inadequate power and water supply. Remote villages cannot send out the agriculture and horticulture surpluses due to inadequate transport facilities and high transportation costs. No marketing network for the rural people in the state as a whole to dispose of the surplus products apart from very few daily markets and periodical markets. There are inadequate cold storage facilities in the state to accommodate the perishable commodities. Therefore, development of transport, generating sufficient electricity, more cold storage facilities, more processing units, development of market yards, are essential. Mere increase in production and productivity is not enough without effective marketing system in Mizoram. While planning and implementing rural development programmes, foremost importance should be given in the above mentioned development sectors in the state. Good coordination of various development departments like Agriculture, Horticulture, Soil and Water Conservation, Power and Electricity, Veterinary, etc. is essential. The role of block level bureaucracy—the block development officer, extension officer and village level workers is also crucial, being the nearest to the rural people, to inspire them to take up various developmental schemes and the necessity of its successful implementation by utilising the resources available and in initiating the proposals for development under various sectors as agriculture, village and small scale industries, livestock, fisheries, horticulture etc. The block administration should seek out technical inputs and logistic support from the development departments while implementing the programmes which require their assistance.

Notes and References

1. Hluna, J.V. "Socio-economic Development in Mizoram: Problems and Prospects, A seminar paper presented in UGC Sponsored State Level Seminar organized by Govt. J. Buana College, Lunglei, Mizoram. 22-23rd September, 2010.
2. http//: mizoram.gov.in, viewed on 11.10.10.
3. *Virthli* Daily News paper, Lunglei, 19th April 2010.
4. Statistical Abstract, Department of Agriculture and Minor Irrigation, Government of Mizoram, 2002-2003, p. 73.
5. Pachuau, Rintluanga (1994): *Geography of Mizoram*, R.T. Enterprise, Aizawl, p. 131.
6. Das, Kalpana, (2004,): *Rural Development in Mizoram*, *op. cit.* p. 34.
7. Pachuau, Rintluanga, (1994): *Geography of Mizoram*, *op. cit.* p. 131.
8. *Statistical Handbook*, Lunglei District 2003, p. 7.
9. *Ibid* p. 9.
10. Statistical Abstract 2002-03, *op. cit.* p. 14.
11. *Statistical Handbook*, Economics and Statistics, Lunglei District 2003, p. 17.
12. *Ibid*. pp. 10-11.
13. *Ibid*. p. 7.
14. Potential Linked Credit Plan, Lunglei District, NABARD, Aizawl, 2005-2006, p. 4.

15. Directorate of Agriculture and Minor Irrigation, Government of Mizoram, Aizawl, 2006-07.
16. Potential Linked Credit Plan, Lunglei District, *op. cit.* p. 8.
17. Statistical Abstract, *op. cit.* p. 66.
18. *Ibid.* p. 78.
19. Souvenir, Dawngliana, CMS (ed.), Indian Republic Golden Jubilee, Lunglei, 2000, p. 138.
20. Potential Linked Credit Plan, Lunglei District, *op. cit.* p. 18.
21. *Ibid.*
22. *Ibid.*
23. Statistical Abstract, *op. cit.* p. 8.
24. Work Plan for Development of Agriculture and Soil Conservation and Credit and Ccoperation in Mizoram, 2005-2006, p. 5.
25. Lianzela. (1995): *Four Decades of Planning in Mizoram*, Published by Khuangkungi, Aizawl, p. 38.
26. Mizoram District Gazetteers (1989), Department of Art and Culture, Government of Mizoram, Aizawl, p. 106.
27. Lianzela (1995), *Four Decades of Planning in Mizoram*, *op. cit.* p. 41.
28. *Mizoram District Gazetteers* (1989): *op. cit.* p. 107.
29. Statistical Abstract, *op. cit.* p. 4.
30. Souvenir, (ed.) Dawngliana, CMS, *op. cit.* p. 126.
31. *Statistical Handbook*, Lunglei District, 1992, pp. 38-39.
32. Souvenir, (ed.) Dawngliana, CMS, *op. cit.* p. 126.
33. Potential Linked Credit Plan, Lunglei District, *op. cit.* p. 16.
34. Pachuau, Rintluanga (1994): *Geography of Mizoram*, *op. cit.* p. 67.
35. Potential Linked Credit Plan, Lunglei District, *op. cit.* p. 20.
36. *Horticulture Guide*, (2001): Department of Horticulture, Government of Mizoram, Aizawl, p. 11.
37. Statistical Handbook of Mizoram, Economics and Statistics, Aizawl, 2004, p. 23.
38. *Statistical Handbook*, Lunglei District, 2003, p. 24.
39. Lianzela (1995): *Four Decades of Planning in Mizoram*, *op. cit.* p. 33.
40. Potential Linked Credit Plan, Lunglei District, *op. cit.* p. 20.
41. *Ibid.* p. 21.
42. *Horticulture Guide* (2001): *op. cit.* p. 3.
43. *Ibid.*
44. Souvenir, Dawngliana, CMS (ed.), *op. cit.* p. 13.
45. Statistical Abstract (2003), *op. cit.* p. 42.
46. *Ibid.* p. 48.
47. Potential Linked Credit Plan, Lunglei District, *op. cit.* p. 20.
48. Singh, S.N.(2002): Mizoram, Mittal Publcations, New Delhi. p. 66.
49. *Ibid.* p. 67.
50. Mizoram District Gazetteers (1989), *op. cit.* p. 111.

51. Foods and Civil Supply Department, Lunglei District (2003).
52. Mizoram District Gazetteers (1989), *op. cit.* p. 112.
53. Singh, S.N. Mizoram (2002), *op. cit.* p. 68.
54. *Ibid.*
55. Foods and Civil Supply Department, Lunglei District.
56. Potential Linked Credit Plan, Lunglei District, *op. cit.* p. 28.
57. *Ibid.*
58. *Ibid.*
59. Souvenir, Dawngliana, CMS, (ed.) Indian Republic Golden Jubilee, Lunglei, p. 82.
60. Potential Linked Credit Plan, Lunglei District, *op. cit.* p. 30.
61. District Animal Husbandry and Veterinary Officer, Lunglei.
62. Potential Linked Credit Plan, Lunglei District, *op. cit.* p. 30.
63. *Ibid.* p. 8.
64. *Ibid.*
65. Souvenir, Dawngliana, CMS (ed.), Indian Republic Golden Jubilee, Lunglei, *op. cit.* 81.
66. Potential Linked Credit Plan, Lunglei District, *op. cit.* p. 34.
67. District Fisheries Development Officer, Lunglei.
68. Statistical Handbook of Mizoram 2004, p. 14.
69. District Fisheries Development Officer, Lunglei.
70. District Fisheries Development Officer, Lunglei.
71. Statistical Handbook of Mizoram 2004, *op. cit.* p. 15.
72. Singh, S.N. (2002): *Mizoram*, Mittal Publications, New Delhi, p. 68.
73. Sen, J.D. "Industrial Development in Mizoram: Progress and Achievement of Industries Department", *Mizoram Souvenir*, Sl. No. 1, Aizawl, 1989, p. 54.
74. Potential Linked Credit Plan, Lunglei District, *op. cit.* p. 5.
75. P.W.D. Road Development Plan of Mizoram, Abstract Statement, Government of Mizoram, p. 14. Quoted in Pachuau, Rintluanga. Geography of Mizoram, *op. cit.* p. 81.
76. Under PMGSY, rural connectivity in the district is going on implemented by the state PWD.
77. Mizoram District Gazetteers (1989), *op. cit.* p. 138.
78. Pachuau, Rintluanga (1994), *Geography of Mizoram*, *op. cit.* p. 79.
79. Souvenir, Dawngliana, CMS (ed.), *op. cit.*, p. 78.
80. Lianzela (1995), Four Decades of Planning in Mizoram, *op. cit.* p. 45.
81. *Ibid.*
82. Public Health Engineering Department, Lunglei.
83. Potential Linked Credit Plan, Lunglei District, *op. cit.* p. 37.
84. Mizoram District Gazetteers (1989), *op. cit.* p. 139.
85. *Ibid.*
86. Pachuau, Rintluanga (1994), *Geography of Mizoram*, *op. cit.* p. 75.
87. *Statistical Handbook*, Lunglei District, 1992, p. 24.

88. Potential Linked Credit Plan, Lunglei District, *op. cit.* p. 5.
89. *Ibid* p. 36.
90. Mizoram District Gazetteers (1989), *op. cit.* p. 143.
91. *Statistical Handbook*, Lunglei District, 1992, p. 26.
92. Potential Linked Credit Plan, Lunglei District, *op. cit.* p. 37.
93. *Ibid.* p. 36.
94. Souvenir, Dawngliana, CMS (ed.), *op. cit.*, p. 28 (d).
95. District Planning Machinery, Lunglei District, Draft Annual Plan for 2006-2007.
96. Kabra, K.C. (2008): *Economic Growth of Mizoram: Role of Business and Industry*, Concept Publishing Company, New Delhi, p. 342.

6

Block Level Bureaucracy: Their Role and Responsibilities

This chapter deals with the grassroots level bureaucracy and their role and responsibilities in rural development. Section-I deals with recruitment, role of the block development officer. Section-II outlines the role of extension officers and their role and responsibilities. Section-III examines the perceptions of block level bureaucracy on their working conditions.

INTRODUCTION

With the launching of the Community Development Programme (CDP), its implementation was characterised by division of the entire country into small manageable blocks based on a geographical area consisting of about 100 villages with a population of 60,000 to 70,000. The whole of India eventually covered with the network of the operational unit—the Community Development (CD) blocks. Today the entire rural India is delimited into CD blocks which are around 5000. 'Block' was created as the chief local area of administration, operation and implementation of the multipurpose rural development programme. With the integration of National Extension Service with the CD blocks, the CDP became complicated for the old bureaucratic functionaries who were not trained for the same and overstrained as well. Hence, a new type of bureaucracy—the 'block level bureaucracy' was introduced. The idea of the creation of the 'block' and the 'block level bureaucracy' were to develop and make the administration closer to the rural people for convenient and in a concentrated manner of administration in comparatively smaller areas. The block level bureaucracy, also portrayed as 'rural bureaucracy', 'block level functionaries' and 'grassroots level bureaucracy' was introduced mainly with the purpose of motivating and assisting the rural people headed by generalist head—project executive officer (now block development officer) to be assisted by a number of assistant development officers, village level workers specialised and trained in some branches of rural development programme. This administrative set up was organised giving topmost priority on trained personnel for the first time to help the rural people on modern technologies mainly in agriculture and allied sectors. The grassroots level bureaucracy has enormous present-day significance in the rural development of India in general and Mizoram in particular. In a state where panchayati raj institutions not introduced the role and responsibility of the Block Development Officer (BDO) in particular, is enormous.

Recruitment of Block Development Officer

The method for the recruitment of the block development officer is not uniform in all the states of Indian Union. In this connection, the Study Team for the Study of Community Project and National Extension Service, appointed by the Committee on Plan Projects (COPP) has stated.[1]

> "A much debated question is whether the BDOs should form a separate cadre or a pool of officers drawn from different cadres. Arrangements vary in the different states but the consensus of opinion seems to be (and we agree with it) that it would best to enlarge the junior administrative cadre to include all BDOs posts, to ensure that at least 75 per cent of this cadre is recruited directly by open competitive examination and to provide that 25 per cent of the cadre can be filled by promotion from various junior cadres such as officers of the cooperative, panchayat and revenue departments and the social education officer's cadre wherever it is not merged in any education department cadre. Officers recruited directly from the open market should be posted as BDOs after their initial training and before they have spent more than two

> or three years in the revenue department so that they are not imbued with what is known as the Revenue Bureaucratic Spirit."

The Government of India has considered the above recommendations of the COPP and they agree with in principle. If it is accepted by the state governments, the arrangement will be in keeping with the objective of transforming the existing administrative services. This will also provide opportunity to the sub-ordinate officers of the development departments to get promoted to the junior administrative cadre by establishing their suitability for holding the post of BDO. These officers, if found fit as BDO, will be eligible to get promoted to the junior administrative cadre or alternatively they may get promoted to superior posts in their parent departments.

The study team recommended 25 per cent of the BDOs post can be filled by promotion, which will provide opportunity to the subordinate officers of the development departments to get promoted to junior administrative cadre by establishing their suitability for holding the posts of BDO. At present,[2] the posts of BDO are filled through–

(i) Direct recruitment through state public service commission, and
(ii) Promotion or transfer from existing state administrative service.

In certain States like Assam, Bihar, Uttar Pradesh, Jammu and Kashmir, Orissa, Karnataka, Punjab, Haryana, the block development officers are directly recruited through the State Public Service Commission. In other States like Andhra Pradesh, Gujarat, Maharashtra, Kerela, Madhya Pradesh and Rajasthan, the BDOs are appointed either by promotion or transfer from the existing state service. In Mizoram, the posts of BDOs are filled from the State Administrative Service. The Mizoram Civil Service (MCS) Junior Grade Officers are appointed as BDOs in Mizoram from 1972 when Mizoram became Union Territory.[3]

The qualification prescribed for the post of BDO is also differ from State to State. But usually, persons in the age group 25-35 and in possession of Bachelor's degree in arts, science, agriculture, veterinary science are eligible for appointment as the BDOs. When the appointments are made emphasis is made on administrative experience, social service or experience of revenue administration.

Assam laid emphasis on social service as an essential qualification, Karnataka on three to five years of administrative experience in the departments of revenue, Haryana and Punjab on field experience in a block.[4] In Andhra Pradesh, recruitment is made from the revenue and non-revenue departments on 40:60 basis and in Uttar Pradesh, all posts are filled through competitive examination held by the State Public Service Commission.[5] The persons with revenue administration are usually given preference over others.[6] The Conference on Community Development[7] held at Mount Abu expressed general agreement with the proposals of the COPP Team regarding recruitment and selection of BDOs and emphasized that no separate cadre for BDOs should be created by the states and that IAS and State Civil Service Officers should actually work as BDOs for one year as a part of their normal field training. The conference recommended that the Ministry of Community Development should once again address the state governments explaining their views including the points brought out above more fully so as to help to evolve a uniform system of recruitment of BDOs.

Thus, there is no uniform method of recruitment of the posts of BDOs and it varies from State to State. But because of the key position held by the BDOs he should be an officer of adequate capability, experience, sufficient ability and familiarity with rural administration.

Training of Block Development Officer

The block development officer needs comprehensive training for performing his duties as an extension worker, as a programme planner, as a programme executive and a coordinator, evaluator and as a captain of the team of functionaries and most important is, as an agent to motivate, encourage and assist village families to develop a change in the attitude of the people especially the poor. There is such a large variety of programmes and complex details of various provisions in the schemes that any functionary is bound to get out of date, unless he participates in training courses periodically.[8] This need has been recognised by both by the union and the state governments. A number of Orientation and Study Centres, Extension Education Institutes, Extension Training Centres, Gram Sevak Training Centres and Gram Sevika Training Centre were started.[9] In 1958, the Government of India set up the Central Institute for Research and Studies in Community Development (later renamed as the National Institute of Rural Development) for training and orientation of senior officers and people's representatives.[10]

The main purpose of imparting this basic training in community development is to ensure that all the functionaries, who have to work at the block level, get a common understanding of the objectives, methods and ways of measuring progress of the CDP with an objective of promoting all-sided development of the village community, including their economic, political, social, cultural and moral development.[11]

The block development officer generally obtain one or two months training in the orientation and study centres along with other extension officers and a job course of six month's duration in the social education organisers training centres for specialised training. The orientation course is of a very general and preliminary nature which acquaints the participants with such subjects as the philosophy, history, organization and programme contents of the CDP, the methodology of extension and the analysis of the rural situation.[12] The method of instruction is mainly through lecture and syndicate studies where the participants are divided into a number of small groups—each of which is allotted one subject for detailed discussion and deliberations in order to develop a deep understanding of the subject which helps them in the field. The participants of the course are trained to handle such functions of their office as programme—planning and execution, administrative, coordination, maintenance of the office records, evaluation, etc.[13]

In Mizoram, as the MCS, junior grade officers are being appointed as BDOs, receive post entry training when they join as MCS officers at the Administrative Training Institute, Aizawl. The State Institute of Rural Development located at Kolasib, Mizoram conducts the training on guidelines of the centrally sponsored programmes, as well as training for the rural development functionaries.[14] There is no provision of training for the promoted BDOs in Mizoram. Those who were hold the posts of Administrative Officers used to get two months foundation course at

Administrative Training Institute, long before they were conferred MCS and then as BDO.[15]

Role and Responsibilities of the Block Development Officer

The block development officer is responsible for the entire administration of the block. He needs to look after the office work as well as extension works in the block.

Being the head of the block office, the BDO look after office management, replies and receive letters, submits monthly, quarterly and annual reports to the higher authorities regarding the activities and achievements of the block under various developmental programmes. Normally, the BDOs receives 15-20 letters in a day from Directorate of Rural Development, District Rural Development Agency (DRDA), Deputy Commissioner, State Level Monitoring Cell (SLMC), etc.[16] He is the drawing and disbursing officer of the block. He receives funds under different schemes and programmes of rural development. The money is deposited in the personal ledger account of the BDO. There is a statistical inspector, who compiles statistical information regarding the progress of various programme and help the BDO in his work of responding and sending of reports, achievements, and progress of the on going programmes.

The block development officer is the manager of the team of the development officers—the extension officer's—agriculture, animal husbandry, industry, minor irrigation and cooperation, who are specialists in their respective fields. The extension officers are to work under the supervision of the BDO. The BDO has the responsibility for efficient implementation of the various development programmes in his block.[17] To implement those programmes efficiently, the BDO needs the technical experts and it is his responsibility to inculcate team spirit among the various officers and to see that the technical personnel remain free to be able to devote themselves fully for efficient implementation of programmes relating to their respective field.[18]

The block development officer coordinates various technical functions in the block and all correspondence between the district level officers of development departments and their field personnel passes through him.[19] It is also the responsibility of the BDO to ensure coordination between the work of different extension officers and help in overcoming departmental rivalries.[20] He needs to convene regular meetings attended by extension officers village level workers to discuss specific problems and progress of the on going programmes and the problems and constraints in their work. The BDO also coordinates various meetings as a convener of Block Level Coordination Committee, Block Level SGSY Committee, and the Block Level Vigilance Committee. He is to see that all the technical officers and representatives of financial institutions remain present. These committees meets once in a month and difficulties relating to various poverty eradication programmes are settled in the meeting.[21] These committees can be used to discuss emerging problems including infrastructure gaps and initiatives needed to be taken to solve them. He prepares agenda for the block meetings, maintains the minutes of the meetings and to implement the decision of the meetings with the team of his functionaries.

The block development officer also act as the Convener of the Block Level SGSY Committee which is consists of Project Director, DRDA as Chairman, Project Officer (Self-employment), member, all Branch Managers of the implementing bank branches in block, block level/sub division level officers of the concerned line departments, one NGO representative. The main task of the committee is to draw up and implement a realistic action plan under the SGSY for the block. The meetings of this committee shall be convened by the BDO. The Lead Bank Officer, DDM, NABARD and the Lead District Officer, RBI may attend the meetings as special invitees. They may attend as many meetings as possible in each block, so that they are familiar with the ground level problems and can help in sorting them out.[22]

The block development officer also works as a planning officer. He prepares developmental plans of the block and submits it to the District Planning Machinery to be discussed and approved by the District Planning Board.[23] As planning constitutes the central institutional kingpin of developmental efforts in India,[24] the block has emerged as a multi-disciplinary agency for the formulation and implementation of local plans to be drawn up taking into account the resources likely to be allocated and locally available and the projects are selected considering the felt needs of the people.[25] He is responsible for various programmes to be planned and implemented keeping in view the resources and schematic guidelines with local participation in a decentralised manner.[26] The development officers and village level functionaries are required to be engaged by the BDO in various field works and helps in the preparation of the annual action plan of the block.[27] The BDO needs to prepare plans, keeping in mind which are realistic and achievable and should laid emphasis on attainment of self-reliance and removal of poverty and ensure substantial expansion in employment opportunities.

Generating rural employment has been the core objective of community development programmes and strategy designed with an aim to improve the economic and social life of the rural poor living below the poverty line. Thus, various rural employment programmes have been introduced especially from Fourth Five Year Plan onwards as a strategy for employment generation for the unemployed in rural areas. Mention may be made of Intensive Rural Employment Programme (IREP) started in November 1972, Drought Prone Area Programme (DPAP) for organizing labour intensive and production oriented works to generate employment, National Rural Employment Programme (NREP) started in 1980, Rural Landless Employment Guarantee Programme (RLEGP) launched on 15th August 1983. In 1990's, new programmes like Employment Assurance Scheme (EAS) introduced in 1993-94 for employment generating programmes. The recent ongoing employment generating programmes like EAS, Food for Work under SGRY, Jawahar Gram Samridhi Yojona (JGSY), SGSY, etc. are executed through blocks under the supervision of the BDOs. The successful implementation of all these programmes depends upon efficient, timely technical and administrative support to be rendered by the BDO and his team of technical officers. The employment generating programmes are to be implemented by the BDO according to the schematic guidelines in the block and he is the key in its successful implementation with the help of his technical staff and village level workers. It is the responsibility of the BDO to identify the potentials of the block and develop infrastructure for generating employment on a sustained basis for eradication of poverty.

The block development officer can play a very important role in emergency situations like floods, unseasonal rains, cyclone, fire, etc. A thorough understanding of natural calamities and arrangement of relief and rehabilitation is essential for the BDO to tackle the situation. He has to remain ready with advance planning and needs to assess and report it to the appropriate authority and to see that essential commodities being allotted to the affected area are reaching the people it meant for. Although Mizoram is not affected by regular natural calamities like cyclone, flood, etc., there are heavy rains causing landslides, all over Mizoram and floods in Lungsen block.[28] The BDO report it to the Deputy Commissioner of the exact date and happenings of the calamities and arrange the necessary requirements. There is also Block Level Disaster Committee, which evaluate the situation in which the BDO plays a key role.[29] It is the duty of the BDO to arrange, safe drinking, water, medicine, distribution of essential commodities, food and clothing, administration of assistance sanctioned by the government, providing 'Food for Work' programme, revising of action plan under such circumstances with the help of his team of functionaries. It is also the responsibility of the BDO to take precautionary measures against epidemics and health hazards that may occur due to natural calamities.

Education plays an important role in human development. The National Policy on Education (NPE) 1986 called for "special emphasis on the removal of disparities and to equalise educational opportunity," especially for Indian women, Scheduled Tribes (ST) and the Scheduled Caste (SC) communities. To achieve these, the policy called for expanding scholarships, adult education, recruiting more teachers from the SCs, incentives for poor families to send their children to school regularly, development of new institutions and providing housing and services. The NPE called for a "child-centered approach" in primary education and launched "Operation Blackboard" to improve primary schools nationwide. The policy also called for the creation of the "rural university" model, based on the philosophy of Indian leader Mahatma Gandhi, to promote economic and social development at the grassroots level in rural India. Sarva Shiksha Abhiyan (SSA), launched in 2001 is the most recent initiatives of the Government of India. Free and compulsory education to all children up to the age fourteen is constitutional commitment in India now. The Parliament of India has recently passed Right to Education Act through which education has become fundamental right of all children of age group 6-14 year.[30] The BDO while preparing annual action plan on community assets should give priority on construction of school buildings and necessary infrastructure for the same. Although the percentage of literature is very high in Mizoram, the percentage of literacy in backward blocks like Lungsen and Bunghmun is relatively low.[31] The block development officer can make a contribution in access of education particularly in remote villages. Under various programmes initiated by the government like the Operation Blackboard, Finance Commission Award, Local Area Development Grant, the BDO should contribute to the creation of infrastructure development.[32] The gigantic problem of poverty is linked to education. Poverty in India is widespread. According to the 2005 World Bank estimate, 42 per cent of India's population falls below the international poverty line. Among the causes ascribed for the high level poverty in India are its history under British rule, large population, and low literacy.[33] The BDO should play an important role in promotion of education in his block while implementing rural development programmes.

In the field of health care, the block development officer as head of the general administration at the block, should take initiatives to ensure and supervise the programmes on safe drinking water, primary health care, disease control measures, nutrition schemes, prevention of malaria, leprosy, immunisation programme, sanitation, environment protection, school health programmes, etc. Government of Mizoram has undertaken various steps to achieve the goal of "Health for All" during the last two decades. A vast network has been built up for providing health services in both urban and rural areas. As on March 2007, Mizoram has a health care network of 10 hospitals, 10 Community Health Centres, 56 Primary Health Centres and 366 Sub-Centres.[34] There is a National Malaria Eradication Programme, which is under implementation in the district. Mizoram is a malaria-prone state especially in the months from May to September.[35] The BDO needs to take measures for cleanliness of inhabited areas and other preventive measures like spray of DDT, distribution of mosquito nets and by educating the people about its prevention measures. He should utilise the available funds for employment generating programmes by construction of sub-centre buildings, organise health camps and keep in touch with the medical staff posted in the block. The BDO has a regular interaction with the Village Councils through which the BDO may discuss primary health care and make conscious of the importance of family planning, tackling of epidemics and malaria, etc. regularly. The BDO should provide logistic support to the medical staff to enable them to visit remote villages and also aware about the immunization programmes through the Village Councils he regularly interacts.

To eradicate poverty and to secure social and economic justice to the poorest of the poor people of rural India, *Social security and welfare schemes* has been introduced in India in recent years by the Government of India like National Old Age Pension Scheme, the National Family Benefit Scheme.[36] The term social security stands for the provision made by any public body for the economic security and thus social welfare of individuals and their families, especially in the case of income losses. Such income loses may occur due to unemployment, work injury, maternity, sickness, old age or death. In the Indian context, social security is a comprehensive approach designed to prevent denial, promise the individual of a basic minimum income for himself and his dependants and to protect the individual from any uncertainties. The State bears the primary responsibility for developing appropriate system for providing protection and assistance to its workforce. Social security is increasingly viewed as an integral part of the development process.[37] The schemes of social security and welfare for unorganised sector—the rural poor are to be implemented under the supervision of the BDO. Under these schemes, the Government of India gives pension and paid the sum of Rs. 10,000 in the death of a breadwinner of the bereaved family under National Benefit Scheme.[38] The BDO should see that the list of genuine beneficiaries get the assistance and money going to the genuine beneficiary. The field verification and identification are to be made by the village level workers and extension officers under the supervision of the BDO.

The block development officer can play an important role in implementing *Public Distribution System* (PDS). Public distribution of foodgrains has been an important component of planning in India. The Indian PDS is a national food security system that distributed subsidised food to India's poor. Major commodities distributed include wheat, rice, sugar, and kerosene. Surpluses of food from increased crop yields (as a result of the Green Revolution and good monsoon seasons) are managed by the Food Corporation of India, established by the Food Corporation Act 1964, implements national policy for farm price support, operations, procurement, storage, preservation, inter-state movement and distribution operations. PDS has a network of about 478,000 fair price shops, perhaps the largest distribution network of its type in the world, operated by the Union Government and State Governments.[39] With the help of the Inspector of Civil Supply, the BDO administers the PDS by distributing the allocations with the identification of families to be covered under the scheme carefully and accurately, regular visits to the fair price shops and random verification of cards, make the essential commodities adequately available in time, take initiatives to effectively operate the Vigilance Committees for monitoring the implementation of the PDS, ensuring distribution of quality of the essential commodities etc. Controlled and low prices of essential commodities increase the real income of the poor and also increase the purchasing power.[40] Being closer to the rural people, involvement of the BDO in public distribution system will be very helpful for the rural people in Mizoram where the villages are scattered due to geographical location. At present, there is no Inspector of Civil Supply of Civil Supply in all the rural development blocks in Mizoram and the BDO is not involved in PDS.

The Block Development Officer and Village Councils

As the Panchayati Raj Institutions (PRIs) are not introduced in Mizoram, the Village Councils are the democratic local-self government responsible for carrying out the welfare and developmental activities in its jurisdiction. In fact, Village Councils are the vital part of developmental works, without which government cannot perform any developmental work.[41] The block development officer entrust the Village Councils in the identification of beneficiaries under various anti-poverty alleviation programmes like IRDP, Employment Assurance Scheme, SGSY, SGRY (Food for Work), and in selection of sites for the construction of drainage, retention walls, drinking water supply scheme, etc. The Village Councils are also entrusted to making list of BPL families, estimation of production and in preparation of Annual Action Plans for which the Village Level Workers (VLWs) helps in it. The Village Councils are entrusted to supervise the works undertaken in his respective area and handed over the cash and food component to the President for necessary action. The BDO frequently meet the Village Council President or sent his personnel's to enquire the works undertaken and the President reports it to the BDO. The Village Council President is being conveyed by the BDO in the introduction of new schemes and benefits available under it. The village people actually know the programmes of rural development through President.[42]

Thus, block, being the nodal agency for implementation of various programmes and schemes, the BDO has a closed link with the Village Councils without which he cannot implement the schemes in accordance with the guidelines issued by the government on various programmes.[43]

The Block Development Officer and DRDA

The District Rural Development Agency (DRDA) since its inception in 1980, is visualised as a specialised and a professional agency capable of managing the anti-poverty programmes of the Ministry of Rural Development on the one hand and to effectively relate these to the overall effort of poverty eradication in the district.[44] The function of DRDA includes[45] identification of families below the poverty line, keeping the district level and block level agencies informed about the basic parameters and requirements of the programmes and the task to be performed by all these agencies, preparing plans and schemes to assist the families of rural population for improving their economic conditions and to bring them above the poverty line. It is an agency registered under a Societies Registration Act headed by a Project Director, who would be of the rank of an Additional District Magistrate and the Deputy Commissioner as the Chairman of DRDA.[46] All the centrally sponsored programmes related to anti-poverty programmes of the Ministry of Rural Development are implemented by the DRDA in the district. Block, being the executing unit, the DRDA and the BDO has a close relation. The DRDA facilitate the implementation of the programmes and the BDO executes those programmes in Mizoram and submits the progress reports and accounts for the funds. The BDO has a direct relation with the DRDA as most programmes of anti-poverty programmes are implemented and executed by the BDO.

The block development officer receives money in cheque from the DRDA for various schemes like Indira Awas Yojana and other anti-poverty programmes and maintains accounts and cashbooks. The BDO submits monthly, quarterly and annual reports to the DRDA in the prescribed proforma. The DRDA then send a consolidated report on quarterly basis to the state along with summary of comments on salient observations and follow up actions on issues noted in its inspection reports as the BDO have to visit and inspect 20 *Swarojgaris*, every month and report it to the Chairman DRDA, the Deputy Commissioner.[47]

It was observed that block administration began to be weakened from about the middle of the decade of sixties onwards with the decline of CDP and rise of separate sectoral programmes of rural development. The giving of responsibility for coordinated implementation of various special anti-poverty programmes to the newly created DRDA however implies that block development administration should be strengthened substantially as the DRDA needed its assistance for discharge of some of its responsibility.[48]

The Block Development Officer and District Councils

The Government of Mizoram, District Council Affairs Department has entrusted[49] the subjects/items under various departments of the Government to the Mara, Lai and Chakma Autonomous District Councils with effect from the financial year of 1994-95 which includes agriculture and horticulture, fisheries, public health engineering, industry, sericulture, arts and culture, social welfare, animal husbandry and veterinary, soil conservation, transport, sports and youth services, cooperation, public works, education, rural development, etc. As such the District Councils are having rural development departments looking after the development works of rural areas such as rural housing, maintenance of inter village paths, construction of community hall, village roads wells, etc. However, the state rural development agencies and the block development officer have no administrative relation with the rural development department of the District Councils. As such, implementation of respective programmes is being implemented independently. The District Council with its rural development department is implementing the schemes undertaken by the District Councils. The District Council is having membership in the District Development Committees where DRDA and BDO are part of it, and this is the only relationship with the other rural development agencies such as DRDA and BDOs.[50] Both DRDA and BDO have separate identity and no relation in their developmental works with the District Councils. As both the Autonomous District Councils and state government have equal responsibilities for uplifting the rural people living under the Sixth Schedule area of Mizoram, they should work in cooperation.

Thus, from the above analysis of the role and responsibilities of the block development officer, it is apparent that he holds a key position in the administrative structure of block administration. In fact, he is all in all in the general administration of the block who have closer relation with the rural people. The BDO is also assigned to various other duties by the government, which includes selection of BPL families, census, election duties in time of assembly and parliamentary elections, registration of voters and any other duties assigned by the government from time to time.

THE ROLE AND RESPONSIBILITIES OF EXTENSION OFFICERS

Rural development process requires integration of a variety of activities in the field in which it operates aiming at amelioration of rural poverty, which cannot be implemented by the block development officer alone in isolation. Thus, the CDP envisaged involvement of functionaries of line departments in implementing welfare and developmental schemes under the umbrella of the block.[51] Democratizing the institutional set up at the village further strengthened this approach and block levels with the recommendation of the team for the Study of Community Project and National Extension Service.[52] The Committee recommended "devolution of power to a body which, when created. will have the entire charge of all development works within its jurisdiction, the government ...... reserving to itself the functions of guidance, supervision and higher planning and where necessary, providing extra finance." To secure this the committee envisaged a three-tier system of rural local government, namely Village Panchayat at the village level, the Panchayat Samiti at the block level and Zila Parishad at the district level. The Panchayat Samiti will have two sets of officers—block level and the village level. The block level officers will include the block development officer and various technical or extension officers in charge of agriculture, irrigation, roads and buildings, public health, animal husbandry, cooperation, social education, etc. The Committee recommended the extension officers should be under the technical control of the corresponding district level officers but under the administrative control of the BDO. At the village level, the Village Level Workers (VLW) recruited by the Zila Parishad, which will assign them to the various Panchayat Samitis, and they will be under the administrative control of the block development officer.[53] The BDO prepares the confidential reports of extension officers, sanctions or cancels their leave, gives them necessary guidelines, conveys government instructions to them, and in case of their non-cooperation, reports the matter to the respective district level officers. The control of the BDO over extension officers has resulted in a problem which could cause a deadlock at Samiti level.[54] Therefore, it is imperative for the BDO to meet the extension officers regularly and, as far as possible, refrain from giving them orders which are inconsistent with those issued by the technical departments.[55]

The block development officer, being the head of the block administration, has to maintain a perfect harmony and understanding with extension staff which is engage in field work as well as with the ministerial staff which maintains block records and establishment, for successful implementation of rural development programmes. The block level bureaucracy is expected to perform their duties and responsibilities as a team and the successful implementation of rural development programmes largely depends on how the block administration works with team spirit.

In Mizoram, as the Panchayati Raj Institutions not being introduced, the block development officer is the chief administrative head and development functionary of the block. The BDO is assisted by a number of extension officers and VLWs deputed from development departments. However, the Gram Sevikas are mostly appointed by the Rural Development Department of Mizoram. The main responsibilities and the role of extension officers agriculture, horticulture, veterinary, statistical inspector and junior engineer are discussed below.

Agriculture Extension Officer

Agriculture is the mainstay and basic means of occupation of rural population of Mizoram. Since rural economy was land-based and over dependent on agriculture, rural development cannot be conceived without promoting this very important sector. The CDP since its inception in 1952, gives top priority in the development of agriculture. Thus, the Agriculture Extension Officer (AEO) is being deputed to the rural development blocks from the agriculture department of the state. His main duty is instructing farmers in the latest techniques of farming, improved tools and implements, seeds, fertilizers, providing opportunities to them to meet together for the purpose of learning from each other and developing leadership in agricultural affairs.[56] He should enthuse the farmers to create in themselves a desire to improve the standard of living, do more, better and faster, and more economically and gives necessary technical 'know-how' and also encourage village institutions like cooperatives and panchayats.[57] He also required to supply essentials like improved seeds, fertilizers, plant protection chemicals and equipments as per the programmes of the government on subsidised rate.

The Agriculture Extension Officer is to assist the block development officer in preparing project reports under the beneficiary oriented schemes of the related sectors and avail of opportunities available under the priority sector programmes to promote agriculture for enhancing food grain production.[58] The AEO is also responsible for the implementation of various agriculture related schemes of rural development by utilising the resources available. It is the responsibility of the AEO in helping the BDO in proper utilisation of the agriculture related schemes and develop suitable infrastructure for more result oriented, economic production with less expenditure with the available resources. He is to instruct and guide the VLWs concerning agriculture related programmes and help in agriculture production plans with the help of the progressive farmers and in consultation with the farmers concerned in at least four villages under the charge of each VLW.[59] The COPP Team recommended[60] relating to agriculture are complete survey of agricultural conditions existing in each village of the block, location, identification and training of at least two progressive farmers in each village, preparation of village agricultural plan, demonstration to conserve all available waste materials namely cattle dung, human and cattle urine, vegetable refuse for compost making, introduction of green manuring and fertilisers, arranging ocular demonstrations at least three per VLW, selection of suitable land for the establishment of seed multiplication farm and horticultural nursery in the block and to assist the agricultural department in starting the same, initiation of youth clubs to take up growing of vegetables, fruits, flowers rearing of poultry, goats and sheep and creating a climate for people's participation in the agricultural programme namely, construction of field channels, tree plantation, soil conservation, plant protection, etc. The AEO and VLW in cooperation with panchayats and cooperatives should guard against failure of supply line. Village panchayats should be encouraged to undertake concerted drives for growing fuel and timber trees, adoption of better cropping patterns including double and triple cropping in irrigated areas, construction and maintenance of terraces, drainage or flood protection measures, etc.

In all the beneficiary oriented schemes on agriculture; the AEO helps the BDO in its proper implementation. The beneficiaries—individual and group needs the help of the AEO for useful and able guidance for its success. The cooperation of the BDO and the AEO is vital in the development of agriculture sector in the block and take up the problems, difficulties being faced by the farmers and provide logistic support to the farmers.

In the hilly state like Mizoram where foodgrain production is not self-sufficient and availability of cultivable land is limited, BDOs, the AEOs and VLWs require to be very active and guide the farmers for proper utilisation of the government plans for increased agricultural production in the villages.

Horticulture Extension Officer

The Horticulture Extension Officer (HEO) is on deputation from the Horticulture Department to the blocks to assist the BDO in promoting horticulture production through anti-poverty programmes in the blocks in Mizoram. The HEO assists the BDO in identifying potential beneficiaries for taking up horticulture production under the beneficiary oriented poverty alleviation schemes. He is required to assist the BDO in preparing suitable schemes for beneficiaries below the poverty line and support services in organising those assisted under the horticulture and arranges inputs, bank loans and training for them. He also needs to guide and instruct the VLW's and supplies organic manure, plant protection material, equipment like *budding knife*, *kodali*, vegetable seeds, mushroom spawns, etc. to the farmers on subsidy as per the programmes and schemes of the government. The duties and responsibilities of the HEO are almost similar to that of the AEO at the block.[61]

Veterinary Extension Officer

Promotion of diary and poultry can go a long way in generating employment opportunities for the unemployed rural people. It provides a significant proportion of self-employment opportunities as well as subsidiary occupation to a large section of rural people particularly to the people living in drought prone, hilly, tribal and other less favoured areas, where crop production on its own may not be capable of engaging them fully.[62] Livestock development has been given prime importance in Mizoram as an alternative to jhum cultivation in recent years through various schemes like New Land Use Policy, Mizoram Intodelhna Project and Centrally Sponsored Schemes like Swarnajayanti Gram Swarojgar Yojana (SGSY) and Special SGSY for Lunglei district. The Veterinary Extension Officers (VEO) posted in the blocks from the department of Animal Husbandry and Veterinary are to assist the BDO preparing appropriate schemes for beneficiaries and to provide animal health care under the livestock sector. Livestock have a good market in the district. Along with Mizoram there is a huge market for beef in the other hilly states of North Eastern region. Considering the scope and potential, some exotic beef animals can be introduced in the state for breeding and to study about the adaptability of these beef breeds in this climate.[63] The VEO is required to help the rural poor in providing marketing infrastructure in terms of collection, storage, institutional finance, utilise opportunities for development of fodder farms and other activities keeping in view the schematic guidelines and the resources available. He is required to assist the BDO keeping in view the schematic guidelines and the potentials available under livestock sector in the block. He should ensure proper supervision and care of the livestock's and encourage the unemployed youths, veterinary graduates, to take livestock such as cattle rearing, dairy farming, goat, poultry, duck, sheep rearing, etc. as a source of income, encourage private milk producers, cooperatives in the block. Although the development of this sector in generally undertaken by the Animal Husbandry and Veterinary department, the VEO needs to coordinate the Animal Health Centres at the block and utilise it properly for its support services in organising those assisted under the livestock sector. It is the duty of the VEO to visit the individual and Self-Help Groups benefited under this sector at regular intervals to provide required health services which will also ensure that the beneficiaries actually undertaken the sector they choose for, and report it to the BDO.

Industry Extension Officer

The Industry Extension Officer (IEO) is another very important extension staff under the block generally deputed from industry department of the state. The IEO can play an important role especially in the development of small scale industries in Mizoram. The small scale industries play an important role in overall economic development of the country and contributes significantly to India's Gross Domestic Products and export earnings besides meeting the social objectives including that of providing employment opportunities to millions of people across the country.[64] Small scale and cottage industries are best suited in Mizoram as they require less capital, low levels of technical skills and less managerial experience. The vast natural resources and local raw materials can be exploited more efficiently by setting up small industries in the state. Location aspects of the traditional small scale and cottage industries are mostly rural and semi-urban. Thus they create employment opportunities mainly to the agricultural labourer and local artisans, which, in turn, helps in equal distribution of state income. Besides increasing the income of the rural poor, these industries preserve craftsmanship and old age heritage.[65] The IEO is to outline plans and projects under small scale and cottage industries sector in his block and help the beneficiaries by organising training under this sector. The IEO assists the BDO in development of cottage and small scale industries which includes blacksmithy including tinsmithy, bricks and tile making, carpentry, leather goods, tailoring, khadi spinning and weaving, bee keeping, weaving handloom, village pottery, handicrafts which includes embroidery, knitting, etc. and motivating the rural people to take up small scale industrial units as a source of earning under various rural development schemes. It is his duty and responsibility to aware the people about the ongoing programmes of the government to be implemented and guide the people for setting up and running of small scale and cottage industries. The IEO should also engage in solving the problems face by the beneficiaries under the block, make it to the notice of the BDO and make necessary arrangement for marketing of the products by taking quality control measures.

The industry extension officer need to identify activity, project preparation, avail of finance, visiting the beneficiaries and report to the BDO about the progress of the anti-poverty programmes undertaken under this sector.[66]

Junior Engineer

The Junior Engineer deputed from the Public Works Department[67] is a very important official of the block. All the developmental projects and preparation of plans and estimates and providing necessary technical supervision are done by the Junior Engineer.[68] The BDO required the technical support for the implementation of employment programmes and other developmental projects from the Junior Engineer. The Junior Engineer prepares plans and estimates of the future development schemes selected for approval and keep a record of all construction activities. He prepares plans and estimates of the ongoing programmes and provides infrastructure support like PMGY (Food for Work) and Border Area Development Programme and supervises the works undertaken and report to the BDO. The role and understanding of Junior Engineer, a specialist, and the BDO, the generalist head, is crucial in the process of planning and implementation of rural development. The BDO requires the services of Junior Engineer to supervise the works entrusted to the Village Councils and those entrusted to the contractors under various rural development programmes and the reports are crucial in the successful implementation of the schemes that requires the services of the Junior Engineer.[69]

Statistical Inspector

The Statistical Inspector is an important ministerial staff of the block administration. The Inspector of Statistics is deputed from the department of Economics and Statistics to the rural development block. The block development officer and other developmental officers being in overall incharge of various programmes and fieldwork, it is the duty of the Statistical Inspector to compile together the progress reports of all the schemes and prepare a consolidated report. All the progress reports are prepared by the Statistical Inspector and help the BDO in transmitting it to the DRDA, the Rural Development Directorate, State Level Monitoring Cell, etc. Hence, the services of the Statistical Inspector are very important. Though the BDO sporadically entrusted field work wherever his services requires, generally the Statistical Inspector is engaged at the block office for helping the BDO in responding to higher authority in regard to reports, letters, preparation of draft, plan and estimate of all the poverty amelioration programmes. Without the help of the Statistical Inspector, the BDO cannot prepare and compile a consolidated report to be submitted to the higher authority. In his duties and responsibilities, the VLWs, and the ministerial staff of the block assits.[70]

Village Level Worker

The Village Level Worker (VLW) also known as Gram Sevak in some states of India is the multi-purpose extension agent and this post was created to act as the link between the government and the rural people. He maintains continuous liaison with the rural population in his jurisdiction through direct contract and provides it the necessary information and guidance.[71] The VLW is the pivot of the CDP who is supposed to be friend, philosopher and guide of the villagers.[72] The needs of the development of the villagers and the villages were multipurpose and these had to be tackled in an integrated manner.[73] Thus, a multipurpose VLW was first conceived and given concrete shape by Albert Mayer, the American expert articulated, in 1946, the need for a corps of 'rural animators' very similar to the country agents in the United States, gave them the present nomenclature of 'Village Level Workers', and recruited the first batch for the Etawah Pilot Project.[74]

The village level worker is the last link in the rural development administration.[75] He works under the guidance of the BDO who gives moral support and encouragement and under the proper advice and inputs from the development officers. The role of the VLW was expounded by the Grow More Food Enquiry Committee in its report in 1952, as: "the joint agent for all development activities and who will convey to the farmer the lessons of agriculture.... difficulties of the farmers, arrange and rendering of first-aid in animal and plant diseases."[76]

The village level workers are recruited by a District Level Selection Committee especially set up for this purpose and chaired by the District Collector.[77] They are generally matriculate, must be in the age-group of 18-24 and, above all, must come from the village.[78] The Grow More Food Enquiry Committee stressed that the selection of the Village Level Workers should be made with great care and the primary qualification should be the experience of rural life and interest in it.[79] The Central Committee[80] suggested in the selection of the VLWs who have intimate knowledge of village conditions and the ability to work as a guide to the villagers, genuine interest in the village and experience of working among villagers and a Diploma in Agriculture from an Agricultural School or High School, Final or Matriculate Examination Certificate with Agriculture as one of the optional subjects.

In Mizoram, about 99 per cent of the VLWs were on deputation from the agriculture; horticulture departments of the State who were demonstrators of the concerned departments and general qualification is matriculation. The Gram Sevikas (female VLWs) are normally appointed through direct recruitment.[81]

After the selection of the VLWs, they got training in the institutional training centre for nearly two years with great emphasis on agriculture and practical work in the field.[82] In Mizoram, the VLWs receive training at the training centre, viz., Integrated Training Centre at Hnahthial, Lunglei district.[83]

As recommended by the Grow More Food Enquiry Committee,[84] VLW's are to be appointed for every five or ten villages. As a multipurpose functionary, the VLW have to serve as a common agency concerned with various aspects of rural development and educate the people and inspiring them for better living, educating them to realise that improvement in their conditions can be secured only by their own efforts and assisting them in formulating their needs, assessing their resources provided by governmental agencies for executing the programmes drawn by them.[85] The functions of VLW, in brief as the following.[86]

1. The village level worker as an extension worker in the production field, educating the villagers in better techniques of agriculture and animal husbandry and promoting irrigational and other productive constructional work. He also makes the villagers aware of fertilisers, improved seeds and use of insecticides for self-sufficiency in food production.
2. The village level worker is an extension worker in other fields as well, such as cooperation, panchayat, social institutions and sanitation. Thus, he is supposed to promote human development in his area.
3. He should specially help youth, women and other sections needing special assistance, to organise themselves for their own benefit and contribute to the advancement of the community.
4. The village level worker should serve as the principal and effective channel of communication between the department authorities and the village. As such he is the spokesman of many government departments and the conveyor of village needs and problems to these departments.
5. He should function as the servant of the village and help individual villagers, plans their production, solve their technical difficulties.

Thus, the village level worker has a wide-range of functions to perform. Apart from these functions, the VLW has to perform all the duties assigned to him by the government like census, making list of below poverty line, supervision of works undertaken through various anti-poverty programmes, in time of natural calamities, verification reports, taking surveys of roads, participation in small savings campaign and other functions of emergent nature as assigned by the BDO from time to time.[87]

The village level workers also organises cooperatives, youth clubs, Mahila Mandals and convenes their meetings quite frequently in his circle.[88] He is to explain to the people, the philosophy of CDP and the opportunities available under it.[89]

In Mizoram, the female VLWs (Gram Sevikas) are to organise

village volunteers, to encourage the NGO's like YMA and MHIP to participate in the community development works.[90] The Gram Sevikas (generally 2 Sevikas in a block) mainly concentrate their works on the nearby villages of the block as they do not go and visit generally the remote villages.[91] They concentrate mainly on encouraging women's in various developmental activities and organising groups of women to undertake the programmes and schemes available under the CDP. The Gram Sevikas also maintain the records of the Self-Help Groups; supervise their work, helps in opening of bank accounts and bank credit requirements under various programmes of rural development like Swarnajayanti Gram Swarojgar Yojana (SGSY).[92]

The success and failure of the rural development depends to a great extent on VLWs. Their social mobilization role in particular, is essential in the absence of Panchayati Raj Institutions in Mizoram. But the intentions in which VLW post created for their multipurpose role is not satisfactory in Mizoram.[93]

The block development officer, being the head of the block, is entirely responsible to guide the extension officers and VLWs to get best out of them so that the objective of community development becomes successful. The extension officers and VLWs work under the supervision and control of the BDO who has to coordinate the activities of these officers and, besides, act as the link between them and the district administration.[94]

The Deputy Commissioner and the Block Development Officer

In India, the districts are created by the state governments for administrative convenience, where the total apparatus of public administration deals with a widely embracive sphere of the management of public affairs.[95]

At the apex of the district administration is an officer designated as Deputy Commissioner or District Collector who plays a pivotal role in the administrative set up of the district and exercise varying degrees of supervision over the heads of other departments functioning in the district.[96] With the dawn of independence, governmental responsibilities in the sphere of development and welfare of community life has been increased. Hence, the developmental duties and responsibilities of the Deputy

Commissioner has increased which comprise of dispelling of ignorance, increase of community projects and national extension services, eradication of superstition, spread of cooperative institutions, etc.[97] He is responsible for overall management of the area and to ensure that the various components of administration functions in such a way that the planned results are achieved and the people engaged in these tasks are satisfied.[98]

With the introduction of community development blocks, the BDO stands as general administrator of the block. The Deputy Commissioner, being the overall incharge of the district administration, keeps a close watch on the activities of the block development officer and his developmental works. The influence of the Deputy Commissioner is strengthened by the fact that the confidential reports of the BDOs are to be signed and reported by the Deputy Commissioner in Mizoram. The opinion of the Deputy Commissioner bears considerable weight being the president of various District Development Committees.[99] The Commissioner knows the activities and their achievements on the developmental work as per the government guidelines, mostly from the people he meets almost everyday.[100]

The block development officer needs to submit reports on such cases as drought, floods, cyclone, fire incidents, etc. and list of persons to be provided with the relief, to the Deputy Commissioner.[101] The Deputy Commissioner also assigned the BDO in the electoral process, as Additional Registration Officer.[102] During Parliamentary and Assembly elections, the BDO is required to deal with more with the logistic like safety arrangement for voters and voting centers, maintaining law and orders, transportation of election materials to the voting centers and back, etc. as Executive Magistrate.[103] The BDO is also designated as Additional Charge Officer to help the collector in conducting the census.[104]

The Deputy Commissioner is the Chairman and he is charged with the responsibility of implementing the rural development programmes in the district. As rural development is spread over many departments, their activities needs to be coordinated—a role which the District Collector has to perform.[105] The management of the District Rural Development Agency is basically in the hands of the Collector, with the Additional Collector (development), performing the day to day supervision tasks, because the governing body meetings are normally formalities with government circulars, or the collectors decisions flowing from such circulars, forming the basis for decision making.[106]

Thus, the Deputy Commissioner being the overall in-charge of district administration and the BDO as the general administrator of the block has a close link as both engage in the development of the district as well as the block. The BDO needs to work under the Deputy Commissioner's supervision as well as the Directorate of Rural Development Department in Mizoram. The success and effective implementation of various programmes of rural development depends on how the BDO guide, manage and succeed in maintaining good relationship, coordination and understanding with other staff of the block as well as the amiable relationship with the District Collector and Directorate of Rural Development in Mizoram.

The extension officers being in the middle level position between BDO and VLWs constitute the core staff of the rural bureaucracy. The duties and responsibilities of the extension officers has grown in volume since the commencement of the CDP as the block became the nodal agency for implementation of various poverty amelioration schemes as well as welfare and area development programmes. Extension officers specialised in their respective fields are to perform their duties in implementation, supervision, formulation of projects, collection and maintenance of basic information relating to their specialisation, to be guided by the BDO from time to time. Hence, a cordial relationship between the BDO and the extension officers is crucial for the successful implementation of the rural development programmes.

The block development officer coordinates the work of all the extension officers and extension officers are to receive orders from him on all the administrative matters. The BDO being a generalist head, the extension officers continue to operate under the supervision of district level development departments in all technical matters. Hence, the extension officers are, in administrative affairs, under the control of the BDO and in technical matter, under the control of the district officer of his respective department. Reconciliation between horizontal responsibility of the area specialist and the vertical responsibility of the subject-matter specialist has not yet been satisfactorily brought about and this is overdue.[107]

The block development officer looks after the administrative needs of the block so that the extension officers and village level workers can devote their time and expertise in their respective field for effective implementation of the programmes. The BDO needs to ensure that all the technical personnel in the block works without any conflict. He needs to convene regular meetings attended by the extension officers and the VLWs and help in overcoming departmental rivalries and also to respect the feelings of the technical personnel and should not pin down their initiatives. He also should not give incongruous instructions to technical personnel and guide the extension officers.

PERCEPTIONS OF GRASSROOTS BUREAUCRACY

The researcher made an attempt to comprehend the perceptions of the grassroots bureaucracy on various issues relating to rural development and about their problems, working conditions, etc. The study was done during 2002-2005 through questionnaire and personal interview.

In the context of Mizoram in general and Lunglei district blocks in particular, inadequate staffing of the block functionaries adversely affected the smooth operation of developmental works. With the extension officers of agriculture, veterinary, statistical inspector and junior engineer in a block in the district where there is no extension officers of agriculture, horticulture, veterinary in Bunghmun and Lungsen blocks and an average seven VLWs in each block adversely affected the functioning of the development works. Interestingly, most of the BDOs in Lunglei district do not complain on the non-deputation of the extension officers. It is obvious that the block administration is not being entrusted with any major agricultural, horticultural, industrial schemes of rural development especially after the discontinuation of the NLUP programme.[108] The technical assistance from the development department not ever required and hence there was very rare working relationship with the development departments and the block level extension officers in the state. The extension officers and VLWs once deputed do not have any technical relations with the parent departments. As a result, the departmental officers at the district level have lost the control over subordinate personnel posted to work at the block level and the BDO, the generalist head is the controlling authority.

The extension officers are not entrusted with any major projects to be implemented and very minor works like supervision of the works entrusted to the Village Councils, assisting the beneficiaries sporadically, minor projects on implementation of the Border Area Development Programme, etc. are the only works that assigned by the BDO. Their involvement in agriculture, horticulture, veterinary, industries is nominal. The few existing extension officers and VLWs in the Lunglei district blocks are found not happy as their expertise are not fully being utilised for which they were deputed. Almost all the extension officers and VLWs are trained but not attended any of the national level seminar or orientation course after they were posted in the blocks. At present there is no system of regular, periodic refresher training course for BDOs, extension officers and VLWs in the State.

The existing extension officers had always very cordial relationship among themselves and also with the BDOs. The extension officers had no conflicts with the BDOs in respect to their technical support and the BDOs with the extension staff. It is quite possible because of the pleasant and never grumble nature of Mizo people, as well as their non-involvement in formulation and implementation of any major schemes of rural development at the moment. Due to inadequate staff, the involvement of the field staff in assisting the beneficiaries under the schemes of rural development, formulation and implementation of the projects, helping the Self-Help Groups is bound to affect. Many schemes on rural development are now entrusted to district level development departments like Public Health Engineering, Horticulture, and Veterinary, etc. which are supposed to be implemented at the block level.

Conveying the messages of the government, farmer's lessons, information on the opportunities of the rural development schemes, etc. to the rural people by the extension officers and by VLWs in particular, are normally not done. Most of the VLWs opined that due to physical constraints and too large the area of the blocks, it is not possible and with the agriculture and horticulture department demonstrators do the supply of necessary requirements to the farmers, the duties and responsibilities of the VLWs in particular is very limited. All the block level functionaries wants to lessen political interference in identifying beneficiaries, in creating working environment and overall progress in developmental works in the blocks. Most of the functionaries also favour the introduction of Panchayati Raj Institutions.

Most of the block functionaries, except the BDO, are not happy with the working conditions where the officials have very little scope for promotion, improving qualifications, unattractive salaries and non-availability of facilities for proper schooling of their children, lack of medical facilities. As a result, motivation of these functionaries is generally low. Unlike the extension officers and VLWs, the BDO is deputed for two or three years only who usually have no complain of the working conditions.

There is no administrative relation of the block with the Village Councils. The block administration has no scope for having regular interactions in terms of policy formulation and implementation due to the absence of Panchayati Raj, though most of the BDOs claimed that VLWs help the Village Councils in preparing Village Annual Action Plans. The review of the works, assigned to the extension officers, VLWs and Village Councils are generally done in the staff meetings of the blocks.

Therefore, the block functionaries deserve attention from the policy-makers to consider their problems as well as utilising their expertise and to increase the level of motivation to work hard. Special allowances for postings in difficult and remote areas, children allowances and adequate promotion opportunities are required. They should be entrusted to perform functions of preparation of plans and programmes, identification of potentials of the available resources in the block. For effective implementation of rural development programmes, the block functionaries felt that there should not be political interference; full-fledged staffing and the Village Councils should be given more powers.

Notes and References

1. Report of the Team for the Study of Community Projects and National Extension Service, appointed by COPP, 1957, Ministry of Community Development letter No. 3/7/58-TG2 dated the 12th February 1958 regarding policy and procedure relating to the selection of BDOs, in Summary Record of Annual Conference on Community Development held at Mount Abu (20th to 24th May 1958) Issued by Ministry of Community Development Government of India, 1958. pp. 317-318.

2. Maheshwari, S.R. (2004): *Local Government in India*, Lakshmi Narayan Agarwal, Agra, Revised Edition: p. 100.
3. Based on Personal Interview with Mr. Lalsiama Fambawl, A&PRO, Directorate of Rural Development, Mizoram.
4. Maheshwari, S.R. (2004): *Local Government in India, op. cit.* p. 100.
5. Khanna, R.L. (1972): *Panchayati Raj in India*, Ambala Cantt: The English Book Depot, 1972, pp. 129-130.
6. Maheshwari, S.R. (2004): *Local Government in India, op. cit.* p. 100.
7. Summary Record of Annual Conference on Community Development, Mount Abu, 20th to 24th May 1958, Issued by Ministry of Community Development Government of India, 1958, p. 320.
8. Guidelines, Training of Rural Development Functionaries, Ministry of Rural Development, New Delhi, 1981, p. 1.
9. *Ibid.*

   There are eight Orientation and Study Centres mainly for the training of BDOs and extension officers and another fourteen for the training of Social Education Organizers and Mukhya Sevikas. There are other Centres educated by the respective State Government under the supervision of the Government of India, where training in subject matter and extension methods of VLWs and Refresher Courses for Extension Officers (Agri.) and Extension Officer (Animal Husbandry) is provided. The Extension Officers (Co-operation) are trained at Centres run by the Govt. of India in collaboration with the Reserve Bank of India.
10. The National Institute of Rural Development was established, as an autonomous registered society on November 1, 1965 to fulfil the training needs of the personnel involved in rural development and also to conduct research studies, located at Hydrabad, Andhra Pradesh.
11. Preamble of Syllabus for Basic Training in Community Development, Summary Record of Annual conference on community development, Mount Abu, *op. cit.* p. 296.
12. Bhatnagar, S. (1976): *Rural Local Government in India*, Light and Life Publishers, New Delhi, 1976, p. 148.
13. *Ibid* p. 148-149.
14. State Institute of Rural Development (SIRD) was established at Kolasib in 2001in "Rural Development Department Hmalakna" Kumli chhunga Zokhaw Hmasawnna, Directorate of Rural Development, Aizawl, Mizoram, 2003, pp. 5-6.
15. Based on Personal Interview with Mr. C. Lalzuiliana, BDO, Lungsen Block.
16. Based on Personal Interview with BDOs of Lunglei district.
17. Maheshwari, S.R. (2004): *Local Government in India, op. cit.* p. 101.
18. *Ibid.*
19. *Ibid.*
20. *Ibid.* p. 102.

21. Taradatt (2002): *Development Administration in An Indian State*, Guide Book Evolved for BDO in Orissa. Uppal Publishing House, New Delhi, pp. 52-53.
22. Guidelines, SGSY, Government of India, Ministry of Rural Development, New Delhi, Published for Mizoram State by the State Institute of Rural Development, Mizoram, 2003, p. 32.
23. Chief Planning Officer, District Planning Machinery, Lunglei District, Lunglei, Draft Annual Plan for 2006-2007, No. G.20011/2/2005-DPM (L), 29th June 2005.
24. Roy, Ramasharay, Vinod Kumar, Singh T.M. (1985): *Problems in Rural Development*, Discovery Publishing House, Delhi, p. 1.
25. Taradatt (2002): *Development Administration in An Indian State, op. cit.* p. 51.
26. *Ibid.*
27. The VLWs help the Village Councils in preparing Annual Action Plans in their respective villages.
28. In the year 2001, there was 3020.7 mm rainfalls recorded in the Lunglei district and in 2002, it was 3138.8 mm. (Statistical Handbook Lunglei, 2003, p. 21).

    The relief Expenditure in Lunglei District due to Natural Calamity in the year 2002-2003 was Rs. 9,00,000 lakhs (Director, Relief and Rehabilitation Department, Government of Mizoram, Aizawl)
29. Based on Personal Interview with Mr. C. Lalzuiliana, BDO, Lungsen RD block.
30. http:/www.educationforallindia.com viewed on 11th October 2010.
31. As per the Census of 2001, the percentage of literacy in Mizoram is 88.88, in Lungsen block 49.30 per cent and 48 per cent in Bunghmun block.
32. Taradatt (2002): *Development Administration in An Indian State, op. cit.* p. 100.
33. http://www. ammado.com/viewed on 11th October 2010.
34. Economic Survey 2006-2007, Economic Survey Cell, Planning and Programme Implementation Department, Government of Mizoram, 2007.
35. In the two Hospitals in the Lunglei town the following are the patients treated of Malaria disease in the year 2002-2003. In Civil Hospital, Lunglei—627 indoor and 185 outdoor patients. In Christian Hospital, Serkawn, Lunglei—564 indoor and 1426 outdoor patients.
36. Gram Vikas: Programmes at a Glance, Govt. of India, Ministry of Rural Development, 2001, p. 13.
37. Singh, Bhartendu and Upadhyay, Anish (2010): Social Security Schemes in India in Laskar B.I. (ed.) *Mizoram—the Emerging Issues of Development*, DVS Publishers, Guwahati, pp. 285-286.

38. *Gram Vikas, op. cit.* p. 14.
39. http/en.wikipedia.org, viewed on 27. 11. 10.
40. Sahota, Avtar Singh. (2002): *Poverty Reduction Strategies in a Market Economy*, Kurukshetra, July, p. 13.
41. Thlamuana, Project Director, DRDA in the closing function of Training organized by SIRD for SGSY programme implementation to Village Council Presidents at Lunglei, Virthli, Daily News Paper, 27th August, 2005.
42. The Block Development Officer used to send letters to the President of the Village Councils regarding various new schemes.
43. The Block Development Officers does not sit in the meetings of the Village Councils and no Structural/Organisational relations with it.
44. Guidelines, DRDA Administration, Ministry of Rural Development, Government of India, New Delhi, 1999, p. 1.
45. *Ibid* p. 4.
46. *Ibid.*
47. Taradatt (2002): *Development Administration in An Indian State, op. cit.*, p. 83.
48. Khanna, B.S. (1991): *Rural Development in South Asia India* 1, Deep and Deep Publications, New Delhi, pp. 243-244.
49. The Government of Mizoram (District Council Affairs Department) vide its notification No. B-17012/3/92-DCA, dated 22nd September 1993.
50. Based on Personal Interview with V. Vanthawng, Executive Member, Lai Autonomous District Council, Lawngtlai, Mizoram.
51. Taradatt (2002): *Development Administration in An Indian State*, Guide Book Evolved for Block Development Officer in Orissa, *op. cit.*, p. 131.
52. Report of the Team for the study of community Projects and National Extension Service, Vol. I, New Delhi, Committee on Plan Projects, 1957, p. 7.
53. Maheshwari, S.R. (2004): *Local Self Government in India*, Laksmi Narain Agarwal Educational Publishers, Revised Edition, New Delhi, p. 66.
54. Arora K. Ramesh and Goyal Rajni (2003): *Indian Public Administration*, Wishwa Prakashan, New Delhi, p. 299.
55. *Ibid.*
56. Maheshwari, S.R. (2004): *Local Self Government in India, op. cit.* p. 99.
57. Summary Record of Annual Conference on Community Development held at Mount Abu, 20th to 24th May 1958. Ministry of Community Development, Government of India, pp. 46-47.
58. Taradatt (2002): *Development Administration in An Indian State*,

Guide Book Evolved for Block Development Officer in Orissa, *op. cit.* p. 137.

59. Summary Record of Annual Conference on Community Development held at Mount Abu, *op. cit.* p. 51.
60. Recommendations of the Committee on Plan Projects Team relating to Agriculture to be brought up before the sub-committee No. 1 meeting on 20th May 1958 in Summary Record of Annual Conference on Community Development held at Mount Abu, *op. cit.* pp. 50-51.
61. Based on a Personal Interview with KL. Zothantluanga, VLW, Horticulture, Lunglei RD Block
62. Lianzela, (1998): *Economy of Mizoram*, Mizoram Publication Board, Aizawl p. 27.
63. Kalita, Girin, Sarma, Kalyan and Rahman, Saidur, Scope of Livestock Production in Mizoram, *Livestock International*, Vol. 8 Issue 11, Nov. 2004. A monthly magazine published in India, p. 18.
64. Laskar, B.I. (2009): *Industrialisation in Mizoram*, New Central Book Agency, Kolkata, p. 52.
65. *Ibid* p. 60.
66. At present the Industries Extension Officer has not been deputed in all the blocks of Lunglei district.
67. In Lungsen Block, the Junior Engineer is appointed by the Rural Development Department.
68. Based on a Personal Interview with Z.D. Lalnuntluangi, JE, Rural Development Block, Lunglei.
69. *Ibid.*
70. Based on a Personal Interview with F.P. Thansiama, Inspector of Statistics, Lunglei RD Block.
71. Arora K. Ramesh and Goyal Rajni (2003): *Indian Public Administration*, *op. cit.* p. 300.
72. Madan, G.R. and Tara Madan (1988): *Village Development in India: A Sociological Approach*, Allied Publishers Private Limited, New Delhi, p. 223.
73. Inamdar, N.R. (1992): *Development Administration in India*, Rawat Publications, Jaipur, New Delhi, p. 81.
74. Mayer, Albert (1956): Pilot Projects, India, Berkeley: University of California Press, Quoted in Maheshwari, S.R. (1985): *Rural Development in India*, Sage Publications, p. 198.
75. Maheshwari, S.R. (1985): *Rural Development in India*, *op. cit.* p. 199.
76. Report of the Grow More Food Enquiry Committee, New Delhi: Ministry of Food and Agriculture, 1952, p. 54.
77. Maheshwari, S.R. (1985): *Rural Development in India*, *op. cit.* p. 198.
78. *Ibid.*
79. The Grow More Food Enquiry Committee, Opportunities. *op. cit.* p. 54.

80. Planning Commission, Important Letters—Community Projects Administration, New Delhi: Planning Commission, 1955.
81. Based on a Personal Interview with B. Saptawni, Gram Sevika, Hnahthial RD Block.
82. Maheshwari, S.R. (1985): *Rural Development in India*, op. cit, p. 199: The deputed Village Level Workers in Mizoram got trained at Integrated training Centres of 2 years Basic Agriculture Science training Course and newly appointed VLW's are also trained in the same.
83. Statistical Abstract, Department of Agriculture and Minor Irrigation. Government of Mizoram, 2002-2003, p. 8. A two years basic Agriculture Science Training Course was offered with (1) Agronomy, (2) Horticulture, (3) Soil Science, (4) Plant Protection, (5) Agriculture extension, (6) Animal Husbandry and Veterinary.
84. The Grow More Food Enquiry Committee, *Op. cit.*
85. Report of the Expert Committee on the Training of Project Personnel, New Delhi, Ministry of Community Development, 1957.
86. Maheshwari, S.R. (1985): *Rural Development in India, op. cit.* p. 199.
87. Based on a Personal Interview with A. Lalengkima, VLW, Chawngte RD Block.
88. Bhagwan, Vishnoo and Bhusan Vidhya (1986): *Public Administration*, S. Chand and Company Ltd., New Delhi, p. 696.
89. *Ibid*, p. 695, In Mizoram the VLWs do not attend any meetings of the Village Councils because of no administrative and organisational relations.
90. Based on a Personal Interview with B. Saptawni and Lalhliri Khiangte, Gram Sevikas of Hnahthial RD Block.
91. *Ibid.*
92. *Ibid.*
93. The VLWs that interviewed in the RD blocks of Lunglei district usually do not visit villages regularly and are in the head office only. In Lungsen block, as there are no extension officers, they perform the extension officer's work as well. The VLWs visit the villages only as supervisors of the work and on emergent situation only.
94. Arora K. Ramesh and Goyal Rajni (2003): *Indian Public Administration, op. cit.* p. 299.
95. Khera, S.S. (1997): *District Administration in India*, New Delhi, National Publishing House, pp. 76-77.
96. Bhagwan, Vishnoo and Bhusan Vidhya (1986): *Public Administration, op. cit.* p. 700.
97. *Ibid* p. 702.
98. Dayal, Ishwar, Mathur, Kuldeep and Bhattacharya, Mohit (1976): *District Administration: A Survey for Reorganization*, Macmillan, New Delhi, p. 45.

99. Based on a Personal Interview with Mr. C. Lalzuiliana, BDO, Lungsen RD Block.
100. Based on a Personal Interview with C. Tawnluaia, Deputy Commissioner, Lunglei.
101. Based on a Personal Interview with Mr. C. Lalzuiliana, BDO, Lungsen RD Block.
102. *Ibid.*
103. Taradatt, (2002): *Development Administration in An Indian State*, Guide Book Evolved for Block Development Officer in Orissa, *op. cit.* p. 126.
104. *Ibid.* p. 130.
105. Maheshwari, S.R. (1985): *Rural Development in India, op. cit*, p. 199.
106. Hooja, Rakesh. (1987): *Administrative Interventions in Rural Development*, Rawat Publications, Jaipur, p. 76.
107. Maheshwari, S.R. (2005): *Local Government in India*, Laxshmi Narain Agarwal, Agra, p. 103.
108. The New Land Use Policy is to be implemented by various development departments of the state after its revival during 2008-09.

7

Assessment of Block Level Bureaucracy

This chapter is consists of two parts. Part-I deals with a brief socio-economic profile of the Lunglei, Hnahthial, Bunghmun and Lungsen rural development blocks of Mizoram. Part-II is devoted to an assessment of block level bureaucracy in these blocks.

Introduction

Bureaucracy at the grassroots level plays an important role in rural development process in India. In fact, the success and failure of various rural development programmes depend on the performance of bureaucracy at the grassroots level. Motivating and mobilising people, communicating programmes to them, seeking their cooperation, building up grassroots institutions, all are new ways of administration which development bureaucracy has to adopt.[1] The socio-economic goals which developing countries have set as the index of achievement are, in fact, translated into realities by the bureaucrats. However, the machinery of government and the procedures which have hitherto been followed are not always in consonance with the growing needs. Their role is becoming more complex and it has to combine a variety of skills and capabilities. They are expected to be less legalistic and more result-oriented in their developmental approach.[2]

In India, various rural development programmes initiated by the Union and State Governments since independence are assigned to its dependable machinery—the grassroots bureaucracy for implementation. The 'rural bureaucratic model' devised with the introduction of Community Development Programme (CDP) in 1952 comprising a generalist head—the Block Development Officer (BDO) with a team of Extension Officers and Village Level Workers (VLWs), is the main apparatus of development in the rural areas. With the introduction of Panchayati Raj Institutions (PRIs), rural development programmes are now implemented with the coordination of grassroots bureaucracy.

In case of Mizoram, since PRIs not introduced and the existing Village Councils (no block and district level bodies) are not intense as panchayat bodies, bureaucracy occupies the vital position to implement rural development programmes, to motivate rural people, to arouse popular participation, etc. Much of the success and failure of rural development programmes depend on the commitment of grassroots bureaucracy—the BDO, extension officer and VLWs in Mizoram. The BDO in particular, is the key functionary, as head of the grassroots level bureaucracy for the successful implementation of rural development programmes. The BDO is the most important intermediary between the government and people in the rural areas. By working as a change agent, he introduces the rural people to the complicated process of development and induces change in their attitude without which the socio-economic transformation remains a far cry. The BDO represents a new culture of administration in what is described as a complex, diverse and risk prone atmosphere. All the activities of the BDO are scrutinised by public in general and public representatives in particular. There is hardly any activity in the rural areas where the participation of block administration is not required.[3] Thus, the BDO as a multipurpose functionary in the rural bureaucratic set up is expected to be more prompt, efficient, objective, and more importantly active in motivating rural people. He is a ubiquitous figure today and no one at least, in rural India, remains, or can even afford to remain unaware of his presence.[4]

The introduction of community development programme and the innovation of new grassroots level bureaucracy have passed more than fifty years since then and India has executed about 50 programmes of rural development through successive planning. But in the high tide of liberation of economy and the necessary shifts and structural adjustments the number of rural inhabitants below the poverty line has been fast increasing, and this is now an accepted fact.[5] In Mizoram, the most notable state sponsored programme of rural development is New Land Use Policy (NLUP) launched in 1990-91, revived in 2009-10 and in 2002-2003 another development programme started as Mizoram Intodelhna Project (MIP). Both NLUP and MIP are the major rural development programmes launched to uplift the rural poor to end the practice of shifting cultivation and to attain self-sufficiency in food production and better livelihood, apart from centrally sponsored schemes. Since most of these programmes were initiated to improve the conditions of the villagers, to increase agricultural production by providing alternative means of livelihood to shifting cultivators, Government of Mizoram employ quite a large extension staff to implement and manage the rural development programmes. Moreover, in the absence of PRIs in Mizoram, heavy reliance has been placed on grassroots level bureaucracy to bring about change in the rural sector. It is therefore high time to make an assessment of the block level bureaucracy involved in the implementation of rural development programmes. In this chapter an attempt has been made to assess the performance of grassroots level bureaucracy—BDO, extension officers, VLWs through field survey, of the all four rural development blocks of Lunglei district of Mizoram. But before we make an assessment, it is worth to mention in brief, the socio-economic profile of the blocks.

SOCIO-ECONOMIC PROFILE OF THE RURAL DEVELOPMENT BLOCKS

Lunglei District of Mizoram

Lunglei District of Mizoram has four rural development blocks, viz., Lunglei, Hnahthial, Bunghmun and Lungsen. Let us analyse the socio-economic profile of these blocks to comprehend its socio-economic status under which the block level bureaucracy is working.

Lunglei Block[6]

Lunglei block came into existence on 2nd October 1956 and Mr. C.L. Rema was its first Officer-in-Charge. The area of the block lies in the middle part of Lunglei district and Mizo tribes mainly inhabit it. The general economic condition of the people in the area is poor but the economic status varies from place to place in the block. The crop production per unit area in the traditional cultivation is low. People of this block mostly depend on jhum cultivation. The source of income other then agricultural produce is forest products like timber, fuelwood and bamboo. Domestication of poultry bird and livestock rearing are also source of subsidiary income. However, the people do not earn their living from those sources. A few of them live on private business, daily labour, carpentry, contract works, government jobs and handloom and handicrafts. The entire territory of Lunglei block is mountainous. The total geographical area of the block is 1,117.06 square kilometers with a total population of 65,592. The total number of villages within the area is 60 and the total households in the whole area is 12,464.[7] Families depending on jhum cultivation are 4,351 in carpentry 251 families; business 613 and 72 families are depending on handloom and handicrafts.

Agriculture in Lunglei block is by far, the largest single industry and the mainstay of the people. Because of the lack of sufficient plain lands for cultivation most of the families depends on jhum cultivation. The whole area is characterised by hilly terrain. The main crops of the area are paddy, maize, pulses, and oilseeds.

Lunglei block offers excellent scope for growing different types of horticulture crops such as fruits, vegetables, species, etc. The block produces various horticulture crops such as ginger, chilies, pumpkin, mandarin orange, etc.[8] The block has potentials of chilies and ginger export. Marketing of the horticulture products is done mainly in the Lunglei town super market. Horticulture production as a source of livelihood is encouraged through various rural development schemes both state and centrally sponsored schemes and a horticulture extension officer is deputed to the block.

In the year 1992, the population of cattle (cross bred) 1558 and 200 (indigenous), 44 buffaloes, 11 sheep's, 1808 Pigs (cross bred exotic) in this block.[9] A chilling plant of the government had been completed at Lunglei with a capacity of 5,000 liters. There is one Veterinary Hospital at Lunglei. An extension officer (veterinary) is being deputed to the block office to help the BDO in the implementation of the veterinary related schemes as well as helping the beneficiaries of this sector.

In this mountainous block the aspect of transport and communication has great significance. The Lunglei town is connected with National Highway No. 54 from Aizwal. Another metalled road approaching Tlabung from Lunglei truck able road is passing through the area. Another National Highway, which starts from Lunglei to Tuipang, is passing through the southern part of the block. Jeep able roads connect most of the villages. The largest town of the area Lunglei is 235 kilometers (now about 165 via Thenzawl) away from Aizwal, the capital of Mizoram. But many villages are not connected with all weather roads. Under PMGSY, under Bharat Nirman Programme, rural connectivity is underway in the block and in the entire district. The State Public Works Department is the implementing agency of this programme. Giving top priority on habitations with more than 500 and above followed by less than 500 populations is under implementation in the entire district. At present, there is one post office at Lunglei, 2 sub-post offices, and 23 branches of post offices in the block. There is one Telephone Exchange at Lunglei town with 3954 subscribers of telephone in the Lunglei block.

Lunglei block is agrarian and there is little scope for industrial growth except small enterprises. Small-scale enterprises like vehicle repairing, carpentry, quilt making, tailoring, handloom, etc. are prominent in the block especially in the Lunglei town area. There is a District Industries Center in the Lunglei District Head-quarter which not only gives training on various trades such as knitting and tailoring, handloom weaving, organises study tours for small scale industry owners, as well as giving grants-in-aid for industrial growth in the district. However, there is no industrial extension officer in the block office. There was an extension officer (industries) deputed form District Industries Center when the NLUP scheme was under implementation.[11] There is a Vocational Training Center at Lunglei to impart training to tribal youth on self-employment in different trades and there is Mizoram Polytechnic College, Lunglei. Khawiva Mini Hydel project, Khawiva near Lunglei town is the main source of electricity in the block. There are 12,391 electrified houses out of 14,320 in the Lunglei block.[12]

Commercial banks are very important to uplift the rural economy by providing loans under various development schemes. In the Lunglei block, there are seven banks, which are helping the rural poor in providing loans under various development schemes. These are (1) State Bank of India, Lunglei, (2) State Bank of India,

Tawipui, (3) State Bank of India, Zobawk, (4) Mizoram Cooperative Apex Bank, Lunglei (5) Mizoram Rural Bank, Lunglei, Haulawng, Thingfal and Serkawn.[13]

The average health of the people in Lunglei block is quite good, due to its salubrious climate of the State, thick forest cover and the simple food habit of the people.[14] The block has two hospitals—the Civil Hospital which is located in Chanmari Veng, Lunglei and Christian Hospital located in Serkawn, Lunglei. There are four Primary Health Centres and they are located in Haulawng, Chhiphir, Tawipui 's' and Hauruang villages and the number of sub-center available in the area is 28.[15] The Government is implementing the Integrated Child Development Scheme (ICDS) for full development of the children of the district as a whole. Looking at the transport facilities more medical institutions are required. The block administration through various schemes of rural development involved in providing safe drinking water, construction of urinal sheds, cleanliness drive, etc.

Education plays an important role in the development of rural people. By 2000, there were 64 government, 7 government aided, 18 private primary school, 43 government 19 deficit and 17 private middle schools, three government higher secondary schools, two government, and one private college in the Lunglei block. Besides the Polytechnic College, there is a District Institute of Education Training at Lunglei.[16] The block administration is involved in requisite physical infrastructures like construction of schools buildings and additional rooms, etc. helped by the Junior Engineer, under employment generating programmes.[17]

The strength of the people of Mizoram lies in its high literacy rate and this factor can be a very high motivating factor for the developers and planners to tap the potential of the people.[18] The total number of literate persons in Lunglei block is 38,403 out of which 20,972 are males and 17,432 are females.

Availability of safe drinking water is a major problem as the region is hilly. People are compelled to bring drinking water on their heads from long distance natural sources. The Government of Mizoram is implementing Rural Water Supply Programme, Urban Water Supply Programme and Accelerated Water Supply System to provide safe drinking water with the financial assistance from non lapsable fund of Central Government.[19] In the Lunglei district, by March 2000, 109 village are covered under pipe water supply.[20] In the Lunglei block there were 248 public water points, 74 drilled water points and 4669 water connection by 2002.[21] The block administration, under various schemes is constructing, repairing of water points. The state is implementing the schemes like Rain Water Harvesting in the block, which not only provide safe drinking water but also checks soil erosion around the homestead and helps in preventing landslide.

Various rural development programmes were implemented and some are under implementation. In Lunglei block 5,675 families living under below poverty line out of the 12,464, that is 45.53 per cent.[22] Under IRDP, 201 families were assisted with a total expenditure of 12, 42 lakhs in the year 1996-97 and in 1997-98 another 120 families were benefited with an expenditure of 1.2 lakhs in the Lunglei block. Under JRY, Rs. 24, 26 lakhs had spent to this block and 40678 man-days were generated during the year 1996-97. Under the scheme, DWCRA, 6 groups were formed with an expenditure of Rs. 1.5 lakhs during the year 1996-97 and under IAY, 38 beneficiaries with a total expenditure of Rs. 6.54 lakhs during the year 1996-97. During the year 1997-98, 30 beneficiaries benefited with an expenditure of Rs. 2.4 lakhs under the Million Wells Scheme in the Lunglei block.[23] Under the New Land Use Policy (NLUP), 1278 families were benefited in the Lunglei block in different sectors such as agriculture and allied sector 795 families, industry sector 100 families, veterinary sector 329 families in the year 1994-95.[24] During the period 2000-2001, under the PMGY, 329 families were benefited with an expenditure of Rs. 59.18 lakhs.[25]

Hnahthial Block[26]

The total geographical area of the Hnahthial Rural Development Block is 93,800 hectares. It borders Myanmar in the east and is bounded by East Lungdar and Serchhip block in the north, Lunglei in the west and Sangau block in the south. The total population of the block is 26,658 out of which 13276 females and 13382 males. It is mainly inhabited by Mizo tribes. The total households in the Hnahthial block are 4657 with 22 villages.[27] Hnahthial is the headquarter of this block and it is one of the three towns in Lunglei district. The people of this block mainly depends on jhum cultivation. In 2003, the total number of below poverty line families in the block is 3420 families out of 4657 households, which is 73.43

per cent. Agriculture is the main occupation of most of the people of Hnahthial block. Due to its hilly terrain, agriculture is far more complex in this block as well. Out of the area of 93,800 hectares, 168.00 hectares is only available for good cultivation, 105.00 hectares are moderately good cultivable land and 1,381.00 hectares are fairly good cultivable land. 72,759.00 hectares of land are not suitable for cultivation but well suited for horticultural and pastoral use and 19,387.00 hectares of land are suitable for forestry and wild life. The block has no agriculture extension officer at present.

The Hnahthial block produces various horticultural crops. like ginger, sweet potato, sugarcane, banana, etc. As per Soil Survey Report of 1997, the areas under horticulture are 213.0 hectares in this block. The main drawback faced by the horticultural growers is lack of marketing facilities. The department of horticulture is helping the farmers in the development of horticulture production and its marketing facilities. There is a Horticulture Demonstration Farm at Hnahthial. At present there is no horticulture extension officer deputed in the Hnahthial block.

In the year 1992,[28] the total population of cattle (cross bred) were 43 and indigenous 1886, 63 buffaloes, 2960 (crossbred exotic), pigs, 11777 desi and 23904 improved poultry in the Hnahthial block. The total livestock population was 42230. There is one Piggery Farm at Hnahthial. The Animal Husbandry and Veterinary Department with its dispensaries and Rural Animal Health Centres looking after the health and development of livestock in the district as a whole. There is a veterinary extension officer in the block. However, there still lot to be done in livestock development. The BDO should encourage unemployed youths, veterinary graduates and farmers to take up diary farming activities as a source of income and livelihood.

Development of transport and communication is one of the most important means in achieving development of this mountainous block. Most of the villages in the block are connected with jeep able roads. Some of them are track able during dry seasons. Only 508 kilometers roads are jeep able, 126 kilometers track able roads and 77 kilometers metalled roads length. Most of the roads are not all weather roads. There are two sub post offices and 16 branches of post offices in the block. There is a Telephone Exchange at Hnahthial with 692 subscriber.[29]

Apart from small scale industries like tailoring, knitting, bakery, handloom, carpentry, motor works, which are mostly present in the Hnahthial town, there are very few industries worth to mention in the rural areas apart from rice mills in the block. The rural based artisans needs to be encouraged. By 2001, there were 4175 houses were electrified which is quite satisfactory. There is no industrial extension officer appointed in the Hnahthial block at present.

There are four branches of banks in the block. One State Bank of India branch at Hnahthial, Mizoram Rural Bank at Hnahthial, Mizoram Rural Bank at Pangzawl and Mizoram Rural Bank Branch at Cherhlun.

There is one Community Health Centre 30 bedded, two Primary Health Centres at S. Vanlalphai and Cherhlun, 10 bedded each and 13 Health Sub-Centres at Hnahthial block.[30]

In the year 2001-2002, there were 39 government 2 private schools, 15 government, 9 government aided and 1 private middle schools, 4 government, 5 government aided and 4 private high schools, 1 government higher secondary and a government college in Hnahthial block. There is also an Integrated Training Centre at Hnahthial. In all the 22 villages of the block, primary schools are present and the educational facilities are quite satisfactory which reflects in its high percentage of literacy of 77.96 per cent.

There were 139 public water points in the entire block by 1996-1997. There was 100 house water connection installed at Hnahthial and an Impounding Reservoir at Cherhlun by 2002-2003. Majority of rural people of this block depends on natural source and water points constructed by the development departments of the government. The block administration, under PMGY (Food for Work)' programme gives importance on construction and repairing of water points. In the Hnahthial block, 391 families were assisted with a total expenditure of Rs. 27.78 lakhs under IRDP during the period 1996-97 to 1999-2000. During this period there were 12 groups were formed under DWCRA in rural areas of this block with an expenditure of Rs. 1.50 lakhs and 89 trainees under TRYSEM with an expenditure of Rs. 2.84 lakhs. Under the programme Jawahar Rozgar Yojana (JRY) 6,629 of man day's employment generated with an expenditure of Rs. 7.64 lakhs during the year 1996-97 to 1997-98. Under Indira Awaas Yojana (IAY) 12 beneficiaries in the block with a total expenditure of Rs. 26.66 lakhs during the period 1999-97 to 1999-2000. During 2002-2003, under IAY, there were 67 beneficiaries with 42 new construction and 25 upgradation with an expenditure of Rs. 11.44 lakhs and 149 beneficiaries under PMGY (GA) with an expenditure of Rs. 25.22 lakhs.[31]

Bunghmun Block[32]

Bunghmun Rural Development Block is one of the most backward block within Lunglei district of Mizoram bordering Hnahthial block in the east, Reiek block in the north east, Bangladesh in the west, Lungsen block in the south, West Phaileng block in the north-west. Bunghmun is the block headquarter under the administrative jurisdiction of Tlabung Sub-Division.

The Bunghmun block is characterised by hilly terrain with a geographical area of 1,35,900 hectares. The total population of the block is 16448 out of which 8234 males and 8214 females. There are 35 villages in the block and out of the total household of 2921, 2370 families live below poverty line, which is 81.13. The block is mainly inhabited by Mizo, Bru and Chakma tribes and the Mizo villages are mostly confined on the ridges of the four hill ranges, while the Bru and Chakma villages are located mostly at the foot hills or valley of the ranges—Buarpui range, West Bunghmun range, Puankhai range. People living in these villages mainly depend on jhum while only a few of them are doing wet rice cultivation in the narrow valley land. Hence, 90 per cent of the total area falls under jhum land.

Thus, jhum provided employment to the largest segment of the rural population. Out of the total area of 1,35,900 hectares of land, 1,550 hectares are suitable for cultivation, 2,534 hectares of land are moderately good cultivable land. Few pockets of flat lands by the riverside are kept under wet rice cultivation. Some of the inhabitants take up horticultural crops like orange, sugarcane, banana, etc. The source of income other than agriculture products is forest produces like timber, fuel wood, bamboo and few teak plantations. A few of them live on petty business, daily labour, and carpentry and government jobs. The general condition of the people is poor and the crop production per unit area is low and marketing facilities of agricultural products is also poor due to disruption in transport and communication and the lack of marketing opportunities. As district headquarters is 146 kilometers away from Bunghmun, marketing of agricultural products to the district headquarter is also difficult. The total area under permanent cultivation is about 1940 hectares. There are agricultural circles at Bunghmun and Buarpui under District Agricultural Department for agricultural development of the block. There is no agricultural extension officer in the Bunghmun block.

About 79,362 hectares of land suitable for horticultural crops, pasture, sericulture and social forestry in the Bunghmun block. The main problem faced by the growers is lack of marketing facilities, inadequate all weather roads. Development of horticulture will not really help as a source of livelihood for the rural people of this block unless there is development of road transport and marketing facilities. There is also no horticulture extension officer in the block as well. Most of the area of the block is covered by vegetation. In the year 1992, 799,4 cross bred and 795 indigenous cattle population, 932 goats, 1263 crossbred exotic and indigenous pigs, 2828 desi and 362 improved poultry population were in the block. There is no veterinary extension officer in the block.

If any development requires immediately in this block is transport and communication, which will follow other aspects of development. This block remains cut off from the district headquarter during rainy season. The road constructed by the State Public Works Development are Buarpui to Lunglei road through Thenzawl, Marpara to Bunghmun road and Lunglei to Khawlek while Buarpui to Bunghmun road has been constructed by the BRTF. Lungchem to Sertlangpui road has been constructed by the Rural Development Department. There is no regular bus service especially during rainy season. The area is approachable by light vehicle through Marpara (during the dry season) and through Thenzawl to Bunghmun via Buarpui. Lunglei to Khawlek road (85 kilometers) is also during the dry season. Border road is under construction to connect Marpara and Tlabung parallel along the Khawthlang Tuipui. The distance between Marpara and Bunghmun is 19 kilometers while Bunghmun to Buarpui is 69 kilometers. There are only a sub-post office, 13 branches of post offices and 225 telephone subscribers in 2003.

Industrially, this block is very backward. Because of its rural nature and lack of marketing facilities, industries large and small-scale were not developed. Apart from tailoring, carpentry, rice mills there is no industries in this block. Rural artisans should be encouraged with marketing facilities. Out of the 35 villages in the block 20 villages are electrified as on 21st May 2004.[33]

Bunghmun block is perhaps the only block in India that does not have any type of banks. In the absence of banks, helping poor in financing under different development schemes could not be implemented. The nearest banks of this block hesitate to provide loans because of the fear that recovery of the same may not be possible as banking system is not under the rural development department.[34] Under different programme of rural development which needs credit, only the subsidy portion is provided to the beneficiaries. The bank account is also at State Bank of India, Lunglei branch which cause delay and smooth functioning of the developmental works for this block.[35]

The availability of medical institutions in this backward block is inadequate. There are two Primary Health Centres located at Bunghmun and Buarpui village and 12 Health Sub-Centres. In this backward block, the importance of education is also no way lesser in changing socio-economic scenario with the spread of education. As on May, 2004, there were four high schools, 14 middle schools, 34 primary schools in this block. Bengali schools were opened in some villages where the inhabitants are mainly Chakma tribes and pre-primary and primary schools opened in almost all villages either by the Government of Mizoram or by the Church Organisations. The percentage of literacy of the block is only 48 per cent, the lowest of the four blocks in Lunglei district.

As on May, 2004, the number of public water points was 90, 5 drilled water points and six villages under Gravity Water Supply Scheme. People of this block have no difference and have to depend on natural sources and the BDO is implementing various schemes in construction and repairing of water points in this block.

During the years from 1996-97 to 1999-2000, there were 307 families with an expenditure of Rs. 18.36 lakhs were benefited under the IRDP in the block. During these years 46 youths were trained under TRYSEM with an expenditure of Rs. 1.73 lakhs. Rural housing was also done to a large extent. During the period 1996-97 to 1999-2000, 139 beneficiaries with a total expenditure of Rs. 25 lakhs under Indira Awaas Yojana in the block. During the year 2003-2004, under IAY 22 families were benefited under new construction and 10 families got up gradation with a total expenditure of Rs. 5,84,000.00. Under PMGY (GA) during 2000-

2003, 63 families benefited under new construction and 40 families up gradation with an expenditure of Rs. 17,86,000 lakhs. During 2003-2004, 60 new constructions and 40 up gradation were done under PMGY (GA). During 1996-1997 to 1997-1998, 19,172 man day's employment generated under JRY in the block. During 2001-2002, under the SGRY-1, Rs. 5,94,150.00 lakhs of cash component and 1490 quintals of rice were disbursed under different works of community asset in the development of the block.

Border Area Development Programme (BADP) is under implementation in the Bunghmun block. During 2002-2003 to 2003-2004, under BADP, Rs. 121,98 lakhs were spend against the sanction of Rs. 125.15, lakhs, mainly in the construction and repair of roads, community halls, construction of water supply, etc.

As the general socio-economic condition of the block is poor, poor people of this block flocked to the block office in the hope of monetary and other help. The BDO's role in this block is very crucial in the overall development and eradication of rural poverty. The entire block is rural in nature.

Lungsen Block[36]

Lungsen Rural Development Block is also one of the most backward blocks in the Lunglei district of Mizoram. The total geographical area of the block is 1046.29 square kilometers, with a total population of 29049 out of which 13972 females and 15077 males and largest number of scattered villages of 62 and out of the 5775 households, 5331 families lives in below poverty line which is 92.31 per cent. Lungsen is the block headquarter under the administrative jurisdiction of Tlabung Sub-Division. The block is inhabited by Mizo, Chakma, Bru, Pang, Bawm tribes.

Agriculture is the chief occupation of the people of Lungsen block, 4,640 males and 2,449 females occupation is agriculture, 242 males and 11 females occupation is casual labour, 248 business and 769 males and 91 females occupation was government job. Jhuming is the common practice of the inhabitants. In 1997, 1,825.00 hectares of area of land were available for good cultivation and 6,243.75 hectares with moderately good cultivable land and 16,944.00 hectares with fairly good for occasional or limited cultivation. Dense wood forest and shrubs cover the area. A limited area of the narrow valley has been utilised for permanent wet rice cultivation. There are two agricultural circles one at Lungsen and the other at Tlabung. Under the Lungsen Agricultural Circle 2318 jhum cultivators, 100 wet rice cultivators and under the Tlabung Agricultural Circle 1046 jhum cultivators and 543 wet rice cultivators by 2002-2003.

In the Lungsen block, an area of 60,598.50 hectares of land are suitable for horticultural crops, pasture, sericulture and social forestry and this block has suitable lands for horticultural crops like citrus, banana, maize, soyabean, pulses, ginger, sugarcane, etc. The uplands are also utilised for vegetable cultivations. However, poor road communication network hinders intensive cultivation of the land. Many of the Chakmas shift from village to jhum and back to the same villages every year with no permanent settlement. Plantation of orange, pineapple, and coconut and bananas are found random near by human habitation. There are relatively better marketing opportunities in this block. Tlabung, being a town, having regular transport services from Tlabung to Lunglei as well. There is no horticulture extension officer and agriculture extension officer in the block.

In the year 1992, there were 91 crossbred and 3449 indigenous cattles, 152 buffaloes, 1993 goads, 1942 crossbred exotic and 2481 indigenous pigs, 5093 desi and 17932 improved poultry population in the Lungsen block. Livestock as a means of livelihood and subsidiary to agriculture has not been developed in this block as well despite the efforts of the Government of Mizoram. There is no extension officer of veterinary, in the Lungsen block.

There is a truck able all weather road of 97 kilometers from Lunglei to Tlabung via Lungsen. Lungsen is 58 kilometers from Lunglei town. But the link road to Lungsen from villages are mostly jeep able fair-weather roads. During rainy season many villages are to cover long distances on foot to reach the head-road. The block administration is implementing PMRY (Food for Work) generating employment as well as clearance and repairing of rural roads. There are 3 sub-post offices and 11 branches of post offices for 62 villages in the block and 270 telephone subscribers. Except some of the varieties of tailoring, furniture workshop, saw mills and rice mills there are no industries developed in this block where people could earn their livelihood. No industrial extension officer as well in this block. By 2003, 2248 households were electrified out of 5775 households in the Lungsen block. There are two banks one State Bank of India branch at Tlabung and a branch of Mizoram Rural Bank at Lungsen.

By 2002, there were one Civil Hospital at Tlabung with bed strength of 30, Leprosy Hospital with 20 bedded, one Primary Health Centre at Lungsen 10 bedded and 12 Health Sub-Centres. Although medical facilities in this block are better, in view of its number of villages in the block, there is still very less number of Health Sub-Centres which needs to be increased.

In a socially and economically less progressive area like Lungsen block, the importance of education is no way lesser. By 2003 there were 3 government 2 aided and 3 private high schools, 16 government, 8 aided 4 private middle schools, 39 government 1 aided and 41 private primary schools in the Lungsen block. Literacy rate is generally low in this block where tribes other than Mizo tribe inhabited like Lungsen and Bunghmun. The percentage of literacy in the block is 49.30 per cent. Public Health Engineering Department is implementing Accelerated Rural Water Supply Programme (ARWSP) a centrally sponsored scheme, for providing safe drinking water in the villages.

Let us examine some of the available achievements made in the Lungsen block implemented through BDO. During 1996-1997 to 1999-2000, under the IRDP, there were 331 beneficiaries with a total expenditure of Rs. 19.86 lakhs, under TRYSEM 84 youths trained with an expenditure of Rs. 3.84 lakhs, under DWCRA 14 groups were formed with the total expenditure of Rs. 3.75 lakhs, Under the Indira Awaas Yojona (IAY), 169 beneficiaries in the Block with an expenditure of Rs. 26.54 lakhs. During the year 1996-1997 to 1997-1998, 12379 man-days employment generated with an expenditure of Rs. 7.52 lakhs. During 2002-2003, under PMGY (GA) 63 new houses constructed and 40 upgraded with a total expenditure of Rs. 17.86 lakhs and under IAY during 2002-2003, 42 new houses were constructed and 25 upgraded with an expenditure of Rs. 11.74 lakhs. At present, the programmes like SGRY (Food for Work), SGSY, IAY, are under implementation. During 2002-2003, there were 3 Self-Help Groups and 30 *swarozgaris* under SGSY in the Lungsen block.

However, being the largest and scattered number of 62 villages, proper implementation of the programmes cannot be made due to lack of communication links like all weather roads and postal services.[37] Also there is lack of full strength of block staff in this block where no extension officers at present.

From the above discussion of development of four blocks of Lunglei district of Mizoram it may be said that after independence, with the introduction of CDP, although a good progress in various developmental aspects has been achieved, the achievements that could have been during the last 50 years was not up to the level as expected. The pace of progress has been both inadequate and slow. This is apparent from the high percentage of below poverty line families in all the blocks of the district. Table 7.1 presents the number of below poverty line (BPL) families as on April, 1998.

Table 7.1: Showing Percentage of BPL Families in Lunglei District RD Blocks: 1998

Sl. No.	*Name of RD Block*	*No. of House Households*	*No. of BPL Families*	*Percentage*
1.	Lunglei	4,947	3,823	77
2.	Hnahthial	4,202	3,274	77
3.	Lungsen	3716	2,994	80
4	Bunghmun	2,447	2172	88
	Total (Rural)	**15,312**	**12,268**	**80**
5.	Lunglei (urban)	5,227	2,005	38
	Grand Total	**20,539**	**14,268**	**70**

Source: DRDA Lunglei, Awareness Campaign on IEC, 2000.

The condition of the BPL families has not been improved in a period of five years where the percentage of BPL family in Lungsen block increases from 80 per cent in 1998 to 92 per cent in 2003. The following is the BPL families in all the blocks of the Lunglei district on April 2003, which is presented in Table 7.2.

Table 7.2: Showing Percentage of BPL families in Lunglei District RD Blocks, 2003

Sl. No.	*Name of RD Block*	*No. of Households*	*No. of BPL families*	*Percentage*
1.	Lunglei	12,464	5,675	45
2.	Hnahthial	4,657	3,420	73
3.	Lungsen	5,775	5,331	92
4.	Bunghmun	2,921	2,370	81
	Total	**25,817**	**16,796**	**65**

Source: Village Level Statistics of Mizoram, 2000.

As heavy reliance has been placed on administration and rural bureaucracy to play facilitating, promotional, and various welfare roles, to improve the conditions of the villagers, to supervise and implement all development programmes of the government, but it seems that block level bureaucracy failed to deliver the goods in desired direction. The nearby villages of the towns and block head quarters are in better position in socio-economic condition than those in remote or interior villages. More the villages in remote places, the development are less and consciousness and awareness of the people on rural development programmes was found lacking.

ASSESSMENT OF GRASSROOTS LEVEL BUREAUCRACY

In the above background of the socio-economic scenario of the rural development blocks, an assessment was made covering the Lunglei district blocks which reveals (Table 7.3 to 7.10) the services of the block level bureaucracy and people's (beneficiaries and non-beneficiaries) perception towards these functionaries, whether the villagers were benefited from the rural development programmes, the method of selection of beneficiaries, priorities on which the block development officer needs to concentrate on and how the villagers know information about rural development programmes, purposes on which the grassroots bureaucracy visit the villages and visit regularly or not and also whether the villagers are happy with the selection process of the beneficiaries. The respondents were selected from the beneficiaries and non-beneficiaries of rural development from the villagers covering the entire district through questionnaire and schedule.

The message from Table 7.3 reflects the availability of the block functionaries in the service of the people such as motivating and assisting the rural people. Out of the 30 beneficiaries 33.33 per cent of the respondents in Lunglei block, 40 per cent in Lungsen block, 36.67 per cent in Hnahthial block, 40 per cent on Bunhmun block responded 'no' and 66.67 per cent in Lunglei block, 60 per cent in Lungsen block, 63.33 per cent in Hnahthial block and 60 per cent in Bunghmun block responded 'yes' on the services of the block development officer.

Table 7.3: Showing Performance about the Services of BDO, Extension Officers, VLWs
Number of Respondents

Each block = 30 Beneficiaries and 30 Non-beneficiaries

Total of Four Blocks = 240

	Lunglei Block			*Lungsen Block*			*Hnahthial Block*			*Bunghmun Block*		
	Number of Beneficiaries = 120											
**Grassroots Bureaucracy*	*Yes*	*No*	*No Res.*	*Yes*	*No*	*No Res.*	*Yes*	*No*	*No Res.*	*Yes*	*No*	*No Res.*
(1)	(2)	(3)	(4)	(5)	(6)	(7)	(8)	(9)	(10)	(11)	(12)	(13)
BDO	20 (66.67%)	10 (33.33%)	–	18 (60%)	12 (40%)	–	19 (63.33%)	11 (36.67%)	–	18 (60%)	12 (40%)	–
EO (Agri)	12 (40%)	18 (60%)	–	10 (33.33%)	20 (66.67%)	–	10 (33.33%)	20 (66.67%)	–	5 (16.67%)	25 (83.33%)	–
EO (Hort)	12 (40%)	18 (60%)	–	10 (33.33%)	20 (66.67%)	–	10 (33.33%)	20 (66.67%)	–	5 (16.67%)	25 (83.33%)	–
E.O. (Vety)	8 (26.67%)	22 (73.33%)	–	5 (16.67%)	25 (83.33%)	–	8 (26.67%)	22 (73.33%)	–	5 (16.67%)	25 (83.33%)	–
VLWs	10 (33.33%)	20 (66.67%)	–	5 (16.67%)	25 (83.33%)	–	11 (36.67%)	19 (63.33%)	–	5 (16.67%)	25 (83.33%)	–

(1)	(2)	(3)	(4)	(5)	(6)	(7)	(8)	(9)	(10)	(11)	(12)	(13)
					Number of Non-beneficiaries = 120							
BDO	12 (40%)	18 (60%)	–	10 (33.33%)	20 (66.67%)	–	11 (36.67%)	19 (63.33%)	–	8 (26.67%)	22 (73.33%)	–
EO (Agri)	8 (26.67%)	22 (73.33%)	–	5 (16.67%)	25 (83.33%)	–	9 (30%)	21 (70%)	–	5 (16.67%)	25 (83.33%)	–
EO (Hort)	8 (26.67%)	22 (73.33%)	–	5 (16.67%)	25 (83.33%)	–	8 (26.67%)	22 (73.33%)	–	5 (16.67%)	25 (83.33%)	–
EO (Vety)	8 (26.67%)	22 (73.33%)	–	5 (16.67%)	25 (83.33%)	–	8 (26.67%)	22 (73.33%)	–	5 (16.67%)	25 (83.33%)	–
VLWs	8 (26.67%)	22 (73.33%)	–	5 (16.67%)	25 (83.33%)	–	9 (30%)	21 (70%)	–	5 (16.67%)	25 (83.33%)	–

Source: Questionnaire and Interview Schedule.

* Abbreviations used in Table 7.3: BDO—Block Development Officer, EO (Agri)—Agriculture Extension Officer, EO (Hort)—Horticulture Extension Officer, EO (Vety)—Veterinary Extension Officer, VLWs—Village Level Workers, No. Res—No Response.

But the responses of the non-beneficiaries are different. 40 per cent in Lunglei block, 33.33 per cent in Lungsen block, 36.67 per cent in Hnahthial block and 26.67 per cent in Bunghmun block responded 'yes' and 60 per cent in Lunglei block, 66.67 per cent in Lungsen block, 63.33 per cent in Hnahthial block and 73.33 per cent in Bunghmun block responded 'no'. The responses of the beneficiaries and non-beneficiaries varies which shows that non-beneficiaries in particular are not convinced with the performance of the BDO in all the blocks of the district in comparison to beneficiaries whose responses found quite positive on the services of the BDO.

Table 7.3 also disclose the performances- of two most important, grassroots bureaucratic personnel—the Agriculture Extension Officer (AEO) and Horticulture Extension Officer (HEO). On the services of the AEO and HEO, the responses of beneficiaries were the same for these two officers in all the four blocks. 40 per cent in Lunglei block, 33.33 per cent in Lungsen and Hanahthial block, 16.67 per cent in Bunghmun block responded 'yes' and 60 per cent in Lunglei block 66.67 per cent in Lungsen and Hnahthial blocks and 83.33 per cent in Bunghmun block beneficiaries responded 'no' to the services of AEO and HEO. The responses of the non-beneficiaries are slightly different. On the services of the AEO, 26.67 per cent in Lunglei block, 16.67 per cent in Lungsen block, 30 per cent in Hnahthial block and 16.7 per cent in Bunghmun block non-beneficiaries says 'yes' and 73.33 per cent in Lunglei block 83.33 per cent in Lungsen block 70 per cent in Hnahthial block and 83 33 per cent in Bunghmun block non-beneficiaries says 'no' On the services of the HEO, 26.67 per cent in Lunglei block, 16.67 per cent in Lungsen block, 26.67 per cent in Hnahthial block and 16 67 per cent in Bunghmun block non-beneficiaries says 'yes' and 73 33 per cent in Lunglei block, 83.33 per cent in Lungsen block, 73.33 per cent in Hnahthial block and 83.33 per cent in Bunghmun block non-beneficiaries says'no'.

Table 7 3 reflects again the opinion of both beneficiaries and non-beneficiaries on Veterinary Extension Officer (VEO). Here 26.67 per cent in Lunglei block, 16.67 per cent in Lungsen block 26.67 per cent in Hnahthial block and 16.67 per cent in Bunghmun block beneficiaries says 'yes' and 73.33 per cent in Lunglei block 83.33 per cent in Lungsen block, 73.33 per cent in Hnahthial block and 83.33 per cent in Bunghmun block beneficiaries says 'no' The opinion of the non-beneficiaries is also not much varied. 26 67 per cent in Lunglei block, 16.67 per cent in Lungsen block, 26 67 per cent in Hnahthial block and 16.67 per cent in Bunghmun block non-beneficiaries says 'yes' and 73.33 in Lunglei block, 83.33 per cent in Lungsen block, 73.33 per cent in Hnahthial block beneficiaries says 'no' to the services of the VEO.

The Village Level Worker (VLW) has been portrayed as the pivot upon which a great deal of the success of community development programme revolved. His role as a guide and philosopher of the rural people is significant in a state like Mizoram where the villages are scattered due to geographical location and panchayati raj institutions have not introduced. Table 7.3 reveals the opinion of beneficiaries and non-beneficiaries on VLW. 33.33 per cent in Lunglei block, 16.67 per cent in Lungsen and Bunghmun block, 36. 67 per cent in Hnahthial block beneficiaries responded 'yes' and 66.67 per cent in Lunglei block, 83.33 per cent in Lungsen and Bunghmun block, 63.33 per cent in Hnahthial block beneficiaries says 'no' to the services of the VLW. The responses of the non-beneficiaries are slightly different as 26.67 per cent in Lunglei block, 16.67 per cent in Lungsen and Bunghmun blocks and 30 per cent in Hnahthial block responded 'yes' and 73.33 per cent in Lunglei block, 83.33 per cent in Lungsen and Bunghmun block and 70 per cent in Hnahthial block says 'no' on the services and availability of the VLWs.

Table 7.3 tells the meagre presence and influence of the block personnel's in the services of the rural people in the rural development blocks of Lunglei district. The responses found not much different from both the beneficiaries and non-beneficiaries on the services of the block level functionaries. In a state where various schemes on agriculture and allied activities has been introduced and implemented as alternative to shifting cultivation and economic self-sufficiency, the services of the extension officers and VLWs in particular are not satisfactory and not up to the expectations of the people. There were also some negative and positive response found on the block functionaries where there was no functionaries posted and the presence of some development department functionaries such as agriculture demonstrator, horticulture demonstrator makes confusion as many people does not know whether the demonstrators belong to blocks or development departments.

Table 7.4 shows the opinion of the respondents on whether the villagers were benefited from the rural development programmes. All the beneficiary respondents appreciated the rural development programmes initiated by both the State and Central Government. All the beneficiaries responded 'yes' on whether the village people were benefited from the programmes initiated during the last 10 years. However, majority of the non-beneficiaries have negative response. 86.87 per cent in Lunglei block, 80 per cent in Lungsen block, 83.33 per cent in Hnahthial block and 80 per cent in Bunghmun block responded 'no' and a small section of non-beneficiary respondents—13.33 per cent in Lunglei, 20 per cent in Lungsen, 16.67 per cent in Hnahthial and 20 per cent in Bunghmun block responded 'yes'.

Table 7.4: Showing Opinion of the Respondents on whether the Village People were Benefited from the Rural Development Programmes (last 10 Years)

		Yes	*No*	*Do Not Know*
Lunglei Block	Beneficiaries No. 30	30 (100%)	–	–
Lungsen Block	Beneficiaries No. 30	30 (100%)	–	–
Hnahthial Block	Beneficiaries No. 30	30 (100%)	–	–
Bunghmun Block	Beneficiaries No. 30	30 (100%)	–	–
No. of Non-beneficiaries—120				
Lunglei Block	Non-Beneficiaries No. 30	4 (13.33%)	26 (86.87%)	–
Lungsen Block	Non-Beneficiaries No. 30	6 (20%)	24 (80%)	–
Hnahthial Block	Non-Beneficiaries No. 30	5 (16.67%)	25 (83.33%)	–
Bunghmun Block	Non-Beneficiaries No. 30	6 (20%)	24 (80%)	–

Source: Questionnaire and Interview Schedule.

From the above table, it is evident that there are differences of opinion on the rural development programmes. People appreciated the programmes but at the same time want successful implementation of the programmes for overall development.

Table 7.5 shows who is responsible in the selection of beneficiaries of rural development programmes from 240 number of respondents of both the beneficiaries and non-beneficiaries and it explicates that majority of the beneficiaries in fact, selected as

Table 7.5: Showing Responses on the Method of Selection of Beneficiaries under Various Rural Development Programmes

Method	*Number Responding*	*Percentage*
Selected through Village Councils		
Village Development Council*	154	64.17
Govt. Officials	45	18.75
Legislators and party leaders	25	10.41
Do not know	16	6.67
Total	**240**	**100**

Source: Questionnaire and Interview Schedule.

* The Village Development Council sometimes exists and sometimes dissolved as per the instructions of the government.

per the guidelines of the programmes namely the Village Councils. But there are also quite a large number of beneficiaries of rural development programmes being selected on irregular methods. 10.41 per cent says that selection is being made by the legislators and party leaders, 18. 75 per cent says it is by bureaucrats. The category 'do not know' is 6.67 per cent.

From the above Table 7.5 it is evident that many beneficiaries are selected on irregular methods. The YMA and MHIP the largest Non-Government Organisations (NGO) are being involved in the selection process but the selection of the beneficiaries by the Village Councils is still not final. All the BDOs interviewed reveals that the beneficiary lists are being challenged by the local party leaders and solicit the BDO to change the list, which is, one of the great challenges of the BDOs in Mizoram.

Table 7.6 shows the responses of both beneficiaries and no-beneficiaries together on which are the areas that the block administration needs to give priority. 25.92 per cent of the respondents responded to give priority on agriculture and allied sector, industry etc. 24.17 per cent on road transport communication, 25 per cent on health services and 10.41 per cent education and 11. 25 per cent on other sectors and 6.25 per cent falls in the category of 'no response'.

It is evident from the above that majority of the respondents want the block administration to work on all the development sectors such as agriculture, industry, health and road transport, etc.

Table 7.6: Showing Responses on the Priority on which of the area the block administration (BDO) needs to work in their area

Priority Sectors	*Number Responding*	*Percentage*
Agriculture and Allied sectors, industry etc.	55	25.92
Road Transport, Communication	58	24.17
Health Services	60	25
Education	25	10.41
Others*	27	11.25
No Response	15	6.25%
Total	**240**	**100**

Source: Questionnaire and interview schedule.

* Include non-interference in selection of beneficiaries, cooperative stores, more medical sub-centre in the villages etc.

Table 7.7 shows the responses from which are the sources the village people know about the programmes of rural development. 68.75 per cent of the villagers know of the rural development programmes from the Village Councils. Mass media like radio and newspapers 8.33 per cent, the NGOs 8.75 and others 14.17.

Table 7.7: Showing the Responses from which source the Village People know Information about Rural Development Programme

Source of Information	*Number Responding*	*Percentage*
Village Councils, Govt. Officials*	165	68.75
Mass media	20	8.33
NGOs	21	8.75
Others+	34	14.17
Total	**240**	**100**

Source: Questionnaire and Interview Schedule.

* VLWs, the BDOs, and Extension Officers.

+ Include party leaders, legislators, friends and relatives.

It is apparent from the above Table 7.7 that voluntary organisations and mass media have exercised only a marginal role. It is also to be mentioned here that the Village Councils can know the programmes of rural development when the block functionaries inform them. Then only the Councils let the villagers know the programmes. This is also with the media where the administration to inform the media first and then only it published. Therefore, the role of the block administration is crucial in respect of giving information and awareness to the rural people.

Table 7.8 shows the responses of beneficiaries and non-beneficiaries on whether the village people are happy on the selection process of beneficiaries for rural development programmes. Out of the 30 beneficiaries in Lunglei block, 66.67 per cent responded 'yes' and 33.33 per cent says 'no', in Lungsen block 40 per cent says 'yes' and 60 per cent says 'no', in Hnahthial block, 46.67 per cent says 'yes' and 53.33 per cent responded 'no'. In Bunghmun block 33.33 per cent says 'yes' and 66.67 per cent says 'no'. But the responses of the non-beneficiaries are quite different from that of the beneficiaries. In Lunglei block 20 per cent responded 'yes' and 80 per cent says 'no', in Lungsen block 13.33 per cent says 'yes' and 86.67 per cent says 'no', in Hnahthial block 16.67 per cent says 'yes' and 83.33 per cent says 'no' and in Bunghmun block 20 per cent says 'yes' and 80 per cent responded 'no'.

Table 7.8: Showing Responses of Beneficiaries and Non-beneficiaries whether the village people are happy on the selection process on beneficiaries of Rural Development Programmes

		Yes	*No*	*Do Not Know*
Lunglei Block	Beneficiaries No. 30	20 (66.67%)	10 (33.33)	–
Lungsen Block	Beneficiaries No. 30	12 (40%)	18 (60%)	–
Hnahthial Block	Beneficiaries No. 30	14 (46.67%)	16 (53.33)	–
Bunghmun Block	Beneficiaries No. 30	10 (33.33%)	20 (66.67)	–
No of Non-beneficiaries—120				
Lunglei Block	Non-Beneficiaries No. 30	6 (20%)	24 (80%)	–
Lungsen Block	Non-Beneficiaries No. 30	4 (13.33%)	26 (86.67%)	–
Hnahthial Block	Non-Beneficiaries No. 30	5 (16.67%)	25 (83.33%)	–
Bunghmun Block	Non-Beneficiaries No. 30	6 (20%)	24 (80%)	–

Source: Questionnaire and Interview Schedule.

From the above Table 7.8 manifest that there are differences of opinion of both beneficiaries and non-beneficiaries on the selection process and non-beneficiaries in particular are not happy with the selection process.

Table 7.9 shows the responses on whether block functionaries are visiting the villages regularly. 75 per cent of the respondents says 'no', 4.17 per cent responded 'yes' and 20.83 per cent falls in the category 'do not know'.

Table 7.9: Showing Responses on whether the Block Functionaries Visits the Village People Regularly

Block Functionaries	*Category*	*No. Responding*	*Percentage*
BDO,	Responding 'Yes'	10	4.17
EOs,	Responding 'No'	180	75
VLWs	Do not know	50	20.83
Total		**240**	**100**

Source: Questionnaire and Interview Schedule.

The message from the above Table 7.9 replicates the non-availability of the block functionaries in the villages again. Many remote villages were not visited by the functionaries although it is found that the villagers heard about these functionaries.

Table 7.10 shows the responses on what are the purposes on which the block functionaries visit the villages. 10.41 per cent responded that they visit for awareness, 2.09 per cent responded as they visit for motivating the farmers and imparting agriculture education and 85.41 per cent responded that the functionaries visit only for supervision of work.

Table 7.10: Showing Responses on what are the Purposes the Block Functionaries Visit the Villages

Purpose	*No. Responding*	*Percentage*
Awareness of RD programmes	25	10.41
Motivating the farmers	5	2.09
Impart agriculture education	5	2.09
Supervision of work	205	85.41
Total	**240**	**100**

Source: Questionnaire and Interview Schedule.

From the above Table 7.10, it is evident that the block

functionaries mainly visit the villages to supervise the works entrusted to the Villages Councils or others.

Thus, from the above analysis of the tables, it is apparent that the performance of the grassroots bureaucracy is far from contentment of the rural people when the expectations of the people are very high.

The block development officers of all the blocks in the district has not organized any medical camps, awareness campaigns on rural development during the last 10 years or so. But it must also be said that the block functionaries are working under difficult working condition with acute shortage of personnel's in all the blocks of the district and in Lungsen and Bunghmun blocks in particular.

The SGRY (Food for Work) programme, out of the recent rural development programme in these blocks was the most appreciated programme of rural development before the Mahatma Gandhi National Rural Employment Guarantee Scheme (NREGS) started. NREGS is the most appreciated and popular scheme of rural development now which has already made deep inroads into the lives of the rural people of Mizoram, but far away from raising productivity and creating durable assets in rural Mizoram.

The Village Councils, although involved in the process of rural development, it is not as synchronised as it is under the Panchayati Raj Institutions (PRIs). As per the guidelines of the ongoing programmes like Indira Awaas Yojana, the Gram Sabha selects the beneficiaries from the list of eligible BPL households, restricting the number to the target allotted as per the programme guidelines and selection of the Gram Sabha is final. No approval by a higher body is required.[38] But in case of Mizoram, due to non-existence of PRIs, the selection of beneficiaries is bound to affect. It is reported by the respondents that people from the urban areas frequently made an attempt to produce rural residential certificates bribing the Presidents of Village Councils.[39] However, some Village Councils Presidents found to be very cautious of these attempts. Corruption in implementation of rural development programmes by the Village Councils was also evident especially in PMGY (Food for Work) programme. The Village Council of Chawngte 'L' under Lungsen block was dissolved on the charges of misuse of Food for Work. Fifty-eight quintals of rice and Rs. 7250 was reportedly misused by the Village Council President and for no account book maintained.[40] The Village Councils are dissolved following the complain from the local political party leaders and NGOs, reported to the Local Administration Department. The Circle Assistant of Local Administration Department made a spot verification on such charges and based on the report, the higher authority dissolved the same. The charges, however, made not only against the opposition party ruled Village Councils but also the ruling party.[41]

The Gram Panchayats play a significant role in Swarnajayanti Gram Swarozgar Yojana (SGSY), which first approve the list of BPL families and monitor the performance of the *Swarozgaris* and in particular whether they are repaying the loan regularly. The Panchayat Samiti (Block Level) will approve the key activities that are identified for the blocks. In Mizoram, in the absence of block level elected body; and the Village Councils being at the village level only, it is to be done by the block administration alone.[42]

It cannot be denied that there are no achievements of block administration in the field of rural development in Mizoram in general and Lunglei district in particular. Many developmental works have been undertaken in all the blocks and completed with the active attempt of the block level bureaucracy. But it can also be said that the present developmental works largely confined in construction of water points, clearance, construction of internal roads, urinal sheds, etc. and very far away from creating sustainable livelihood opportunities and durable assets in rural areas. Here, it may be too ruthless to blame the bureaucrats alone for the failure of the rural development programmes in making a positive impact, in creating durable income generating assets, eradication and reduction of rural poverty, etc. But bureaucracy has to take the larger responsibility in case of Mizoram where it plays a decisive role in the absence of PRIs. Block level bureaucracy is the exclusive machinery to implement rural development programmes in the state of Mizoram. The Government of Mizoram set goals for socio-economic development and economic self-sufficiency to achieve from time to time, which are translated into realities by the bureaucrats. But grassroots level bureaucracy in Mizoram is yet to conquer confidence of the village people. Therefore, it is time for bureaucracy to take bigger responsibility and reach to the remote villages as agents of development rather than villagers looming to them for their help and development.

Notes and References

1. Sapru, R.K. (2003): *Development Administration*, Sterling Publishers, New Delhi, p. 304.
2. *Ibid*. p. 304.
3. Taradatt, (2002,): *Development Administration in an Indian State Guide Book Evolved for BDO in Orissa*, Uppal Publishing House, New Delhi, pp. 153-54.
4. Maheshwari, S.R. (2004): *Local Government in India*, Lakshmi Narain Agarwal, (10th edition) Agra, New Delhi, pp. 99-100.
5. Singh, Amita (1998): *Public Administration: The Grassroot Concern*, Mittal Publications, New Delhi, p. 4.
6. Report on Soil and Land Capability Survey of Lunglei RD Block, Lunglei District, Mizoram, Soil Survey Organisation, Department of Agriculture, Jan., 1997, p. 5 (b)
7. Government of Mizoram: (2003): Village Level Statistics, Economics and Statistics Department, Aizawl, p. 67.
8. Government of Mizoram: (2003): Statistical Hand Book, Lunglei District, Mizoram, p. 24.
9. Government of Mizoram, (1992): *Statistical Hand Book*, Lunglei District, Mizoram, p. 11.
10. Government of Mizoram, (2003): *Village Level Statistics, op. cit*. p. 67.
11. Based on Personal interview with Mr. R. Rongenga, BDO, Lunglei Block.
12. Government of Mizoram: (2002): *Statistical Hand Book*, Mizoram, p. 51.
13. Government of Mizoram, (1992): *Statistical Hand Book*, Lunglei District, Mizoram, p. 19.
14. Potential Linked Credit Plan, Lunglei District, Mizoram 2005-06, NABARD, Aizawl. p. 5.
15. Report on Soil and Land Capability Survey of Lunglei RD Block, *op. cit*. p. 5.
16. Government of Mizoram: (2002): Statistical Hand Book, *op. cit*. p. 51.
17. Based on Personal interview with Mr. R. Rongenga, BDO, Lunglei Block.
18. Potential Linked Credit Plan, Lunglei District, *op. cit*. p. 44.
19. *Ibid*. p. 45.
20. Government of Mizoram: (2003): *Statistical Hand Book*, Lunglei District, Mizoram, p. 19.
21. Government of Mizoram: (2002): *Statistical Hand Book*, Mizoram p. 52.
22. Government of Mizoram, (2003): Village Level Statistics, *op. cit*. p. 67.

23. Government of Mizoram, (1998): *Statistical Hand Book*, Mizoram, pp. 144-137.
24. Government of Mizoram, (1994): List of NLUP Beneficiaries, 1994-95 under Lunglei Rural Development Block, Rural Development Department, Aizawl.
25. Government of Mizoram, (2002): *Statistical Hand Book*, Mizoram, p. 70.
26. Report on Soil and Land Capability Survey of Hnahthial RD Block, Lunglei District, Mizoram, Soil Survey Organisation, Department of Agriculture, January, 1997.
27. Government of Mizoram: (2003): Village Level Statistics, Lunglei p. 39.
28. Government of Mizoram, (1992): *Statistical Hand Book*, Lunglei District pp. 11-12.
29. Government of Mizoram, (2002): *Statistical Hand Book*, Mizoram, p. 51.
30. Government of Mizoram, (2003): *Statistical Handbook*, Lunglei, 2003, *op. cit.* p. 36.
31. Project Director, District Rural Development Agency, 2003. Lunglei.
32. Report on Soil and Land Capability Survey of Bunghmun RD Block, Soil Survey Organisation, Department of Agriculture, Mizoram, January, 1997.
33. Report on Block Statistical Data, Rural Development Block, Bunghmun, Lunglei, Mizoram, 2004, p. 1.
34. Based on Personal Interview with Mr. S.K. Bhattacharjee, Lead District Manager, State Bank of India, Lunglei.
35. Based on Personal Interview with Zathangliana, BDO, Bunghmun RD Block, Lunglei.
36. Report on Soil and Land Capability Survey of Lungsen RD Block, Soil Survey Organisation, Department of Agriculture, Mizoram, January, 1997.
37. Based on Personal Interview with Zathangliana, BDO, Bunghmun RD Block, Lunglei.
38. Guidelines for Indira Awaas Yojana (Effective from 01.04. 2004) Ministry of Rural Development, Government of India, New Delhi, p. 5.
39. Based on Personal Interview with Mr. K. Lalthlamuana, Village Council President, Thualthu, Lunglei block.
40. As per Lushai Hills District Council (Village Councils) Act, Section (25) Vide memo B-14021/9/02-LAD/VC/Dt. 30th March'05.
41. Based on Personal Interview with Mr. TC. Lalruata, Circle Assistant, Local Administration Department, Lunglei.
42. Guidelines, SGSY, Ministry of Rural Development, Government, New Delhi, 2003, p. 39.

8

Findings and Suggestions

The main focus of the research was to make an appraisal of the grassroots bureaucracy, their performance and role in the execution of rural development programmes, their difficulties, and perceptions of the people on the rural bureaucracy and suggest ways to overcome the difficulties that arise. This chapter presents the authors findings and suggestions. The major findings of the study have been highlighted hereunder along with suitable suggestions.

With the launching of the Community Development Programme, it was hoped that the living standard of rural people would increase, there would be equity in the socio-economic status, peoples level of confidence and morality would be high and their participation be integral part of rural development and there would be overall economic growth with active assistance and guidance of the rural bureaucracy. But the condition of the rural people to achieve as above has not been improved as was expected even after 50 years since its inception. About 40 per cent of rural population is still living below poverty line under poverty, inequality, unemployment, isolation, low confidence and parochialism. Bureaucracy involved in implementation of rural development could not capture the minds and hearts of the people and people's perception towards bureaucracy is negative.

The effort of the Government of India and State Governments towards rural regeneration progammes has been continuous. But how these efforts has been failing and expected results are not been achieved, now needs to be given topmost priority while planning and implementing rural development programmes. Continuous assessment and evaluation of the rural development programmes by independent bodies is necessary. Independent bodies and institutions should be encouraged and government should spend at least 5 per cent out of the rural development funds to undertake further research for providing feedback to decision-makers for better formulation, effective implementation, identification of reasons for success or failures, and possible modifications where necessary of the project in future so that the fruits of development reach to the rural poor for which it is meant for. Bureaucracy involved in rural development and Panchayati Raj Institutions needs to be evaluated at regular intervals to make them responsible for failure and success of the rural development programmes. Bureaucracy needs to respond promptly to the process of economic and social change.

Both electronic and print media gives very little coverage on the issues, problems and prospects of rural development in India. Media today is urban oriented. In developing countries in particular, including India, research findings on various subjects of development, problems and prospects of development are not given much importance while formulating development plans and programmes. The seminars and workshops that are organised on rural development and its outcomes are usually confined to universities, college's and in books which do not actually reach to the rural people and there is no effective apparatus through which the inferences drawn can be placed before the policy makers and implementing bureaucracy.

Therefore, media should play a responsible role to highlight the problems, prospects and success stories of rural people. Giving importance to the findings of the research works while formulating policies and programmes by policy-makers and bureaucrats is essential which will ultimately help the rural poor. Educational institutions particularly higher education should play an important role in rural development. The existing National Service Scheme should be utilised in rural development. The college and university teachers and students should be involved in motivating, guiding and in identifying the potentials rural people and the area have.

In Mizoram, although two decades of insurgency had severely slowed down the process of rural development, development has been very slow as expected. Inequality in economic status in Mizo society has been evident. It is observed that before 50 years back all Mizo families were more or less equal in terms of economic status. Despite 50 years of planned development, a huge gap of rich and poor is evident now. The communication, marketing system, agriculture and allied sector is still in infantile stage in this state which needs to be looked at. In spite of the fact that the Three District Councils that has been functioning in the southern part of Mizoram, this area is still backward and the living standard of the rural poor has not been improved as it could have been. The District Council's in their respective area need to perform for all round development of rural people. More attention is needed to eradicate poverty, develop education, health, marketing facilities, agriculture and communication. The District Councils may give attention to a particular area to be developed within a particular time and period then again to another area so to achieve desired level of development in every aspect of rural life. There is no relation between the Councils and state rural development functionaries in this area. There is a need of some sort of relations to avoid duplication in their work. The block administration and DRDA while implementing rural development programmes may work in collaboration with the District Councils Rural Development Department to generate better outcome of rural development programmes.

The Village Councils are local self-governing bodies in Mizoram. But the study of Village Councils reveals that the Village Councils does not enjoy such powers which Gram Panchayats under the Panchayati Raj Institutions (PRIs) does. The Councils does not enjoy decision-making power in a larger degree. People's participation in decision-making is not possible in this system of local self-government. To carry out developmental works, its fund position is meagre and the term of three years is too short for a local self-government body. Although the District Councils and Village Councils in Mizoram have been engaged in rural development, bureaucracy override the Councils and there is a huge gap between the District Councils and Village Councils, Village Councils and district level and state administration in the absence of an intermediary body at the block level.

Thus, there is need of a block level elected body, where the villages are scattered due to geographical location, for effective planning, participation and decision-making and in smooth implementation of rural development programmes. Introduction of Panchayati Raj Institutions or extending the powers of the existing Village Councils through legislation, as viable democratic institutions as per with the Constitution (73rd Amendment) Act is needed. This is desirable for ensuring decentralised planning; to enable people's participation in decision-making, making rural development administration responsive to the elected representatives of the people, implementation of the rural development programmes in coordination with rural bureaucracy and its positive role as a socio-economic development body.

Before independence, no significant development was made in the entire state. Till 1972, development of the district was affected due to limited funds while it was a district of Assam. Development planning and implementation of rural development programmes started especially with the community development projects and the creation of blocks and later with the creation of the Rural Development Department in Mizoram. This department since its inception has been working for the poverty amelioration programmes and for all-round development of village life. The Directorate of Rural Development heads the department. This department is a crucial department in respect of its diverse functions of rural development. However, almost all the bureaucratic personnel's in this department, from the directorate to the grassroots level, has been on deputation from the development departments like agriculture, horticulture, etc. As a result of this, it was found that among the bureaucrats, the belongingness and motivation is lacking. Almost all the bureaucrats like to go back in their parent departments. Furthermore, at present, most of the top level bureaucrats at the directorate level do not have any major assignments of works allotted to them. In the absence of major programmes for implementation of rural development like that of New Land Use Policy and Mizoram Intohdelhna Project by this directorate, the activities of the bureaucrats are found to be very limited, which is the wastage of their expertise. The Animal Husbandry and Veterinary Surgeon, was looking after the technical supervision of the programme of Special SGSY (Piggery) Scheme at Lunglei on a frequent visit from Aizawl. The extension officers of horticulture, agriculture in the directorate are not being properly utilised as such. It is also observed that the directorate, have no control over the block administration. As the annual confidential report of a block development officer, the head of the block, is reported by the Deputy Commissioner, the Director of Rural Development department, thus, actually has very insignificant control over the BDOs. As the blocks are scattered through out the state, the directorate at Aizawl actually has very limited control over the block administration. This is one of the serious problem in smooth implementation of rural development programmes.

In this background, this important department should be reorganised in the pattern of other developments departments. Separate rural development service for recruitment of rural bureaucracy may well be introduced. In fact, rural development department is as important as the other line departments. As it needs to guide and shape the technical and general aspects of rural development programmes, the bureaucrats at the directorate level should be of its own. This will, bring unity, spirit and more responsibility and accountability and challenges in their work, which will ultimately help the rural poor. The bureaucrats at the directorate level need to be organised in such a way that their expertise and technical knowledge can best be utilised.

At the district level, District Rural Development Department in each district may be created under the directorate to supervise and monitor the programmes of rural development. This will bring interlink with the directorate and the blocks as well as with District Rural Development Agencies. An officer of Deputy Director's rank of the present directorate may head this office at the district level. It will bring more transparency and effective implementation and supervision of the rural development programmes in which the BDO and extension officers will be very close to the department. It should be well equipped with technical staff required to guide the block functionaries. This will enable as the link between directorate and blocks.

The main aim for planning and development in Mizoram has been to achieve economic self-sufficiency. As such the main objectives of rural development programmes such as NLUP, MUP, BAFFACOS, etc. are to put an end to the practice of wasteful shifting cultivation and is to take up Wet Rice Cultivation (WRC) in all the potential flat lands in order to promote self-sufficiency in food production. But the state will have to go a long way towards achieving its objective. The state is backward in almost all development sectors such as road transport facilities, agriculture and allied activities, etc. Majority of the people lives on agriculture but the production does not supplement as per requirement of the state. The Lunglei district largely depends on essential commodities from outside the state and practically nothing that exporting outside the state. Various schemes of development on land reclamation, minor irrigation, potential area connectivity, efforts on abolition of jhuming, etc. are under implementation and some achievements in these programmes cannot be denied but the achievements does not comprise any record of the impact of the programmes. The researcher found that all the development departments are implementing some of the centrally sponsored programmes assigned to them and there is no state sponsored programmes worth to mention with the exception of New Land Use Policy. There is also no coordination of development departments in the state.

Hence, a perfect coordination of the development departments and extra efforts of all the development departments is required. A special package like NLUP or MIP for agriculture and horti-culture development is required in the state as a whole for more concentrated efforts on developing infrastructure, farm mechani-sation, marketing facilities, potential connectivity, irrigation and supply of fertilisers. Good management of the projects like NLUP at all levels especially at the state level ensuring effective leadership, guidance, direction, execution, appropriate choice of resources and also the integration and coordination of the departments involved is the key for successful implementation of the project. If the programmes like MIP and NLUP fails, the sufficiency in foodgrain production and economic development as a whole, would be a distant dream for years to come in Mizoram.

Lack of good communication facility is the major problem face by the village people of Mizoram. Due to remoteness and scattered nature of the villages and lack of road transport facilities the farmers of the remote villages cannot market their products even to the block headquarters. There is no regulated market and cold storage facilities in the state are inadequate. Although the agro-climatic condition of the Lunglei district and the state as a whole is conducive in livestock development, piggery is the only sector developed in the district. Dairy, poultry, etc. has not been developed as a means of livelihood. Veterinary services in the rural areas are inadequate. The efforts of the government in developing small-scale industries are quite satisfactory but this sector has a direct link with road transport, power, and water resources. Middleman's share has been one of the main reason behind increasing food prices at the retail level. How to eliminate the middleman and thus cut costs and to reach the actual profit to the rural development beneficiaries are not taken into consideration while implementing rural development schemes.

Hence, effective implementation of rural development programmes is vital. More infrastructure development ensuring better link roads, market connectivity, cold storage facilities are required. Initiatives for more farmers' cooperative societies should be encouraged, which will help in eliminating the middleman. Understanding of the technical factors involved while implementing development programmes by the implementing departments, timely supply of appropriate inputs, flow of assistance, marketing of outputs, strict and continuous monitoring will be essential. The rural bureaucracy should be very active and work on the field in reaching the remote villages and see that they do not look at the problems from the office. Demonstrations at regular intervals to impart technical know how and skill to the farmers through training, tours, audio-visuals, seminars to aware and in involving the farmers to join actively in the programme is needed for which trained, skilled, specialised, efficient, impartial and more importantly motivated bureaucracy is required.

With the introduction of the community development programmme, the block development officers were expected to play a very important role in the development of agriculture and allied sector, horticulture, fishery, etc. helping the farmers to take these sectors as sustainable income generation. The block administration headed by the BDO are supposed to encourage the farmers, create enthusiasm, motivate them and make aware of the importance of increasing food grain production and giving all the technical aspects of the agriculture related schemes with the help of the extension officers and village level workers. In the absence of PRIs in Mizoram, the block bureaucracy is the sole implementing agency of rural development programmes. However, the bock level bureaucrats play a very insignificant role in all the development sectors such as agriculture, veterinary etc. The BDO never ever organised any awareness campaign in the Lunglei district blocks to motivate the farmers. The extension officers and village level workers do not visit the farmers related to these aspects at regular intervals. With the introduction of various schemes of rural development, the rural bureaucracy is busy in implementation of those programmes and there is a presence of other development departments as well. Hence, motivating the farmers, organising awareness campaign for the farmers, organising medical camps for the rural poor is perhaps not in the agenda of the rural bureaucracy. The average term of a BDO is about two or three years only to adjust to the working conditions and to have accomplished knowledge of the community development and schematic guidelines. In the Lungsen and Bunghmun blocks, the agriculture horticulture, veterinary extension officers not been appointed for a very long period. The village level workers in these blocks are busy in performing the duties of the extension officers mostly from the block office itself. They are generally not assigned particular villages to be covered by them. In these blocks even the postal services are also not available in some of the villages, which affected the links with the block office. The BDOs and extension officers do not attend the training programmes regularly as organised by the State Institute of Rural Development. One of the reason articulated is due to their involvements in other activities assigned by the authority such as election duties, census, etc.

Thus, the block development officers posting should be at least not less than 4 to 5 years so that they can understand the problems and prospects of the block, acquainted with the working conditions of the block and to have a clear understanding of the guidelines of rural development. The BDOs should not be involved in too much of paper work and should involve in field work. In this respect the post of Additional BDO should be filled to help the BDO. If the BDO starts working on the field, he will be able to motivate the other field staff of the block too. The BDO should be equipped with adequate staff—the extension officers and village level workers and additional BDOs especially in the blocks like Lungsen—the largest of blocks in Lunglei district. This will enable the block administration to function smoothly in all the development sectors. The number of village level workers should be according to the number of villages to be covered. The area of operation for each Village Level Worker (VLW) should be made in each of the block.

The system of deputation of bureaucracy from development departments to block level also failed in Mizoram to induce belongingness in this office. All the extension officers and VLWs like to go back to their parent department. The functions of the

BDOs and his assisting staff mostly found to be confined in the block office only due to excessive paper works, difficult working conditions, lack of sufficient staffs and lack of motivation especially the extension officers and village level workers. As a manager of the team of the development officers, the BDOs have no differences with other block level officers in all the blocks of the Lunglei district. But efforts in motivating the extension officers and village level workers to work hard on the field is perhaps lacking.

Therefore, direct recruitment method of at least 70 per cent from the open market and the rest through promotion can be effective. As Mizoram have a reputation of social service through NGOs, emphasis should be made on this aspect apart from the bachelor's degree in arts, science and agriculture, veterinary science for the post of BDOs including other block functionaries. After the selection, they should be provided basic training in community development to get a thorough understanding of the objectives of the multi-sided rural development. The BDO then get regular orientation courses from State Institute of Rural Development in securing complete understanding of the guidelines of the ongoing rural development programmes. The extension officers and village level workers should also belong to the Rural Development Department with better promotion opportunities. Motivation and training for bureaucracy again are not enough to get best out of the bureaucrats who are to work in a difficult working condition (due to physical constraints like poor communication, remoteness of the villages). The hard working, committed, sincere and honest bureaucrats should be identified and rewarded to encourage and inspire them.

In all the rural development blocks in Mizoram, post of education extension officer, extension officer of civil supply, social education organisers are not created. Involving the block administration in these sectors were not considered. Apart from the construction of the educational institutions, the block bureaucracy does not play any significant role in educational field in their blocks. The block administration is also not involved in public distribution system in the state. Almost all the people of villages particularly, in Mizoram worried of the deadly disease of malaria. People from the remote villages cannot afford to the expenses required in higher centre for treatment whereas the medical sub-centres are not well equipped with complete treatment.

In this context, involving the block bureaucracy being the close links and nearest to the rural people is suggested. Most of the BDOs of the district agreed that there should be extension officers in these sectors. The education extension officer if appointed can inspect and made spot verification of the requirements of the schools and help in planning related to this very important sector. He may make frequent visits in the educational institutions to inspect the presence of the teachers in their working place or not as well. Civil supply officer if appointed can see the requirements of the rural people in the block. The block administration should also be entrusted responsibilities in providing medical first aid to the villagers and also in providing logistic support to the medical staff posted in the blocks. The BDO should organise special health camps and ensure continuous monitoring of the health of the rural people.

The grassroots bureaucracy and local self-government in Mizoram has no structural and organizational relations. The Village Councils are involved in rural development by the bureaucracy on the compulsion of the schematic guidelines and the block development officers used to intimate the president of Village Councils through letters regarding new schemes and follow up action. Although the Village Councils are part of the Block Development Committee, but many Village Council Presidents from remote villages generally does not attend. There is no provision for transport allowance and dearness allowances for Village Councils to attend those meetings which is also the reasons behind the Village Council President's absence. As a result, the only forum to address the problems and prospects of the villages together with the block administration hinders. Therefore, the President of Village Councils who usually attend those meetings should be paid transport allowance and dearness allowances to attend the meetings considering the communication constraints and make those meetings fruitful. The Block Development Committee should be utilised for policy making, planning and implementation of rural development programmes.

The community development envisages involvement of extension officers and village level workers. The block development officer being the generalist head cannot implement rural development schemes alone in isolation. The BDO has to maintain a perfect coordination and understanding with the extension officers and other block level functionaries for effective implementation of the rural development programmes. In Lungsen and Bunghmun blocks the extension officers not been appointed for a long period of time and inadequate village level workers, the study of relations with the BDOs has been limited. Although, in Lunglei and Hnahthial blocks there are few extension officers which are not involved in any major development schemes and hence they does no have any differences with BDOs. But almost all the village level workers, in all the blocks, are not being utilised for the purpose they were appointed for. The village level workers got two years training at the Extension Training Centres, which are not being utilised. Their knowledge on agriculture, agronomy, plant protection, soil science, etc. is hardly being utilised due to its insignificant involvement in these sectors. This may also responsible for lack of motivation, enthusiasm and job satisfaction. The Gram Sevikas are mostly engaged in maintenance of official work in the block office. The purpose for which the Gram Sevikas appointed as well is also not being fully utilised. Proper management and utilisation of the expertise of the existing grassroots bureaucracy is essential which will lead to the benefit of the rural people and the rural area.

Securing people's participation through voluntary organizations is vital to the success of rural development programmes as it increases the suitability and utilisation of the services. It can also function as watchdog of the people and act as link between administration and the people. The largest Non-Governmental Organizations (NGOs) in Mizoram—Young Mizo Association (YMA) and Mizoram Hmeichhe Insuihkhawm Pawl (MHIP), Mizo Upa Pawl (MUP) which the Government of Mizoram considers as partners of development. These NGOs are being involved in the selection of beneficiaries, selection of BPL families' etc. by the government. However, rural development is not in the agenda of these NGOs. These NGOs are not involved in providing loans to the poor, in the development of rural infrastructure, in exploiting the local resources etc. and largely concerned with social and not in economic programmes.

Being very popular and close to the minds and hearts of the people, these organisations should work for the rural poor by providing loans in such sectors as floriculture, small-scale industries like development of weaving and knitting, horticulture etc. and help in the marketing of those products, leading to provide employment to a sizeable number of poor people. The NGOs can also form committees like Forest Protection Committee, Product Marketing Committee, Monitoring Committee, Development Committee and Awareness Committee, etc. This will ensure people's participation and help to aware the people and the beneficiaries of rural development for their sincere effort in the implementation of the programmes and in minimising corruption and political interference at implementation level.

Out of the four blocks, the present study was undertaken in the Lunglei district of Mizoram, Bunghmun and Lungsen blocks are relatively backward blocks. In the Bunghmun block there are no commercial banks and all the schemes, which need credit, cannot be implemented in this block. The immediate need of this block is a commercial bank and better road transport facilities. Without developing road transport facilities, mere implementation of rural development programmes will have very little impact in this block. For sustainable rural development in these blocks, policies should be made to divert some of the schemes to develop road transport sector only within a specific period. Successful implementation of programme like Border Area Development Programme (BADP) in these blocks is very essential by giving highest priority to all weather road connectivity. Spending huge amount of money on construction of market sheets under BADP, for example, will be of no use without marketing links and communication.

Conclusion

In Mizoram the atmosphere is very conducive for effective implementation of rural development programmes, because the state has a reputation of voluntary services for the community, no money lenders, no caste barriers, hard working nature of the people, high literacy rate and being the most peaceful state in the North Eastern States. A special tax policy should be made for more funds in rural development in the state. Special focus in a particular block for given period and then to another block, choosing appropriate technology for rural areas, coordination of various development departments, hard working grassroots bureaucracy is essential. To ensure durable and sustained rural development, accommodating the increasing population, eradication of poverty, supporting the rural people who are just above the below poverty line, efforts have to be made from all angles.

Mizoram, an agricultural state, the topographical isolation, bad communication networks, limited cultivable lands, primitive method of cultivation and insufficiency in food production is still backward. Facilities like transport, communication, irrigation, electricity, and industry for development are not adequate. In this background, trained, skilled, specialised, efficient and impartial bureaucracy is required. The rural development of a tribal state is quite different than that of other plain States of India. Mizoram, a hilly state where the villages are scattered and remote, development of all sectors is also different. The development process, thus, requires extra efforts and zeal from the bureaucracy as well as needs more financial allocations. The policy makers at the national and state level need to make policies which are realistic and achievable within a particular area and in a specific period of time. Proper utilisation of local resources ensuring sustainable development and full utilisation of funds is required.

Lunglei district is one of the most backward district of Mizoram needs topmost priority for all-round development in all sectors of development. In the overall development of the district and success of rural development schemes, the rural bureaucracy is the key. Full-fledged staff in all the rural development blocks and involving them effectively in all sectors of development—agriculture, small-scale industry, veterinary, horticulture, fishery to generate employment for the rural poor is required. In the field of social security, education and health their involvement is also needed. But the importance must be given in motivating the rural bureaucracy to work hard in assisting the villagers in a difficult working condition for which the head of the block administration—the block development officer is entirely responsible in the absence of PRIs.

APPENDICES

Appendix-I

Questionnaire and Interview Schedule for Beneficiaries and Non-Beneficiaries

Notes: 1. Suggestions are welcome. They may please be attached on separate sheets.
2. Please tick mark (✔) the appropriate answer, wherever applicable.

PART-I

INVESTIGATORS SHEET

(i) Name of the Block ....
(ii) Village ....
(iii) Sex ....
(iv) Age ....
(v) Educational Qualification ....
(vi) Marital Status ....
(vii) Community ....
(viii) Mother tongue ....
(ix) Occupation ....
(x) Income per annum ....
(xi) Whether beneficiary or availed benefit of any Rural Development Scheme? Pl mention ....

PART-II

1. Do you feel that your village has developed during the last 10 years or so?
   (i) Yes
   (ii) No
   (iii) Do not know
2. Do you feel the villagers were benefited from the Rural

Development Schemes such as NLUP, MIP, IRDP, SGRY, SGSY, IAY, EAS etc.?
(i) Yes
(ii) No
(iii) Do not know

3. Out of the ongoing rural development schemes, which scheme you like most? Please mention
....

4. Who do you think is responsible in the selection of the beneficiaries?
(i) Village Councils
(ii) Village Development Committee
(iii) Government Officials
(iv) Legislators and party leaders
(v) Do not know

5. Are you happy with the selection process of the beneficiaries?
(i) Yes
(ii) No
(iii) Do not know

6. Does your village have Cooperative Stores, Medical Sub-centers, Veterinary sub-centres?
(i) Yes
(ii) No
(iii) Do not know

7. From which source you know of the rural development programmes?
(i) Village Councils
(ii) Government Officials
(iii) Radio/Newspaper/Propaganda
(iv) Political leaders

8. Have you heard of Village Level Worker (VLW), Gram Sevika, extension officer?
(i) Yes
(ii) No
(iii) Do not know

9. Does the Block Development Officer (BDO), VLW, Gram Sevika, extension officers of your block visit your village regularly?
(i) Yes

(ii) No
(iii) Do not know

10. Do you know on which are the purposes the BDO, VLW, Gram Sevika, extension officer visits your village?
    (i) Awareness of rural development schemes
    (ii) Motivating the farmers
    (iii) Imparting agricultural education, aware of fertilizers etc.
    (iv) Supervision of works only
11. Did the BDO organise awareness camps, medical camps in your village?
    (i) Yes
    (ii) No
    (iii) Do not know
12. Do you think that the BDO, extension officers, VLWs, Gram Sevikas are available for the services of the people and helpful for you?
    (i) For beneficiary? Please tick (✔) (a) Yes or (b) No
    Block Development Officer (a) Yes (b) No
    Agriculture Extension Officer (a) Yes (b) No
    Horticulture Extension Officer (a) Yes (b) No
    Veterinary Extension Officer (a) Yes (b) No
    Village Level Workers, Gram Sevikas (a) Yes (b) No
    (ii) If you are a non-beneficiary? Please tick (✔) (a) Yes or (b) No
    Block Development Officer (a) Yes (b) No
    Agriculture Extension Officer (a) Yes (b) No
    Horticulture Extension Officer (a) Yes (b) No
    Veterinary Extension Officer (a) Yes (b) No
    Village Level Workers, Gram Sevikas (a) Yes (b) No
13. What are the areas the BDO should concentrate for the development of your village/area. Please mention.

Appendix-II

Questionnaire for Grassroots Bureaucracy

PART-I

INVESTIGATORS SHEET

(I) Name of the Respondent and Designation ....
(II) Age..
(II) Sex ....
(III) Designation ....
(IV) Educational Qualification ....
(V) Name of the Block ....
(VI) Since when working ....
(VI) Previous post held ....
(VI) Department from which deputed ....

PART-II

1. Do you feel that there is excessive paper works and how many letters do you receive and to reply in a day?

   ....

2. Do you enjoy your work?

   ....

3. Being a Generalist head, do you find any difficulty or differences with the specialists?

   ....

4. Are the functionaries cooperative and technically trained to discharge their duties?

   ....

5. What are the problems and difficulties do you face in implementation of the rural development schemes?

   ....

6. Are you following the central guidelines of schemes in regard to beneficiary selection?

   ....

7. What kind of training you attended before and after joining this post? Please mention.

   ....

8. What kind of training did you get before joining, if you are promoted to this post?

   ....

9. Have you attended any orientation programme, seminar on rural development? Please mention if attended

   ....

10. What kind of cooperation do you find from the line departments?

    ....

11. What kind of works do you assigned to the VLWs. and extension officers?

    ....

12. What is your role in Village Action Plan?

    ....

13. What are the areas that your block is progressing?

    ....

14. Do you find any political interference in your work?

    ....

15. Do you feel that the area of your block is too large?

    ....

16. What is your relation with the Village Councils, DRDA, Deputy Commissioner? Kindly mention.

    ....

17. How do you help, motivate and encourage the villagers/ beneficiaries?

....

18. What is your role in development sectors—agriculture, horticulture, veterinary, small scale industries, etc.?

....

19. What suggestions do you have to make the Village Councils more viable?

....

20. What is your impression on implementation of the rural development programmes?

....

21. What are the problems in identifying the beneficiaries in your block?

....

22. What suggestions do you have to offer to improve the working condition in your block?

....

Bibliography

Books

Arthur, Devis K. (1949): Bureaucratic Patterns in the Navy Officer Corps, Social Forces.

Arora, K. Ramesh and Goyal, Rajni (1995): *Indian Public Administration*, Wishwa Prakashan, New Delhi.

Avasthi, Amreshwar, Maheshwari, Shriram (1999): *Public Administration*, Lakshmi Narain Agarwal, New Delhi.

Avasthi, A.P. (2002): *Indian Government and Politics*, Lakshmi Narain Agarwal, Agra.

Basu, Rumki (2000): *Public Administration*, Sterling Publishers Private Limited, New Delhi.

Bhatnagar, S. (1976): *Rural Local Government in India*, Light and Life Publishers, New Delhi.

Bhagwan, Vishnoo and Bhusan Vidhya (1986): *Public Administration*, S. Chand and Company Ltd., New Delhi.

Bhattacharya, Mohit (2007); *Public Administration*, The World Press Private Limited, Kolkata.

Chamber, Robert. (1983): *Rural Development: Putting the Last First*, Longman Group Ltd., London.

Chatterjee, N. (1975): *The Mizo Chief and His Administration*, Aizawl.

______, (1975) Zawlbuk As a Social Institution in the Mizo Society, Tribal Research Institute, Aizawl, Mizoram.

Choudry, D. Paul (1978): *New Partnership in Rural Development*, M.N. Publishers, New Delhi.

Das, Kalpana (2004): *Rural Development in Mizoram*, Mittal Publications, New Delhi.

Dayal, Ishwar, Mathur, Kuldeep and Bhattacharya, Mohit. *(1976): District Administration: A Survey for Reorganization*, Macmillan, New Delhi.

Devis, K Arthur (1949): Bureaucratic Patterns in the Navy Officer Corps, Social Forces.

Dey, Bata K. (1978): *Bureaucracy Development and Public Management in India*, Uppal Publishing House, New Delhi.

Deogaonkar, S.G. (1980): *Administration for Rural Development in India*, Concept Publishing Company, New Delhi.

Dubhashi, P.R. (1985): *Essays in Public Administration*, NBO Publishers Distributors, New Delhi.

Dwevedi, O.P. and R.B. Jain (1985): *India's Administrative State*, Gitanjali Publishing House, New Delhi.

Fadia, B.L. and Fadia, Kuldeep (2007): *Public Administration*, Sahitya Bhawan Publications, Agra.

Hminga, C.L. (1987): *The Life and Witness of the Churches in Mizoram*, Serkawn.

Hooja, Rakesh (1987): *Administrative Interventions in Rural Development*, Rawat Publications, Jaipur.

http://en.wikipedia.org/wikipolitics

http://www. britannica.com/bps/rural

http://www.en.wikipedia.org/wiki/rural

http://www. websters-online-dictionary

http://www. ers.usda.gov/briefing/rurality

http://www. britannica.com/bps/development

http://www. websters-online-dictionary/development

http://www. longmansdictionary/development

http://www. en.wikipedia.org/wiki/rural

http/en.wikipedia.org/Ministry of Consumers Affairs

http://en.wikipedia.org/wiki/History_of_panchayati_raj_in_India.

http://en.wikipedia.org/wikipolitics.

http://web.worldbank.org.

http//:mizoram.gov.in.

http:/www.educationforallindia.com.

http://www. ammado.com

Inamdar, N.R. (1992): *Development Administration in India*, Rawat Publications, Jaipur, New Delhi.

Johnson, Bruce F., and Kilby Peter (1973): 'Agricultural Strategy', Rural-Urban Interactions and the Expansions of Income Opportunities, Paris, OECD.

Kabra, K.C. (2008): *Economic Growth of Mizoram: Role of Business and Industry*, Concept Publishing Company, New Delhi.

Khanna, R.L. (1972): *Panchayati Raj in India*, Ambala Cantt: The English Book Depot.

Khanna, B.S. (1991): *Rural Development in South Asia India* 1, Deep and Deep Publications, New Delhi.

Khera, S.S. (1997): *District Administration in India*, National Publishing House, New Delhi.

Kothari, C.R. (1991) (edited): *Rural Development in India: Retrospect and Prospect, Rural Development*, Vol. 1, Strategy for Rural Development, Manak Publications (P) Ltd, New Delhi.

Lalkima, C. (1997) *"Social Welfare Administration in a Tribal State-A Case Study of Mizoram"*, Spectrum Publication, Guwahati, Delhi.

Laskar, B.I. (2010): *Industrialization in Mizoram*, New Central Book Agency (P) Ltd, Kolkata.

______, ed (2010): *Mizoram: The Emerging Issues of Development*, DVS Publishers, Guwahati.

Lele, Uma. (1975): *"The Design of Rural Development: Lesson from America"*, John Hopkins, Baltimore.

Lianzela (1994): *Economic Development of Mizoram*, Spectrum Publications, Guwahati.

______, (1995): *Four Decades of Planning in Mizoram*, Published by Khuangkungi, Aizawl (1998) Economy of Mizoram, Mizoram Publication Board, Aizawl.

Madan, G.R. and Tara Madan (1988): *Village Development In India A sociological Approach*, Allied Publishers Private Limited New Delhi.

Maheshwari, S.R. (2000): *State Government in India*, Macmillan India Ltd., Delhi.

______, (2004): *Local Government in India*, Lakshmi Narayan Agarwal, Agra.

______, (1985): *Rural Development in India*, Sage Publications, New Delhi.

Malsawma, H.L. (2002): *Sociology of The Mizos*, Spectrum Publications, Guwahati: Delhi.

Murthy, N.L. and Narayana, K.V. (ed.) (1989): *Rural Economy of India*, Mittal Publications, New Delhi.

Nag, Chittaranjan (1999): *Post-Colonial Mizo Politics, 1947-1998*, Vikas Publication Pvt. Ltd, New Delhi.

Naidu, S.P. (2004): *Public Administration*, New Age International Publishers, New Delhi.

Nanda, B.R. (ed.) (1995): *Mahatma Gandhi 125 Years*, Indian Council For Cultural Relations, New Delhi.

Nandini, Durgesh (1992): *Rural Development Administration*, Rawat Publications, New Delhi.

Pachuau, Rintluanga (1994): *Geography of Mizoram*, R.T. Enterprise, Aizawl.

______, (2009): *Mizoram: A Study in Comprehensive Geography*, Northern Book Centre, New Delhi.

Patel, K.V. (1987): *Rural Economics*, Himalaya Publishing House, Bombay.

Pfiffner M. John and Presthus V. Robert (1960): *Public Administration*, Ronald Press, New York.

Prasad, R.N. (1987): *Government and Politics in Mizoram 1947-1986*, Northern Book Center, New Delhi.

Prasad, R.N. and Agarwal, A.K. (1991): *Political and Economic Development of Mizoram*, Mittal Publications, New Delhi.

______, (ed.) (2003): *Modernisation of The Mizo Society*, Mittal Publications, New Delhi.

______, (ed.) (1995): *Landmarks: A Study of Public Administration in Mizoram*, IIPA, Aizawl Local Branch, Mizoram.

Purushotham, P.W., Karamatullah, M. (1993): "*Development Administration: A Rural Perspective*", Kanishka Publishing House, Delhi.

Rao, V. Venkata, Thansanga, H., Hazarika, Niru. (1987): *A Century of Government and Politics in North-East India*, Volume III, Mizoram, S. Chand and Company (Pvt) LTD, New Delhi.

Rastogi, A.K. (2002): *Rural Development Strategy*, Wide Vision, Jaipur.

Ray, Animesh (1982): *Mizoram Dynamics of Change*, Pearl Publishers, Calcutta.

Roy, Ramashray, Vinod Kumar, T.M. and Singh V.B. (1985): *Problems in Rural Development*, Discovery Publishing House, Delhi.

Sapru, R.K. (2003): *Development Administration*, Sterling

Publishers Pvt. Ltd., New Delhi.

Seetharam, M. (1990): *Citizen Participation in Rural Development*, Mittal Publications, New Delhi.

Setty, E.D. (2002): *New Approaches to Rural Development*, Anmol Publications Private Limited, New Delhi.

Sharma, Arvind K. (2004): *Bureaucracy and Decentralisation*, Mittal Publications, New Delhi.

Sharma, MP and Sadana, B.L. (2008): *Public Administration in Theory and Practice*, Kitab Mahal, Allahabad.

Sharma, S.K. and Malhotra, S.L. (1977): *Integrated Rural Development Approach, Strategy and Perspectives*, New Delhi.

Shepherd, Andrew, (1998): *Sustainable Rural Development*, Macmillan Press Ltd., London.

Singh, Amita (1998): *Public Administration: The Grassroot Concern*, Mittal Publications, New Delhi.

Singh, Hoshiar (1985): *Rural Development in India*, Printwell; Jaipur.

Singh, Katar (1999): *Rural Development: Principles, Politics and Management*, Sage Publications India Pvt. Ltd. New Delhi.

Singh, Kh. Menjor (2001): *Economic Reforms in India: Problems and Prospects*, Mittal Publications, New Delhi.

Singh, Shiv Raj (1989): *Bureaucracy and Rural Development*, Mittal Publications, New Delhi.

Singh, S.N. (1994): *Mizoram*, Mittal Publications, New Delhi.

Sipra, Sen. (1992): *Tribes of Mizoram*, Gian Publishing House, New Delhi.

Taradatt, (2002): *Development Administration in an Indian State*, Guide Book Evolved for BDO in Orissa, Uppal Publishing House, New Delhi.

Government Publications and other Documents

Government of India: Community Development, Publication Division, 1951.

______ : Planning Commission, First Five Year Plan, Publications Division, Ministry of Information, New Delhi, 1952.

______ : Report of the Team for the Study of Community Projects and National Extension Service, Vol. 1, Committee on Plan Project, 1957.

Government of India: Summary Record of Annual Conference on

Community Development held at Mount Abu, 20th to 24th May 1958, Issued by Ministry of Community Development, 1958.

______ : Community Development, Panchayati Raj and Cooperation, 1959.

______ : Report of the Committee on Special Multipurpose Tribal Blocks, Ministry of Home Affairs, New Delhi, March, 1960.

______ : Albert, M., Etawah, Experiment Report of the Pilot Development Projects, 1961.

______ : Guidelines, Training of Rural Development Functionaries, Ministry of Rural Development, New Delhi, 1981.

______ : Guidelines, DRDA Administration, Ministry of Rural Development, New Delhi, 1999.

______ : Ministry of Rural Development. (May 2001) "Gram Vikas Programmes at a Glance, New Delhi.

______ : SGRY Guidelines, Ministry of Rural Development, Department of Rural Development, Krishi Bhawan, New Delhi, 2004.

______ : SGSY Guidelines, Ministry of Rural Development, New Delhi, 2004.

______ : Bharat Nirman, A Time-bound Plan, 2005.

______ : NREGA Operational Guidelines, Ministry of Rural Development, New Delhi, 2008.

Government of Mizoram: Mizoram District Gazetteers, Department of Art and Culture, Aizawl, 1989.

______ : Department of Rural Development; Project Report on New Land Use Policy, Aizawl, 1990.

______ : Economics and Statistics Department, Block Statistics 1992.

______ : District Council Affairs Department, vide its notification No. B-17012/3/92-DCA, dated 22nd September 1993.

______ : Report on Soil and Land Capability Survey of Lunglei, Hnahthial, Lungsen, Bunghmun RD Blocks, Lunglei District, Soil Survey Organisation, Department of Agriculture, January, 1997.

______ : NLUP Sekibuhchhuak: A Bulletin of Commisionerate of Rural Development, Vol. II, Issue No. 4, October-December, 1997.

______ : NLUP Sekibuhchhuak': A Bulletin of Commisionerate of Rural Development, Vol. II, Issue No. 5, October-December, 1998.

______ : Notification No. B/16011/1/86-RD/Pt, Rural Development Department, Aizawl, November 3, 2000.

______ : Department of Economics and Statistics, Statistical Hand Books Aizawl, Mizoram—1998, 2000, 2001, 2002, 2003, 2004, 2008.

______ : Statistical Abstract, Department of Agriculture and Minor Irrigation, Mizoram, Aizawl 2002-2003.

______ : Economics and Statistics Department, Village Level Statistics of Mizoram 2003.

______ : Department of Relief and Rehabilitation, Aizawl, Mizoram, 2003-2004.

______ : Statistical Handbook, Lunglei District, Economics and Statistics Department, District Research Officers Office, Lunglei District, Lunglei, 2003, 2007.

______ : A Brief Note on Schemes being taken up by Rural Development Department, Aizawl, October, 2005.

______ : Rural Development Department Hmalakna Kum Li Chhunga Zokhaw Hmasawnna, Directorate of Rural Development, August 2003. (Programmes initiated by RD Department and Achievements during the last four years).

______ : Department of Agriculture, Crop Husbandry and Minor Irrigation, Revised Annual Plan, 2005-2006.

______ : Chief Engineer, Public Works Department, Action Plan for PMGSY Roads under Bharat Nirman Programme, Lunglei District, 2005-2006.

______ : District Planning Machinery, Lunglei District, Draft Annual Plan for 2006-2007.

______ : Directorate of Agriculture and Minor Irrigation, Land Utilisation, 2006-07.

______ : Economic Survey, Economic Survey Cell, Planning and Programme Implementation Department, 2006-2007.

______ : The Prospect of Rural Village, Department of Economics and Statistics, Lungei, Mizoram, 2009.

______ : Minute, Matter of Dissolution of MIP and Launching of NLUP, Department of Agriculture, Aizawl, 5 February 2010.

Potential Linked Credit Plan, Lunglei District, NABARD, Aizawl, 2005-2006.

Report of the Royal Commission on Agriculture, 1928.

Rural Development Sector Policy Paper, World Bank, Washington D.C., 1975.

Souvenir, Indian Republic Golden Jubilee, Lunglei, 2000.

Reports, Acts, Rules and Regulations

Administrative Report of the North Lushai Hills for the year 1895-96, Government of Assam, Shillong, 1896.

Administrative Report of the Lushai Hills (selected only).

Lushai Hills (Change of Name) Act, 1954.

Lushai Hills District (Change of Name) Act, 1954.

Lushai Hills District (Village Councils) Act, 1953 (amended upto date) Section 25, Sub Section (1).

North East Area (Reorganisation) Act, 1971.

Sixth Schedule of the Constitution of India (Amendment) Act, 1988.

Sixth Schedule of the Constitution of India, Art (2), *275.*

The Assam-Lushai Hills District (Acquisition of Chiefs) Act 1954.

Journals, Papers, Thesis

Bhargava, B.S., "Balwant Rai Mehta and Balwant Rai Mehta Committee Report (1957)", *Local Government Quarterly*, July-September, Mumbai: All India Institute of Local Self Government. Mumbai, 2009.

Bawitlung, Vanlalringa, "The System of Administration in South Mizoram from the Earliest to 1890": *Historical Journal Mizoram,* vol. iv, Issue I, Mizo History Association, July 2003.

Ensminger, D., "Rural Development: What is it? Its contribution in nation-building" Paper presented in East-West Center's Conference on Integrated Communication for Rural Development, Honolulu, 1974.

Haokip, T.T., "Traditional Self-governing Institutions and Democratic Governance in NE India", *Local Government Quarterly*, July-September, All India Institute of Local Self Government, Mumbai, 2009.

Hluna, Dr. J.V. "Socio-economic Development in Mizoram—Problems and Prospects", A seminar paper presented in UGC Sponsored State Level Seminar organized by Govt. J. Buana College, Lunglei, Mizoram. 22-23rd September, 2010.

Kalita, Girin, Sarma Kalyan and Rahman Saidur, Scope of Livestock Production in Mizoram, *Livestock International*, Vol. 8, Issue 11, November 2004, India.

Maheshwari, S.R., 'Rural Development in India', *The Indian Journal of Public Administration*, Vol. Xxx, No. 4, 1984.

Mandal, Amal, Poverty Eradication in Rural India Reflection on Methodology, *Kurukshetra*, Vol. 51 No. 10 August 2003.

Naithani, Pankaj. Replicating An Established Rural Development Model, *Kurukshetra*, Vol. 49, October 2000.

Roa, U.R., Crisis in Agriculture, *The Mizoram Post*, Aizawl, 9th September, 2006.

Sahota, Avtar Singh, Poverty Reduction Strategies in a Market Economy, *Kurukshetra*, Vol. 50, No. 9, July 2002.

S.B.I. Monthly Review: Evaluation of the Impact of IRDP Assistance: A study conducted in ten Lead Districts of SBI Vol. 24, No. 8, August, 1985.

Sinha, Harendra: Block Administration without Panchayati Raj Institutions—An Assessment in Lunglei District of Mizoram, *Kurukshetra*, New Delhi, October, 2010.

——: "NLUP towards Economic Self-sufficiency in Mizoram", A seminar paper presented in UGC Sponsored State Level Seminar organised by Govt. J. Buana College, Lunglei, Mizoram. 22-23rd September, 2010.

Shah, Dilip, Tribal Development Planning and Performance, *Kurukshetra*, Vol. 51, No. 8, June 2003.

Virthli, *Daily Newspaper*, Lunglei, Mizoram.

Zorema, J., The Bureaucracy, The Chiefs and Indirect Rule in the Lushai Hills of Assam: 1898-1952, A Thesis submitted for Doctor of Philosophy to North Eastern Hill University, Shillong, 2002.

Index